Praise for This Book

By the time I'd finished reading—devouring, actually—the first edition of *IAftWWW* in 1998, the pages were—literally—dripping yellow highlighter ink. I don't think I've ever learned as much from another book. And now with Jorge's help, Lou and Peter have pulled off another remarkable feat: they've taken a groundbreaking book written for a world that's being replaced by another one with head-spinning speed (do they still even make highlighter pens?) and reinvented it brilliantly, proving that the principles they made so clear in the first place are still...the important principles.

—Steve Krug, author of
Don't Make Me Think:
A Common Sense Approach to Web Usability

I was one of the rare people with the job title "information architect" when the first edition of this book came out. At the time, it seemed like a meaningful validation of my work, and I feel no less so about seeing the fourth edition come out. Nearly 20 years later, information architecture is more meaningful and necessary than ever, and so is this book.

—Karen McGrane,
managing partner,
Bond Art + Science

The Web isn't just for browsers anymore. It's the thread tying our digital lives together. That's just one lesson from this essential classic, reframed and renewed for our omni-channel, internet-of-everything age. If you've never read it, now is the time. And if you think you know it already, you're definitely due for an update.

—Andrew Hinton,
author, *Understanding Context,*
senior information architect, The Understanding Group

Awesome to see this canonical IA textbook updated with an eye towards cross-channel information architecture. Jorge Arango was the perfect third author to add a perspective from the emerging new school of IA. Kudos to O'Reilly for realizing the need to bring this important book back into the conversation.

—Abby Covert,
president of the IA Institute

I'm fascinated by the ways that imprimatur corresponds with permission. The fact that O'Reilly continues to deepen its investment in IA by way of this fourth update to the polar bear book gives all of us permission to continue being curious about and building skills around IA. If this stuff weren't important, or used to be but is no longer a thing, or was just a subset of UX, why bother with another edition?

I'll tell you why: because it is impossible to know what "good" means in design without the frameworks for understanding provided by and through the process of information architecture.

This book helps you get there.

—Dan Klyn,
cofounder and information architect,
The Understanding Group

Once again, the polar bear book proves just how vital information architecture is to how we design interactive products and services. This book offers a fresh look at a fundamental topic. It's timeless, definitive, and indispensable."

—Jim Kalbach, author of
Mapping Experiences (O'Reilly, 2015)

The polar bear book has always been my go-to recommendation for a solid introduction to information architecture for the Web. With the new material now included on mobile, meaning-making, system design, and the importance of context—as well as updates to the fundamentals of IA—this is the first book I recommend to anyone involved in designing electronic information spaces of any kind.

—Andy Fitzgerald, PhD,
frog design

The fourth edition of a book that almost twenty years ago changed the way we work with information is a slimmer, more compact, and more focused read that takes us all the way from the Web to the ever-expanding world of cross-channel design.

—Andrea Resmini,
senior lecturer, Jönköping University

FOURTH EDITION

Information Architecture
For the Web and Beyond

*Louis Rosenfeld, Peter Morville,
and Jorge Arango*

Beijing · Boston · Farnham · Sebastopol · Tokyo

Information Architecture: For the Web and Beyond

by Louis Rosenfeld, Peter Morville, and Jorge Arango

Printed in the United States of America.

Published by O'Reilly Media, Inc., 1005 Gravenstein Highway North, Sebastopol, CA 95472.

O'Reilly books may be purchased for educational, business, or sales promotional use. Online editions are also available for most titles (*http://safaribooksonline.com*). For more information, contact our corporate/institutional sales department: 800-998-9938 or *corporate@oreilly.com*.

Acquisitions Editor: Mary Treseler
Editor: Angela Rufino
Production Editor: Matthew Hacker
Copyeditor: Jasmine Kwityn
Proofreader: Rachel Head

Indexer: Judith McConville
Interior Designer: David Futato
Cover Designer: Ellie Volckhausen
Illustrator: Rebecca Demarest

February 1998:	First Edition
August 2002:	Second Edition
December 2006:	Third Edition
September 2015:	Fourth Edition

Revision History for the Fourth Edition
2015-09-01:   First Release
2015-10-30:   Second Release

See *http://oreilly.com/catalog/errata.csp?isbn=9781491911686* for release details.

978-1-491-91168-6

[LSI]

Table of Contents

Part II.   Basic Principles of Information Architecture

Part III.   Getting Information Architecture Done

Preface

The town may be changed,
But the well cannot be changed.
It neither decreases nor increases.
They come and go and draw from the well.

—I Ching

The first edition of this book—then titled *Information Architecture for the World Wide Web*—was published in 1998. This was a full 9 years before the iPhone changed the way we share pictures of our kids with our family and friends, 6 years before Facebook reintroduced long-forgotten high school friends into our lives, 6 years before the term "folksonomy" was coined (and 10 years before its currency devalued), and 12 or so years before many of us first heard the term "Internet of Things." There was no "Web 2.0" back then; we were still trying to figure out Web 1.0!

Those of us who have been structuring and designing websites since the "early days" have experienced astonishing changes in our industry. We've seen the underlying technologies of the medium—including HTML itself, along with JavaScript—evolve from what were at first primitive content-delivery mechanisms into full-featured interactive application stacks. We've seen device form factors evolve from indirect experiences where we controlled an abstract pointer with a mouse, to the direct, intimate experience of manipulating information by touching elegant slabs of glass with our fingers. We've seen Internet access go from being a slow, discreet activity that we engaged in by sitting at a desk, in front of a bulky computer tethered to a copper wire, to something we do everywhere at any time by pulling out a blazing fast, sensor- and camera-laden minicomputer/telephone from our pocket. And now we've started to see that power permeate into everyday objects and environments, fundamentally transforming everyday experiences we've long taken for granted. Change is relentless, ubiquitous, exhilarating—and a little scary.

One constant amidst all this change is that every year humanity produces and consumes more information than before. This information glut can make it increasingly challenging for people to find the stuff they're looking for, and make sense of it once they do—especially now that users can interact with information using a wide range of devices and services. Information architecture is the area of practice that helps alleviate this problem. The concepts, methodologies, and techniques that have been so effective in structuring websites can also be applied to broader, more heterogeneous information ecosystems such as those we have today.

Earlier editions of this book were focused on one type of such information ecosystems: websites (in their various manifestations, including intranets and corporate portals.) This fourth edition has a new subtitle: *For the Web and Beyond*. This is an acknowledgment that the information ecosystem landscape is richer and more complex today. Many people's experience of interacting with information increasingly occurs via smartphone apps and other channels that do not involve a traditional web browser. Additionally, as system components and sensors keep getting smaller and cheaper, two-way access to information is becoming a key part of everyday objects like thermostats and doorknobs, which aren't perceived as traditional computing devices at all. While many of these experiences will not require the same types of semantic structures that traditional websites did, they are still key components in information ecosystems and thus subject to many of the same design principles presented in previous editions of the book. When considering the subject of our designs in the abstract—as *information environments* instead of websites—we can see that the design principles that inform these semantic structures have broad applicability beyond design for the Web.

The *I Ching* is an ancient Chinese oracle, and arguably the oldest interactive information environment in the world. Its text presents 64 patterns that describe—and teach us how to deal with—different aspects of change. One of these patterns, "The Well," represents those things in life that are constant and which steadfastly replenish and refresh us, even as the chaos of impermanence alters the world around us. We have approached this fourth edition of the "polar bear book" with the recognition that information architecture is one such "well": as long as we are dealing with the design of information environments for use by human beings, we will have a need for tools and techniques that allow us to structure that information to make it easier to find and understand. We have gone back to first principles to identify those that can be used in any situation to help bring consistency, coherence, and understandability to digital products and services, regardless of their manifestations in space and time. Our hope is that even as technologies and techniques come and go, you will be able to continue drawing from the well of information architecture for many years to come.

What's New in the Fourth Edition

Information Architecture: For the Web and Beyond focuses on information architecture as a set of tools and techniques for dealing with tough information organization problems—by *anyone* involved in *any* aspect of design, regardless of their job title. We have gone through the first three editions and brought forward those principles of information organization that are universal and timeless. We've cast these in the context of current practice by updating the examples and illustrations. We've avoided discussions of particular software packages; it's all changing too quickly for this information to have much value in the long term. Instead, we've focused on tools and techniques that have stood the test of time and which are not dependent on particular technologies or vendors. Finally, we've updated Appendix A to include the most useful information architecture resources available today.

Organization of This Book

This book is divided into 3 parts and 13 chapters, progressing from abstract fundamental concepts to processes, tools, and techniques you can use to put them into practice. It breaks down as follows.

Part I, "Introducing Information Architecture," provides an overview of information architecture for those new to the field and experienced practitioners alike, and comprises the following chapters:

Chapter 1, The Problems That Information Architecture Addresses
This chapter sets the stage by describing the main challenges we face today when dealing with complex information environments.

Chapter 2, Defining Information Architecture
This chapter offers definitions and analogies, and explains why information architecture is not easy to identify in everyday life.

Chapter 3, Design for Finding
This chapter helps us better understand people's information-seeking needs and behaviors.

Chapter 4, Design for Understanding
This chapter explains how information architecture can create the right contexts for people to understand information.

Part II, "Basic Principles of Information Architecture," presents the fundamental components of an architecture, illustrating the interconnected nature of these systems. It comprises the following chapters:

Chapter 5, The Anatomy of an Information Architecture
This chapter helps you visualize the nuts and bolts of an architecture and introduces the systems covered in subsequent chapters.

Chapter 6, Organization Systems
This chapter describes ways to structure and organize sites to meet business goals and user needs.

Chapter 7, Labeling Systems
This chapter presents approaches for creating consistent, effective, and descriptive labels for a site.

Chapter 8, Navigation Systems
This chapter explores the design of browsing systems that help users understand where they are and where they can go within a site.

Chapter 9, Search Systems
> This chapter covers the nuts and bolts of searching systems, and describes approaches to indexing and the design of search result interfaces that can improve overall performance.

Chapter 10, Thesauri, Controlled Vocabularies, and Metadata
> This chapter shows how vocabulary control can connect these systems and improve the user experience.

Part III, "Getting Information Architecture Done," covers the conceptual tools, techniques, and methods to take you from research to strategy and design to implementation of an information architecture. It comprises the following chapters:

Chapter 11, Research
> This chapter explains the discovery process necessary to create a foundation of understanding for your information architecture.

Chapter 12, Strategy
> This chapter presents a framework and methodology for defining the direction and scope of your information architecture.

Chapter 13, Design and Documentation
> This chapter introduces the deliverables and processes required to bring your information architecture to life.

We end with the Coda, which wraps things up.

Appendix A presents a selective list of pointers to the most useful information architecture resources available today.

Audience for This Book

Who do we hope to reach with this fourth edition of the polar bear book? Because we assume that any interactive product contains *information*, this book is for anyone who's responsible for defining how interactive products and services work: user experience designers, product managers, developers, and more. The job titles don't really matter; what matters is that your work results in products and services that are interactive, information dense, and used by at least one person besides yourself.

Previous editions of the book delved into the subject of information architecture as a career path. We have eschewed these discussions in the fourth edition in favor of treating information architecture as an area of practice. You do not need to have the words "information architect" on your business card in order to benefit from the ideas in this book.

Conventions Used in This Book

The following typographical conventions are used in this book:

Italic

> Indicates new terms, URLs, email addresses, filenames, and file extensions.

`Constant width`

> Used for program listings, as well as within paragraphs to refer to program elements such as variable or function names, databases, data types, environment variables, statements, and keywords.

 This element signifies a general note.

Contacting the Authors

Please direct all suggestions, kudos, flames, and other assorted comments to us via email:

- Peter Morville, Semantic Studios (*morville@semanticstudios.com*)
- Lou Rosenfeld, Louis Rosenfeld LLC (*lou@louisrosenfeld.com*)
- Jorge Arango, Futuredraft (*jorge@futuredraft.com*)

Safari® Books Online

 *Safari Books Online* is an on-demand digital library that delivers expert content in both book and video form from the world's leading authors in technology and business.

Technology professionals, software developers, web designers, and business and creative professionals use Safari Books Online as their primary resource for research, problem solving, learning, and certification training.

Safari Books Online offers a range of plans and pricing for enterprise, government, education, and individuals.

Members have access to thousands of books, training videos, and prepublication manuscripts in one fully searchable database from publishers like O'Reilly Media, Prentice Hall Professional, Addison-Wesley Professional, Microsoft Press, Sams, Que, Peachpit Press, Focal Press, Cisco Press, John Wiley & Sons, Syngress, Morgan Kaufmann, IBM Redbooks, Packt, Adobe Press, FT Press, Apress, Manning, New Riders, McGraw-Hill, Jones & Bartlett, Course Technology, and hundreds more. For more information about Safari Books Online, please visit us online.

How to Contact Us

Please address comments and questions concerning this book to the publisher:

O'Reilly Media, Inc.
1005 Gravenstein Highway North
Sebastopol, CA 95472
800-998-9938 (in the United States or Canada)
707-829-0515 (international or local)
707-829-0104 (fax)

We have a web page for this book, where we list errata, examples, and any additional information. You can access this page at *http://bit.ly/info_architecture_4e*.

To comment or ask technical questions about this book, send email to *bookquestions@oreilly.com*.

For more information about our books, courses, conferences, and news, see our website at *http://www.oreilly.com*.

Find us on Facebook: *http://facebook.com/oreilly*

Follow us on Twitter: *http://twitter.com/oreillymedia*

Watch us on YouTube: *http://www.youtube.com/oreillymedia*

Acknowledgments

This book exists because of the generosity and intelligence of the many teachers, colleagues, clients, friends, and family members who helped us form and nurture these ideas, and gave us the wherewithal to share them with you. We can't thank all of them here, but we will briefly acknowledge those who have been most influential in bringing this fourth edition to life.

We have been very lucky to work with an amazing team of technical reviewers whose generosity is a true mark of the information architecture community: Abby Covert, Andrea Resmini, Andrew Hinton, Andy Fitzgerald, Carl Collins, Danielle Malik, Dan Klyn, Dan Ramsden, John Simpkins, Jonathan Shariat, Jonathon Coleman, and Kat King. Their input has made this book better in many ways; we are very grateful for their contributions.

As always, the team at O'Reilly Media has been a pleasure to work with. Our editors Angela Rufino and Mary Treseler helped keep us on track, and were supportive and energizing throughout the writing process. We owe many, many thanks to Angela, Mary, and the entire production crew at O'Reilly.

We are grateful to Chris Farnum and ProQuest for providing sample wireframes for Chapter 13.

Finally, some personal thanks from each of us.

Lou thanks his teachers from the University of Michigan's School of Information—especially Joe Janes, Amy Warner, Vic Rosenberg, Karen Drabenstott, and the late Miranda Pao—and Mary Jean, Iris, and Nate for sharing the apartment with an occasionally very cranky author.

Peter thanks Susan, Claudia, Claire, and a dog named Knowsy.

Jorge thanks his partners at Futuredraft—Brian O'Kelley, Chris Baum, and Hans Krueger—for giving him the opportunity to hone his craft among giants, the fine folks at KDFC ("The Bay Area's listener-supported classical radio station") for keeping him company at ungodly hours, and his family—Jimena, Julia, Ada, and Elias—for allowing him the time and space to work on the book...and the reason to do so.

Louis Rosenfeld
Brooklyn, NY

Peter Morville
Ann Arbor, MI

Jorge Arango
San Leandro, CA

PART I

Introducing Information Architecture

Information is more abundant today than ever before. With smartphones, activity monitors, smart watches, tablets, and new Internet-enabled appliances of every kind, we also have many more ways of interacting with it than before. This abundance and pervasiveness makes our lives better in many ways, but it also introduces new challenges. With so much information available in so many places, it can sometimes be difficult to cut through the noise to *find* the information you need and *understand* it once you have found it.

Information architecture (IA) is a design discipline that is focused on making information findable and understandable. Because of this, it is uniquely well suited to address these challenges. IA allows us to think about problems through two important perspectives: that information products and services are perceived by people as *places made of information*, and that these information environments can be *organized for optimum findability and understandability.*

This first part of the book explains what IA is, what problems it solves, and how it can help you create more effective products and services. Part II and Part III will then show you how.

Let's get started!

CHAPTER 1

The Problems That Information Architecture Addresses

And it really doesn't matter
If I'm wrong, I'm right
Where I belong I'm right
Where I belong
—"Fixing a Hole,"
Lennon–McCartney

In this chapter, we'll cover:

- How information broke free from its containers
- The challenges of information overload and contextual proliferation
- How information architecture can help people deal with these challenges

Marla was in the mood for The Beatles. She walked over to the shelf where she kept her LP records and looked through her collection. Fortunately, Marla was very organized: her record collection was neatly sorted alphabetically by the artist's name. Alice Cooper, Aretha Franklin, Badfinger... and there, next to her Beach Boys albums, were The Beatles. She pulled the *Sgt. Pepper's Lonely Hearts Club Band* vinyl disc out of its sleeve and put it on the turntable, and relaxed as the music started.

For most of our history, the information we have interacted with has existed in a one-to-one relationship with the artifacts that contain it.

Marla had only one *Sgt. Pepper's* album, and if she wanted to listen to it, she needed to know exactly where it was on the shelf. If she was traveling and didn't bring her record with her, she couldn't listen to it. Because the information (the music) was physically embedded in containers (vinyl discs), and she only had one copy of each, she had to define "one right way" to organize her records. Should they be ordered alphabetically based on the artists' first names, as shown in Figure 1-1, or their last names? What about albums in which the composer mattered more than the performer, as in her copy of Holst's *The Planets*? Then there were compilation albums, containing music by many artists. Should they be listed under "Various Artists"? And when she bought a new album, she needed to remember to store it in the right place in the collection. It all got very complicated very quickly. Perhaps she shouldn't bother with organizing them at all... but then she wouldn't be able to find them easily when she was in the mood for a particular artist.

Figure 1-1. Marla's music is embedded in physical objects—vinyl records—so she must choose how to organize them on the shelf

Now meet Marla's son, Mario. Instead of vinyl discs, Mario's record collection consisted of compact discs (CDs). Because the music in the discs was stored digitally, he could now randomize the order in which the songs were played. He'd been promised that the music would also sound better, and the discs would last longer than the previous technology. It was great! However, even though the music was stored digitally, his plastic discs were not that different from his mother's collection: the music was still tied to the individual physical discs that contained it. He still had to choose whether to organize the discs by the artist's name or the album's name; he couldn't do both.

But then, in 2001, Mario got an iMac. The colorful computer's advertising campaign invited him to "Rip, Mix, Burn" his music—in other words, liberate it from the plastic discs that contained it and get it into his computer ("Rip"). Once there, it would sound just as good as the CDs, but now he could explore it any way he pleased: he could browse his collection by artist, genre, album title, song title, year produced, and more. He could search it. He could save backup copies. He could make playlists that combined the music from various albums ("Mix") and record songs onto blank discs ("Burn") to share with friends (much to the chagrin of the people who'd produced the music).

As shown in Figure 1-2, Mario was no longer limited to the one-to-one relationship between information (the music) and containers (the discs) that his mother had to deal with. He was no longer constrained to deciding between sorting the albums alphabetically by artist name or album name; he could now do both simultaneously. He could make multiple perfect copies of his songs, and bring them with him on his laptop when he traveled. Mario stopped thinking of his music as something tied to its container. It had dematerialized.

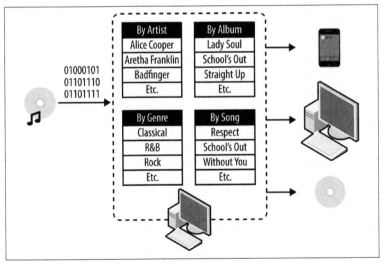

Figure 1-2. Being digital, Mario's music collection can be organized in more than one way and can live in multiple devices simultaneously

Hello, iTunes

The tool that Mario used to do all of this, iTunes, is shown in Figure 1-3. Digital music had been around for a long time before iTunes, but this was the first time that many people encountered it in the mainstream. Originally a third-party application called SoundJam, iTunes was acquired by Apple in 2000 to become the default music player included with Macintosh computers. In its initial release, iTunes served a clear purpose: it allowed Mario to create and manage a music library for use in his own computer ("Rip, Mix, Burn"). He spent a long weekend importing his collection of 40 CDs into his Mac and organizing his music, and put the discs away for good. From now on, his music would be all-digital.

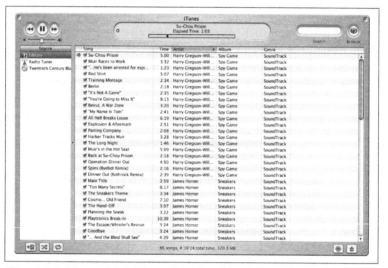

Figure 1-3. iTunes 1.0 browsing by Artist and Album (image: http:// bit.ly/et_tu_itune)

The first version of iTunes had a few distinct modes—for example, there was a "ripping" mode that showed progress when the user was extracting music from a CD into the computer—but its focus was clearly on allowing people like Mario to find and play music from their own collections. As a result of this reduced feature set, it had a very simple user interface and information structures. Mario loved it, and playing music became one of his favorite uses for his Mac.

However, iTunes started to become more complex over time. Each new release of the app introduced amazing new features: smart playlists, podcast subscriptions, Internet radio station streaming, support for audiobooks, streamed music sharing, and more. When Apple released the iPod, Mario rushed to get one. iTunes was now about more than just managing music on his Mac: it was also about managing the library on his portable music player. In 2003, Apple introduced the iTunes Music Store. Now Mario could enter a separate mode within iTunes that allowed him to purchase music, using a categorization scheme that was different from the one he used to organize his own library. By 2005, the iTunes Music Store had more than 2 million songs available, a far cry from the 40 albums that Mario had in his collection to begin with. But Apple didn't stop there: soon it started selling TV shows and then movies through the (now renamed) iTunes Store. TV shows, movies, and music were presented as distinct categories within the store, and each "department" had its own categorization scheme: rock, alternative, pop, hip-hop/rap, etc. for music; kids & family, comedy, action & adventure, etc. for movies; and so on.

iTunes was not just where Mario listened to and organized his music anymore. Now it was where he went to:

- Buy, rent, and watch movies
- Buy, rent, and watch TV shows
- Preview and buy music
- Buy applications for his iPod
- Search for and listen to podcasts
- Browse and subscribe to "iTunes U" university courses
- Listen to streaming radio stations
- Listen to audiobooks
- Browse and listen to music shared by others in his household

Each of these functions introduced new content types with particular categorization schemes. iTunes still had a search box, as it had on day one, but search results were now much more difficult to parse, because they included different (and incompatible) media types. Was the result for "Dazed and Confused" referring to the movie, the movie soundtrack, the Led Zeppelin song, or one of its myriad covers?

Later, when Mario bought his first iPhone, he was surprised to discover that the functionality that he was used to having in iTunes on the Mac (music, movies, TV shows, podcasts, etc.) had now been "unbundled" into various apps, as shown in Figure 1-4. On the iPhone, iTunes is not where you play music; for that there is an app called (appropriately) "Music." However, there are no "Movies" or "TV Shows" apps; there is one app ("Videos") that plays both. This is not where Mario can see the videos he has shot himself, though; for that he has to go to the "Photos" app. There is also an app on the phone where Mario can buy movies, music, and TV shows, called "iTunes Store"—the only reference to iTunes on the phone—and another where he can buy iPhone apps, called "App Store." All of these apps offer functionality that is available within iTunes on the Mac, and all of them have different content organization structures. Later on, Apple introduced a service called iTunes Match, which allowed Mario to upload his music collection to Apple's "cloud"; now he also had to keep track of which songs were actually on his phone and his Mac, and which were on Apple's servers.

Mario bought Apple products in part because of the company's reputation for excellent design. He'd heard that Apple "controls the hardware and the software," and was thus able to provide a unified, coherent experience across all of its products. Yet managing his media across his Mac and his iPhone was neither unified nor coherent. Also, over time, Mario became a consumer *and* an organizer of an information ecosystem; he had to deal with the information structures designed into the system by Apple and his own organization schemes for his personal music collection, which were now transcending many device form factors and contexts. Mario couldn't quite put his finger on it, but he could tell that something big was amiss with the design of these products, even though he found them visually appealing.

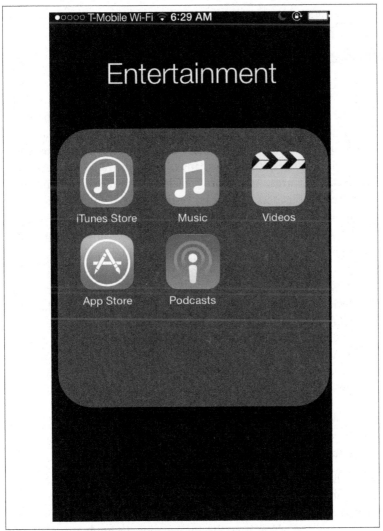

Figure 1-4. iOS's unbundled iTunes apps

The Problems Information Architecture Addresses

Mario was experiencing two problems:

- The tool he used to manage and navigate his simple library of 40 or so music albums had changed into one that dealt with hundreds of millions of different data objects of various types (songs, movies, TV shows, apps, podcasts, radio streams, university lectures, and more), each with different organization schemes, business rules (e.g., restrictions on which device he is allowed to play back his rented movie on within the next 24 hours), and ways of interacting with the information (e.g., viewing, subscribing, playing, transcoding, etc.).

- The functions provided by this tool were no longer constrained to Mario's computer; they are now available across multiple devices, including his iPhone, iPod, Apple TV, CarPlay, and Apple Watch. Each of these devices brings with it different constraints and possibilities that define what they can (and cannot) do with these information structures (e.g., "Siri, play 'With a Little Help from My Friends'"), and Mario doesn't experience them as a consistent, coherent interaction model.

Let's look at these challenges in a bit more detail.

Information Overload

People have been complaining about having to deal with too much information for centuries. As far back as Ecclesiastes (composed in the 3rd or 4th century BCE), we read that "of making many books there is no end." However, the information technology revolution that started around 70 years ago has greatly increased the information available to us. The phrase "information overload" was popularized by futurist Alvin Toffler in the 1970s.[1] Toffler called out the increased rate and pace of information production, and the resulting reduction in the signal-to-noise ratio, as problems that we'd have to deal with in the future. (As you can see from Mario's example, this

---

[1] Alvin Toffler, *Future Shock* (New York: Random House, 1970).

future is now!) The career of Richard Saul Wurman—originator of the term "information architect"—is based on using design to address information overload. His book *Information Anxiety*[2] is considered a classic in the field.

In the 19th and 20th centuries, electronic media such as the telegraph, telephone, radio, and television allowed more information to reach more people over greater distances than ever before. However, the process really sped up in the second half of the 20th century with the appearance of digital computers and their eventual connection into what became the Internet. Suddenly, massive amounts of information could be shared with anyone in the world. The Internet —and the World Wide Web, especially—were conceptualized as two-way, interactive media. For example, you could not only receive email, but also send it. Sir Tim Berners-Lee meant for the Web to be a read/write medium; the first web browser, called WorldWideWeb (with no spaces), gave as much prominence to editing web pages as it did to browsing them. Compared to previous information media, publishing on the Web was fast, cheap, and efficient. As a result, the amount of information being published today in information environments like Facebook, Twitter, and WordPress dwarfs anything that has ever come before.

It's important to note that while every advance in information technologies has increased the overall amount of information available and has made it possible for more people to publish and have access to information, the resulting glut has also led to the creation of new technologies to help people organize, find, and make better use of information. For example, the invention of the movable type printing press in the 15th century made more books and pamphlets available more cheaply to more people. This, in turn, led to the creation of technologies such as encyclopedias, alphabetic indexes, and public libraries, which allowed people to better manage and make sense of the new information sources.[3]

It should not be surprising, then, that some of the great success stories of the early Web, such as Google and Yahoo!, were companies

2 Richard Saul Wurman, *Information Anxiety* (New York: Bantam, 1989).

3 For more on this topic, see Ann Blair's Boston Globe article "Information overload, the early years" (*http://bit.ly/information_overload*).

founded to help users find information online.[4] Still, there is much more information out there than we can manage, and the findability techniques that were effective in the late 1990s (e.g., Yahoo!'s curated hierarchical directory) are ineffective today.

With the rise of app-centric Internet-connected mobile devices such as smartphones, it has become fashionable for pundits to postulate the demise of the World Wide Web. However, instead of making the Web irrelevant, these devices have given more people access to the information available on the Internet. For many applications, the data sources that feed apps tend to be indistinguishable from (if not identical to) those that power the Web. If anything, the mobile revolution has increased access to the information available in the world.

So, back to Mario. Instead of the 400 or so songs in his record collection, he can now peruse the iTunes Store's (*http://en.wikipedia.org/wiki/ITunes_Store*) collection of 37 million songs. Not that he can flip through it like he could with his CDs (or even at his local Tower Records[5]); here, he's going to need a bit of help to find what he's looking for.

More Ways to Access Information

While the information explosion has been happening for a long time, the second problem Mario faces is newer: the relentless miniaturization of electronics, combined with widespread adoption of wireless communications technologies, has resulted in a proliferation of small, inexpensive Internet-connected devices that are transforming the way that we interact with information and with one another.

As we mentioned earlier, there was a time when information existed in a tightly coupled relationship with the artifacts that conveyed that information. Recall Marla's record collection. The music in her copy of *Sgt. Pepper's* was set into a singular vinyl disc that sat on her shelf. Marla's copy was a reproduction: many more people had similar vinyl discs with that particular music on it. However, this particular

---

4 Google's stated mission (*http://www.google.com/about/*) is to "organize the world's information and make it universally accessible and useful."

5 R.I.P.

container (the disc) and the information (the music) were irrevocably tied together after being manufactured.

Going back further—to a time before mechanical reproductions—we find an even tighter relationship between information and its containers. Think of early books: making handwritten copies—the only reproduction technique available before the invention of printing—was an extremely onerous process. It wasn't easy or cheap to make copies, so individual instances of information artifacts such as books were even more valuable. Because of the rarity and cost of these early books, reading them was an activity reserved for particular classes of people (e.g., scholars, monks, aristocrats, etc.) in specific times and places (e.g., an abbey library during daylight hours).

Now consider an ebook, such as you would read on a Kindle. These "books" are not tied at all to their containing devices; a single Kindle ereader can contain hundreds of ebooks, and conversely, each individual Kindle ebook can be downloaded and read on a wide variety of different devices, ranging from smartphones to dedicated ereaders to desktop computers. You can have the same book open in more than one device at a time, as either a text file or an audiobook, and your reading position—along with your highlights and annotations—is synchronized instantaneously between devices. The presentation of these books varies from device to device depending on the features and limitations of each, with the text itself being an invariant that is reformatted, reflowed, and reconfigured to fit its new environment. (Perhaps you are reading or listening to these words on such a device!)

Whereas physical books—especially the expensive, handwritten ones—had constraints on when and where you could use them, ebooks have no such limitations. You are as likely to be reading an ebook while taking a bath as while standing in line at the supermarket. The result is that the information (e.g., the text of the book) is decoupled not only from the artifact that contains it (e.g., the paper book), but also from the contexts in which we access it (e.g., the quiet abbey library).

Another important difference between physical media (like printed books) and their digital counterparts is that the latter are part of a system that can gather information about their usage, including highlights, annotations, and reading patterns, and provide additional functionality based on this metadata. For example, Kindle apps include a feature called "popular highlights" that allows the reader to identify the passages of a book that have been most often highlighted by other Kindle readers (Figure 1-5). Decoupling information from its physical containers has also made it cheaper to reproduce and distribute, and this in turn has made it more available to more people. Fortunately, the days when information was only accessible to monks in abbey libraries are long gone.

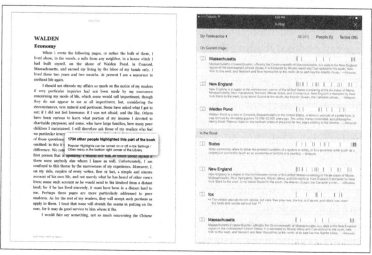

Figure 1-5. The Kindle iPad app includes features that use metadata to allow you to explore books in interesting new ways that were previously impossible

Obviously, contextual proliferation is not just happening for books; we are experiencing it with all of our information technologies. As mentioned earlier, if Marla wanted to bring *Sgt. Pepper's* along with her on a trip, she needed to bring the physical vinyl disc with her, and her music library back home would have a gap where that particular album used to be. On the other hand, when Mario wants to bring *Sgt. Pepper's* on a trip, all he needs to do is drag a copy of the bits that represent the album from his computer onto his iPhone. Both devices now have exact replicas of the information, and neither music library is reduced as a result of the operation.

The next logical step in the dematerialization of information is for it to permeate our surroundings and become an ever-present feature of our personal interactions with the world. We can already see the beginnings of this ambient digital information layer in what is being referred to as the "Internet of Things"—the proliferation of small Internet-connected devices into everyday contexts and activities—and in "wearable" computers, whose constant proximity to our bodies allows them to record health and activity data, serve us small morsels of information in the form of just-in-time notifications, and activate or enable functions in the environment. Devices like the Fitbit activity monitors and the Nest thermostat serve as two-way information conduits between our physical environments and cyberspace, learning from our behavior patterns and adjusting themselves accordingly to suit our needs.

A fascinating example of this trend toward blurring of physical and information spaces was an innovating marketing campaign (*http://bit.ly/virtual_shops*) carried out in 2011 by South Korean supermarket chain Home Plus. In a bid for increased market share, Home Plus appealed to smartphone-wielding commuters by plastering subway stations with photographs of shelves full of groceries. Customers could walk up to these virtual shelves and order their groceries by snapping photos of QR codes associated with products (Figure 1-6.) Delivery would happen within minutes or hours, saving commuters time. As a result of the campaign, sales increased 130% in three months, and registered users increased 76%.

Figure 1-6. Commuter shopping Home Plus's virtual supermarket shelves (image: http://bit.ly/virtual_subway_store)

To summarize, we are not only having to deal with more information than ever before, we are also doing so in a wide variety of different physical and psychological contexts. This will take getting used to: we bring different expectations to a web search entered on a computer keyboard in a quiet office than one tapped into a five-inch glass screen in a football stadium or spoken into a car's Bluetooth audio system while driving at 50 miles per hour. Increasingly, organizations have to consider how users will access their information in these and many other wildly different contexts. They will obviously want these experiences to be consistent and coherent regardless of where and how the information is being accessed.

So, Mario is not only faced with finding new music to listen to from a collection of over 37 million songs; he's having to do so using multiple devices—notebook computer, smartphone, TV set-top box, and more—that provide very different ways of interacting with the information, and in a wide variety of different contexts. Mario is going to need a lot of help from the people who design these products and services.

Enter Information Architecture

Part of the reason Mario is confused is that while most software applications are designed to solve very specific problems, the successful ones tend to outgrow their problem-set boundaries to encompass more and more functionality over time. As a result, they lose clarity and simplicity. As we saw, while iTunes started its life as a tool to enable the digitization and management of music collections in personal computers, it grew to become a *media platform* that encompasses the original music ripping, playing, and organizing functionalities plus other media types (movies, podcasts, audiobooks, university courses, other software applications), other modes of access (buying, renting, streaming, subscribing, sharing), and various device/interaction paradigms (Microsoft Windows computers, iPods, iPads, Apple Watches, Apple TVs). In other words, iTunes went from being a tool to being an *ecosystem*.

Given the information and device class proliferation we mentioned earlier, this is a situation many organizations are already struggling with. What is needed is a systematic, comprehensive, holistic approach to structuring information in a way that makes it easy to find and understand—regardless of the context, channel, or medium the user employs to access it. In other words, someone needs to step out of the product development trenches and look at the broader picture in the abstract, to understand how it all fits together so that information can be easier to find and to understand. Information architecture can be used as a lens to help teams and individuals gain this perspective.

Places Made of Information

As we've said before, the experience of using digital products and services is expanding to encompass multiple devices in different places and times. It's important to recognize that we interact with these products and services through the use of language: labels, menus, descriptions, visual elements, content, and their relationships with one another create an environment that differentiates these experiences and facilitates understanding (or not!). For example, the language employed by a recipe app on a mobile phone is bound to be different from that employed by an auto insurance company's website. These differences in language help define them as distinct "places" that people can visit to accomplish certain specific tasks: they create a frame for the information they convey, allowing us to understand it relative to concepts we already know.

In his book *Understanding Context*, information architect Andrew Hinton argues that we make sense of these experiences much like we do physical places: by picking up on particular words and images that define what can and can't be done in the environment—be it an idyllic open field in the English countryside or a web search engine. Digital experiences are new (and very real) types of places made of information; the design challenge lies in making them be coherent across multiple contexts. As Andrew says, "Information architecture is a discipline well-suited for attending to these challenges. It has been working with them in one way or another for decades."[6]

---

6 Andrew Hinton, *Understanding Context* (Sebastopol, CA: O'Reilly, 2014), 252.

Coherence Across Channels

How does information architecture achieve this coherence? To begin with, it does so by asking designers to think about these challenges in the abstract. Where other design disciplines are focused on specific instances of an artifact—the label on a bottle of detergent, the look and feel of an app's user interface—information architecture asks designers to define semantic structures that can be instantiated in multiple ways depending on the needs of different channels. A navigation structure that works well in a desktop web page should function differently when presented on a five-inch touchscreen, but the user's experience with both should be coherent (Figure 1-7).

In their landmark book *Pervasive Information Architecture*, Andrea Resmini and Luca Rosati argue for consistency as a critical component of what they call a *pervasive information architecture*—that is, one that is experienced across multiple channels and contexts. As they explain it:

> Consistency is the capability of a pervasive information architecture to serve the contexts it is designed for (internal consistency), and to preserve this logic across different media, environments, and uses (external consistency)...Consistency needs to be designed with the context it is addressing clear in mind, and in respect to the several media and environments that the service or process will span.[7]

In other words, when an organization serves its users via multiple channels, the users' experiences across those channels should be consistent and familiar. For example, a person using a bank's mobile app should experience consistent semantic structures when using the bank's website or calling the bank's phone-based service. While the capabilities and limitations of each channel are different, the semantic structures employed in each of them should be familiar and consistent. In order for this to happen, they must be abstracted from actual implementations.

---

7 Andrea Resmini and Luca Rosati, *Pervasive Information Architecture: Designing Cross-Channel User Experiences* (Burlington, MA: Morgan Kaufmann, 2011), 90.

Figure 1-7. CNN's website uses a responsive layout that adapts page elements to fit different screen sizes, while offering a coherent experience

Systems Thinking

Because of this emphasis on abstracting solutions to complex challenges, information architecture also requires that the designer think systemically about the problems at hand. Where other design disciplines focus on the design of particular artifacts, information architecture is concerned with defining the semantic systems that the individual artifacts—apps, websites, voice interfaces, etc.—will be working within. Peter's book *Intertwingled* is an impassioned plea for systems thinking in the design of complex information environments. He calls out the dangers of low-level thinking when trying to design these new types of products and services:

> In the era of ecosystems, seeing the big picture is more important than ever, and less likely. It's not simply that we're forced into little boxes by organizational silos and professional specialization. We like it in there. We feel safe. But we're not. This is no time to stick to your knitting. We must go from boxes to arrows. Tomorrow belongs to those who connect.[8]

You can't design products and services that work effectively and coherently across various interaction channels if you don't understand how they influence and interact with one another and with various other systems that affect them. As mentioned earlier, each interaction channel brings to the mix different limitations and possibilities that should inform the whole. A high-level, comprehensive understanding of the ecosystem can help ensure that its constituent elements work together to present coherent experiences to users. As a discipline, information architecture is ideally suited to this task.

That said, the focus of information architecture is not only on high-level, abstract models: the design of products and services that are findable and understandable requires the creation of many low-level artifacts as well. Traditionally, many people think of website navigation structures when they think of information architecture, and this view isn't entirely off: navigation menus and their ilk are certainly within the remit of what information architecture produces. It's just that you can't get there without having explored the more abstract territory first. Effective information environments strike a balance between structural coherence (high-level invariance) and

---

8 Peter Morville, *Intertwingled: Information Changes Everything* (Ann Arbor, MI: Semantic Studios, 2014), 5.

suppleness (low-level flexibility), so well-designed information architectures consider both.

Having a systems-level view that is informed by (and that informs) day-to-day design activities is also a good way of ensuring that you are solving the right problems. In his book *Introduction to General Systems Thinking*, computer scientist Gerald Weinberg uses the following story to illustrate what he calls *fallacies of absolute thought*:

> A minister was walking by a construction project and saw two men laying bricks. "What are you doing?" he asked the first.
>
> "I'm laying bricks," he answered gruffly.
>
> "And you?" he asked the other. "I'm building a cathedral," came the happy reply.
>
> The minister was agreeably impressed with this man's idealism and sense of participation in God's Grand Plan. He composed a sermon on the subject, and returned the next day to speak to the inspired bricklayer. Only the first man was at work.
>
> "Where's your friend?" asked the minister.
>
> "He got fired."
>
> "How terrible. Why?"
>
> "He thought we were building a cathedral, but we're building a garage."[9]

So ask yourself: am I designing a cathedral or a garage? The difference between the two is important, and it's often hard to tell them apart when your focus is on laying bricks. Sometimes—as in the case of iTunes—designers start working on a garage, and before they know what's happening, they've grafted an apse, choir, and stained-glass windows onto it, making it hard to understand and use. Information architecture can help ensure that you're working on the plans for a great garage (the best in the world!)—or a cathedral, if such is the problem you're trying to solve. In the rest of the book, we'll show you how.

9 Gerald Weinberg, *An Introduction to General Systems Thinking* (New York: Dorset House, 2001) 61.

Recap

Let's recap what we've learned thus far:

- Historically, information has shown a tendency to dematerialize, going from having a one-to-one relationship with its containers to being completely detached from its containers (as is the case with our digital information).

- This has had two important effects in our time: information is more abundant than ever before, and we have more ways of interacting with it than ever before.

- Information architecture is focused on making information findable and understandable. Because of this, it is uniquely well suited to address these issues.

- It does this by asking the designer to think about problems through two important perspectives: that our products and services are perceived as places made of information, and that they function as ecosystems that can be designed for maximum effectiveness.

- That said, information architecture doesn't operate solely at the level of abstractions: for it to be effective, it needs to be defined at various levels.

In Chapter 2, we will give you a deeper overview of the discipline of IA, and will have a shot at defining the damned thing.[10]

---

10 "Defining the damned thing"—or DTDT, as it is often shortened on Twitter and mailing lists—is an ongoing source of contention in the IA community, to the merriment of some and annoyance of others. When you make a living labeling things, squabbles about conceptual boundaries are an occupational hazard.

CHAPTER 2

Defining Information Architecture

We say nothing essential about the
cathedral when we speak of its stones.
—*Antoine de Saint-Exupéry*

In this chapter, we'll cover:

- A working definition (or four!) of information architecture
- Why it's so hard to point to something and say, "that's a great IA"!
- A model for effective IA design

If you're new to information architecture, at this point you may be wondering what this is all about. This chapter has answers for you! And if you have been working in one of the UX design disciplines for a while, you may be thinking, "But isn't information architecture about making sitemaps, wireframes, and website navigation menus?" Well, yes—these are important elements of information architecture design. But there is much more to this story! In this chapter, we'll give you a broader picture of what information architecture is—and isn't.

Definitions

Let's start by clarifying what we mean by information architecture:

1. The structural design of shared information environments
2. The synthesis of organization, labeling, search, and navigation systems within digital, physical, and cross-channel ecosystems
3. The art and science of shaping information products and experiences to support usability, findability, and understanding
4. An emerging discipline and community of practice focused on bringing principles of design and architecture to the digital landscape

Were you expecting a single definition? Something short and sweet? A few words that succinctly capture the essence and expanse of the field of information architecture? Keep dreaming!

The reason we can't serve up a single, all-powerful, all-purpose definition is a clue to understanding why it's so hard to design good digital products and services. We're talking about the challenges inherent in language and representation. No document fully and accurately represents the intended meaning of its author. No label or definition totally captures the meaning of a document. And no two readers experience or understand a particular document or definition or label in quite the same way. The relationship between words and meaning is tricky at best.[1] And here's the paradox of defining information architecture: by defining and clarifying semantic concepts, IA makes them more understandable and findable, but at a cost, because definitions are so imperfect and limiting at the same time. The definition of IA itself is a great illustration of this paradox.

We'll now descend from our philosophical soapbox and get down to basics. Let's expand on our definitions to explore some basic concepts of information architecture:

---

1 For a humorous perspective on the trickiness of the English language, see Bill Bryson's *The Mother Tongue: English and How It Got That Way* (New York: William Morrow, 1990).

Information

We use the term "information" to distinguish information architecture from data and knowledge management. Data is facts and figures. Relational databases are highly structured and produce specific answers to specific questions. Knowledge is the stuff in people's heads. Knowledge managers develop tools, processes, and incentives to encourage people to share that stuff. Information exists in the messy middle. With information systems, there's often no single "right" answer to a given question. We're concerned with information of all shapes and sizes: websites, documents, software applications, images, and more. We're also concerned with metadata: terms used to describe and represent content objects such as documents, people, processes, and organizations.

Structuring, organizing, and labeling

Structuring involves determining the appropriate levels of granularity[2] for the information "atoms" in your product or service, and deciding how to relate them to one another. Organizing involves grouping those components into meaningful and distinctive categories, creating the right contexts for users to understand the environment they are in and what they're looking at. Labeling means figuring out what to call those categories and the navigation structure elements that lead to them.

Finding and managing

Findability is a critical success factor for overall usability. If users can't find what they need through some combination of browsing, searching, and asking, then the system fails. But designing for the needs of users isn't enough. The organizations and people who manage information are important, too. An information architecture must balance the needs of users with the goals of the business. Efficient content management and clear policies and procedures are essential.

Art and science

Disciplines such as usability engineering and methodologies such as ethnography bring the rigor of the scientific method to the analysis of users' needs and information-seeking behaviors.

---

2 Granularity refers to the relative size or coarseness of information chunks. Varying levels of granularity might include journal issue, article, paragraph, and sentence.

We're increasingly able to study patterns of usage and subsequently make improvements to our websites. But the practice of information architecture will never be reduced to numbers; there's too much ambiguity and complexity. Information architects must rely on experience, intuition, and creativity. We must be willing to take risks and trust our intuition. This is the "art" of information architecture.

Just Because You Can't See It, Doesn't Mean It Isn't There

One of the challenges people have with information architecture is that they can't easily point to it. How many times have you heard someone say, "Boy, that website's information architecture is really terrific!" or, "I can't find anything in this app! Its information architecture sucks!" Our bet is, not many. But the fact that you can't readily *see* the information architecture in things doesn't mean it's not there. As de Saint-Exupéry said, sometimes what is essential is invisible to the eye.

To illustrate, think of the game of chess. Perhaps the image that comes to your mind is of a chessboard like the one shown in Figure 2-1, with beautifully sculpted wooden pieces, and a goblet of brandy sitting near a flickering fireplace. That beautiful chessboard is a common instantiation of the game we call chess. However, chess is more than that. You could argue that what makes chess "chess" is a set of information structures that relate to one another according to predefined rules.

To begin with, chess has a taxonomy of pieces that represent army units: pawns, rooks, bishops, knights, kings, and queens. In play, there are two sets ("armies") of such pieces: "black" and "white." These armies face each other in a field that consists of an eight-by-eight grid of alternating light- and dark-colored squares. This field—the chessboard—creates a context (a "place") for the battle to take place.

Figure 2-1. A chess board with pieces in the opening position (image: http://bit.ly/opening_chess_position)

The different types of pieces can move and interact in different ways in this board; there are lots of rules that determine how the armies can interact. Differences in the pieces' range, scope, and numbers determine their relative worth to each army (Table 2-1).

Table 2-1. The different types of chess pieces, including their relative values and starting amounts

Name	Amount per army	Relative value
Pawn	8	1
Knight	2	3
Bishop	2	3
Rook	2	5
Queen	1	9
King	1	—

(The king is invaluable: its capture ends the game.)

So think back to the beautiful wooden chess set. If chess can be reduced to these basic information structures, perhaps you're suspecting that the wooden pieces and board are somewhat superfluous and that you should be able to play chess with many different types of sets. You'd be correct: in fact, chess can be played in many different ways that do not involve carved wood—or any types of physical pieces—at all. For example, you may have heard of correspondence chess, which is played via postal mail using pen and paper (Figure 2-2).

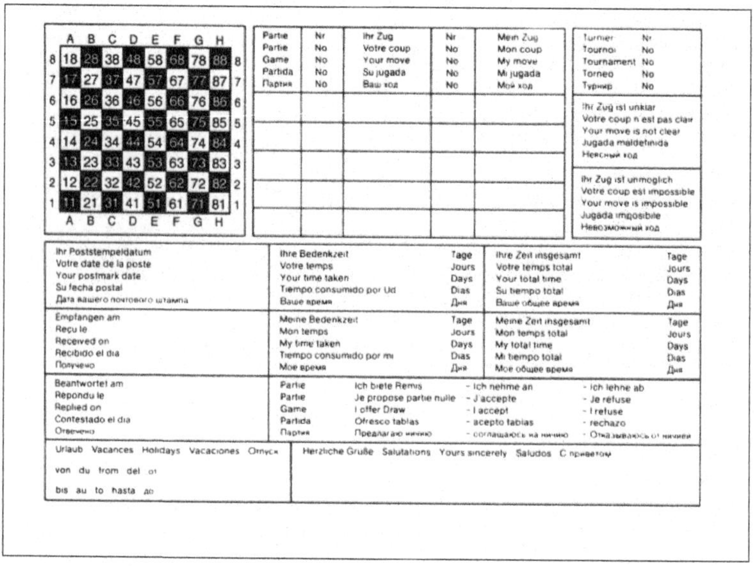

	Partie	Nr	Ihr Zug	Nr	Mein Zug		Turnier	Nr
	Partie	No	Votre coup	No	Mon coup		Tournoi	No
	Game	No	Your move	No	My move		Tournament	No
	Partida	No	Su jugada	No	Mi jugada		Torneo	No
	Партия	No	Ваш ход	No	Мой ход		Турнир	No

Board grid (columns A B C D E F G H):

```
  A  B  C  D  E  F  G  H
8 18 28 38 48 58 68 78 88 8
7 17 27 37 47 57 67 77 87 7
6 16 26 36 46 56 66 76 86 6
5 15 25 35 45 55 65 75 85 5
4 14 24 34 44 54 64 74 84 4
3 13 23 33 43 53 63 73 83 3
2 12 22 32 42 52 62 72 82 2
1 11 21 31 41 51 61 71 81 1
  A  B  C  D  E  F  G  H
```

Ihr Zug ist unklar
Votre coup n'est pas clair
Your move is not clear
Jugada maldefinida
Неясный ход

Ihr Zug ist unmöglich
Votre coup est impossible
Your move is impossible
Jugada imposible
Невозможный ход

Ihr Poststempeldatum	Ihre Bedenkzeit		Tage	Ihre Zeit insgesamt	Tage
Votre date de la poste	Votre temps		Jours	Votre temps total	Jours
Your postmark date	Your time taken		Days	Your total time	Days
Su fecha postal	Tiempo consumido por Ud		Días	Su tiempo total	Días
Дата вашего почтового штампа	Ваше время		Дни	Ваше общее время	Дни

Empfangen am	Meine Bedenkzeit		Tage	Meine Zeit insgesamt	Tage
Reçu le	Mon temps		Jours	Mon temps total	Jours
Received on	My time taken		Days	My total time	Days
Recibido el día	Tiempo consumido por mi		Días	Mi tiempo total	Días
Получено	Мое время		Дни	Мое общее время	Дни

Beantwortet am	Partie	Ich biete Remis	- Ich nehme an	- Ich lehne ab
Répondu le	Partie	Je propose partie nulle	- J'accepte	- Je refuse
Replied on	Game	I offer Draw	- I accept	- I refuse
Contestado el día	Partida	Ofresco tablas	- acepto tablas	- rechazo
Отвечено	Партия	Предлагаю ничью	- соглашаюсь на ничью	- Отказываюсь от ничьей

Urlaub Vacances Holidays Vacaciones Отпуск	Herzliche Grüße Salutations Yours sincerely Saludos С приветом
von du from del от	
bis au to hasta до	

Figure 2-2. Correspondence chess postcard (image: Schach Niggemann GFDL, http://www.gnu.org/copyleft/fdl.html, or CC-BY-SA–3.0, http://creativecommons.org/licenses/by-sa/3.0/, via Wikimedia Commons)

Or perhaps you're more familiar with chess as a video game, an example of which is shown in Figure 2-3. This variant is played on a computing device with the board and pieces rendered as pixels on a screen, with the game mechanics adjusted to conform to the device's user interface particularities.

Figure 2-3. Deep Green chess, played on an iPhone with a touchscreen interface

Chess can also be played in a computer terminal console, with the most minimally symbolic user interface imaginable (Figure 2-4).

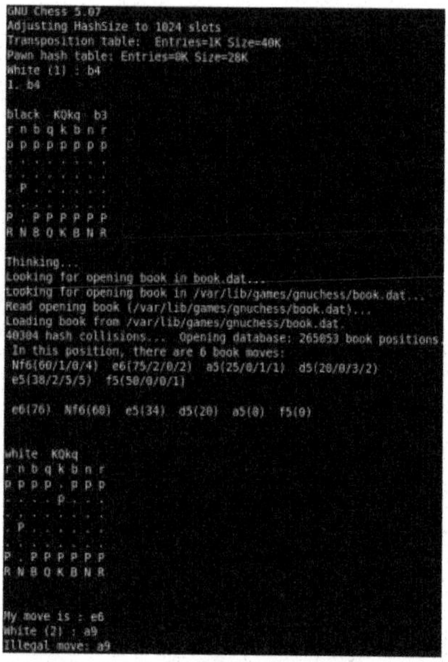

Figure 2-4. GNU Chess, played with a command-line interface

And of course, there are also countless variations of physical chess sets, ranging from our beautiful wooden set, to cheap "travel" sets with minimally rendered graphics on magnetic pieces (Figure 2-5), to the "Jewel Royale Chess Set" that is valued at almost $10 million.

These incarnations of chess are all physically very different from one another, yet they are all still chess. Why? Because they make possible and express the underlying information structures and rules of chess. Expressing and supporting these information structures is what *makes* all of these incarnations chess; their physical form and interaction mechanisms are merely matters of interaction or industrial design. In many ways, this abstract idea of chess is more "real" —but less tangible—than the physical (or virtual) chess sets that we interact with, because it is what makes chess different from other games.

Figure 2-5. Intense game of chess unfolding on a cheap magnetic travel set (image: http://bit.ly/magnetic_chess; cropped)

It's worth noting that nobody set out to explicitly create this "information architecture" of chess—the game, its piece types and rules, its lore, etc. have evolved over centuries. This is also true of the ways we've organized other information structures that afford understanding over time: it's only in retrospect that we can point to them and say, "that's a damned good information architecture!"

Toward a Damned Good Information Architecture

Users. Content. Context. You'll hear these three words again and again throughout this book. They form the basis of our model for practicing effective information architecture design. Underlying this model is a recognition that you can't design useful information architectures in a vacuum. An architect can't huddle in a dark room with a bunch of content, organize it, and emerge with a grand solution. It simply won't hold up against the light of day.

Websites, intranets, apps, and other information environments are not lifeless, static constructs. Rather, there is a dynamic, organic nature to both the information systems and the broader contexts in which they exist. This is not the old world of yellowing cards in a library card catalog. We're talking complex, adaptive systems with emergent qualities. We're talking rich streams of information flowing within and beyond the borders of departments, business units, institutions, and countries. We're talking messiness and mistakes, trial and error, survival of the fittest.

We use the concept of an "information ecology"[3] composed of users, content, and context to address the complex dependencies that exist in these information environments. And we draw upon our trusty Venn diagram (see Figure 2-6) to help people visualize and understand these relationships. The three circles illustrate the interdependent nature of users, content, and context within a complex, adaptive information ecology.

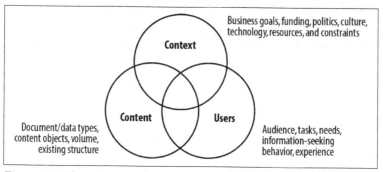

Figure 2-6. The infamous three circles of information architecture

In short, we need to understand the business goals behind the project and the resources available for design and implementation. We need to be aware of the nature and volume of content that exists today and how that might change a year from now, and we must learn about the needs and information-seeking behaviors of our major audiences.

---

3 For more about information ecologies, read *Information Ecology* by Thomas Davenport and Lawrence Prusak (Oxford: Oxford University Press, 1997) and *Information Ecologies* by Bonnie Nardi and Vicki O'Day (Cambridge, MA: MIT Press, 1999). Nardi and O'Day define an information ecology as "a system of people, practices, values, and technologies in a particular local environment."

Good information architecture design is informed by all three areas, and all three are moving targets. Users can vary in their attitude, demographics, psychographics, tasks and information needs, information-seeking behaviors, and more. Content can vary in quality, currency, authority, popularity, strategic value, cost, and more. And organizational context can vary based on mission, vision, goals, organizational politics, organizational culture, degree of centralization or autonomy, and more. The particular mix of variables differs from one information environment to another, and within the same environment it varies over time.

Even so, this is an oversimplified view of reality. Is it still useful? Absolutely. We've been using this model for 20 years. It's held up well in all sorts of environments, from global websites of Fortune 100 corporations to standalone intranet applications within small nonprofits. More importantly, we find these three circles incredibly helpful whenever we're confronted by a difficult question. After mouthing the trusty phrase "It depends"—as all smart practitioners of information architecture do—we develop our answer by deconstructing the question into three parts that coincide with our three circles. When asked what are the most important qualities that we should bring to the table, the answer becomes quite simple: some knowledge of users and their needs (which might come from exposure to human–computer interaction and a variety of other fields), content (think technical communication and journalism), and context (read a book on organizational psychology).

The three circles help with other tough questions, too, such as:

- What research and evaluation methods should we be familiar with?
- What kinds of people should be part of the team that designs the information architecture?
- What kinds of books and blogs should we read to keep up with the field and its practice?
- What should go into the IA strategy that we propose to a new prospect?

The answer to each starts with a balance among the three areas: users, content, and context.

Should technology have its own circle? Maybe. But we find that technology usually gets too much attention. Also, we increasingly find that much of what falls under the rubric of technology can be expressed within the "context" circle. After all, what technology brings to the table are new possibilities and constraints that give shape to the final product, and this is squarely within the realm of the context we're designing for.

Incidentally, we think it's important to have a good sense of humor about this stuff. Perhaps you've already figured this out. The work we do involves high levels of abstraction, ambiguity, and occasionally absurdity, and to some degree we're all still making it up as we go along.

If there's one thing that many years of information architecture consulting has taught us, it's that every situation is unique. We don't just mean that websites are different from intranets or that extranets should vary by industry. We mean that, like fingerprints and snowflakes, every information ecology is unique. The Toyota intranet is vastly different from that of Ford or GM. Fidelity, Vanguard, Schwab, and E*TRADE have each created unique online financial-service experiences. Despite all the copycatting, benchmarking, and definitions of industry best practices that have surged throughout the business world in recent years, each of these information systems has emerged as quite distinctive.

That's where our model comes in handy. It's an excellent tool for learning about the specific needs and opportunities presented by a particular project. Let's take a look at how each of our three circles contributes to the emergence of a totally unique information ecology.

Context

All digital design projects exist within a particular business or organizational context. Whether explicit or implicit, each organization has a mission, goals, strategy, staff, processes and procedures, physical and technology infrastructure, budget, and culture. This collective mix of capabilities, aspirations, and resources is unique to each organization.

Because of this, information architectures must be uniquely matched to their contexts. The vocabulary and structure of your websites and your apps is a major component of the evolving conversation between your business and your customers and employees. It influences how they think about your products and services. It tells them what to expect from you in the future. It invites or limits interaction between customers and employees. Your information architecture provides perhaps the most tangible snapshot of your organization's mission, vision, values, strategy, and culture. Do you really want that snapshot to look like that of your competitor?

The key to success is understanding and alignment. First, you need to understand the business context. What makes it unique? Where is the business today, and where does it want to be tomorrow? In many cases, you're dealing with tacit knowledge. It's not written down anywhere; it's in people's heads and has never been put into words. We'll discuss a variety of methods for extracting and organizing this understanding of context. Then, you need to find ways to align the information architecture with the goals, strategy, and culture of the business. We'll discuss the approaches and tools that enable this custom configuration.

As mentioned in Chapter 1, you also need to understand the contextual differences imposed by the channels that the user will be using to interact with your organization. Will they be experiencing your services primarily via apps on mobile phones, or via a website in a desktop-based browser? Both platforms have things they can do well, and things they can't. For example, smaller screens mean less space, which in turn implies shorter labels and navigation menus. Devices with small screens are also used at different times and places than those with larger screens. If your service will be used via more than one channel, you need to consider how these channels will overlap and interact with one another. All of these factors form part of the context that will shape your information architecture.

Content

We define "content" very broadly to include the documents, applications, services, schemas, and metadata that people need to use or find in your systems. To employ a technical term, it's the "stuff" that makes up your sites and apps. Many digital systems are heavily textual; among other things, the Web is a wonderful communication tool, and communication is built upon words and sentences trying to convey meaning. Of course, we also recognize it as a tool for tasks and transactions; a flexible technology platform that supports buying and selling, calculating and configuring, sorting and simulating.

But even the most task-oriented ecommerce website has "content" that customers must be able to find.

As you survey content across a variety of digital systems, the following facets will bubble to the surface as distinguishing factors of each information ecology:

Ownership

Who creates and owns the content? Is ownership centralized within a content authoring group or distributed among functional departments? How much content is licensed from external information vendors? How much is produced by the users themselves? The answers to these questions play a huge role in influencing the level of control you have over all the other dimensions.

Format

Websites and intranets have become the unifying means of access to all digital formats within many organizations. Databases, product catalogs, discussion archives, technical reports in MS Word, annual reports in PDF, office supply purchasing applications, and video clips of the CEO are just a few of the types of documents, databases, and applications you'll find on a given site.

Structure

All documents are not created equal. An important memo may be fewer than 100 words. A technical manual may be more than 1,000 pages. Some information systems are built around the document paradigm, with the fully integrated document as the smallest discrete unit. Other systems take a content component or digital asset approach, leveraging some form of structural markup (e.g., XML or JSON) to allow management and access at a finer level of granularity.

Metadata

To what extent has metadata that describes the content and objects within your system already been created? Have documents been tagged manually or automatically? What's the level of quality and consistency? Is there a controlled vocabulary in place, or have users been allowed to tag the content? These factors determine the extent to which you're starting from scratch with respect to both information retrieval and content management.

Volume

How much content are we talking about? A hundred applications? A thousand pages? A million documents? How big is the system?

Dynamism

What is the rate of growth or turnover? How much new content will be added next year? And how quickly will it go stale?

All of these dimensions make for a unique mix of content and applications, which in turn suggests the need for a customized information architecture.

Users

The most important thing to know about users is that when we are talking about "users" we are talking about *people*. These are human beings with desires, needs, concerns, and foibles—just like you and us. We use the word "users" as shorthand to mean "the people who will use your information environment."

When we worked on the first corporate website for Borders Books & Music, back in the mid-1990s before Amazon became a household name, we learned a lot about how customer research and analysis was applied to the design and architecture of physical bookstores.

Borders had a clear understanding of how the demographics, aesthetic preferences, and purchasing behaviors of its customers differed from those of its main competitor, Barnes & Noble. It was no mistake that the physical layout and the selection of books differed significantly between these two stores, even within the same town. They were different by design. And that difference was built upon an understanding of their unique customer or market segments.

Differences in customer preferences and behaviors within the physical world translate into different information needs and information-seeking behaviors in the context of websites and apps. For example, senior executives may need to find a few good documents on a particular topic very quickly. Research analysts may need to find all the relevant documents and may be willing to spend several hours on the hunt. Managers may have a high level of industry knowledge but low navigation and searching proficiency. Teenagers may be new to the subject area but skilled in handling a search engine.

Do you know who's using your system? Do you know how they're using it? And perhaps most importantly, do you know what information they want from your systems? These are not questions you can answer in brainstorming meetings or focus groups. As our friend and fellow information architect Chris Farnum likes to say, you need to get out there in the real world and study your "users in the mist."

Recap

Let's recap what we've learned in this chapter:

- There's more than one way to define information architecture, and that's OK.

- Information architecture is not something you can easily point to; it is mostly abstract and exists below the surface, in the deep semantic structures of products and services. This is OK, too!

- Our model for practicing effective information architecture design considers three things: users, context, and content.

- The particular mix of variables changes not just from one information environment to another, but also for a single information environment over time.

As we mentioned in the introduction to Part I, IA is focused on making information environments *findable* and *understandable*. These are related, but different, objectives. In the next chapter, we'll look more closely at designing for findability. Onward!

CHAPTER 3

Design for Finding

*I've had thank-you emails from people whose lives have
been saved by information on a medical website or who
have found the love of their life on a dating website.*
—*Tim Berners-Lee*

In this chapter, we'll cover:

- Different models for how people look for information
- People's information-seeking behaviors
- How we learn about these behaviors

Information architecture is not restricted to taxonomies, search
engines, and the other things that help users find stuff in an information environment. Information architecture starts with people
and the reason they come to your site or use your app: they have an
information need.

This is a truism, but there's more to it than meets the eye. Information needs can vary widely, and each type of information need
causes people to exhibit specific information-seeking behaviors. It's
important that you understand those needs and behaviors, and
shape your designs to correspond accordingly. There is no goal
more important to designing information architecture than to satisfy peoples' needs.

For example, if your information environment is a web-based staff
directory, looking up a staff member's phone number is probably a
very common information need among your users; in fact, this type

of need may describe most of your users' finding sessions. When confronted by such a need, people will likely perform a search, and you'd be wise to make sure your information architecture supports searching by name. On the other hand, if your product helps non-savvy investors learn about and select mutual funds for investment, your users may satisfy this need through some other means. They might benefit from a step-by-step tutorial, or they may wish to wander by browsing through categories.

Seeking something you know is there, like your colleague's phone number, is quite a different information need than learning about a topic like small-cap mutual funds, and your system's information architecture should be designed with those differences in mind. These kinds of needs lead to different information-seeking behaviors; not surprisingly, searching for something you know exists involves a very different behavior than browsing for the unknown. Distinguishing between these needs and behaviors and determining which are your users' highest priorities is an extremely valuable pursuit—it helps you determine where to invest your efforts and resources as you design your architecture.

The "Too-Simple" Information Model

There are different models of what happens when people look for information. Modeling needs and behaviors forces us to ask useful questions about what kind of information users want, how much information is enough, and how they actually interact with the architecture.

Unfortunately, "too simple" is the most common information model, and it's also the most problematic. It looks something like Figure 3-1.

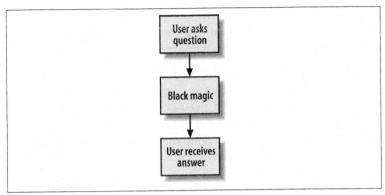

Figure 3-1. The "too-simple" model of information needs

Or, expressed as a simple algorithm:

1. User asks a question.
2. Something happens (i.e., searching or browsing).
3. User receives the answer.
4. Fin.

Input, output, end of story. This is a very mechanistic and ultimately dehumanizing model for how people find and use information. In fact, in this model, the user, like the site or app itself, is just another system—predictable in behavior, rational in motivation.

Why do we have a problem with this "too-simple" model? Because it rarely happens this way. There are exceptions—for example, when people know what they're looking for, as in the staff directory scenario. Here, users have a question for which there is a right answer, they know where to find the answer, they know how to state the question, and they know how to use the system to do so.

But people don't always know exactly what they want. Have you ever visited a website just to poke around? By exploring the site, you're trying to find information of a sort; you just don't know exactly what you're looking for. Even when you do, you may not have the language to express it: is it "skin cancer," or "melanoma"?

People often complete their efforts at finding information in a state of partial satisfaction or outright frustration. Example: "I was able to find information on synchronizing my iPhone, but nothing specific on syncing to Lotus Notes." Or, during the process of finding, they may learn new information that changes what they're looking for altogether. Example: "I realized that a Roth IRA is ideal for me, even though when I started I was trying to learn about retirement plans."

We also dislike the "too-simple" model because it narrowly focuses on what happens while the user is interacting with the information architecture. The information need's context—all the related stuff that happens before and after the user ever touches the keyboard—gets left out. It also assumes an ignorant user who brings little, if any, prior knowledge to the table. So, the model essentially ignores any context for this scenario.

Finally, by oversimplifying, this model cedes so many great opportunities to understand what goes on in users' heads and observe the richness of what happens during their interactions with an information architecture.

This model is dangerous because it's built upon a misconception: that finding information is a straightforward problem that can be addressed by a simple, algorithmic approach. After all, we've solved the challenge of retrieving data—which, of course, is facts and figures—with database technologies such as SQL. So, the thinking goes, let's treat the abstract ideas and concepts embedded in our semistructured textual documents the same way.

This attitude has led to the wasting of many millions of dollars on search engine software and other technological panaceas that would indeed work if this assumption were true. Many user-centered design techniques carry this misconception forward, assuming that the process of finding is simple enough to be easily measured in a quantifiable way. So we think we can measure the experience of finding by how long it takes, or how many mouse clicks it takes, or how many viewed pages it takes to find the "right" answer, when often there *is* no right answer.

OK, enough complaining about this model. Let's take a closer look at information needs and seeking behaviors so that we can build better models.

Information Needs

When someone visits a website to find something, what does she really want? In the "too-simple" model, she wants the "right answer" to her question. Indeed, right answers are found from searching databases, which store facts and figures and answer questions that really do have right answers, such as "What is the population of San Marino?" To many of us, database searching is the most familiar model of searching.

But digital systems store much more than highly structured data. Not surprisingly, text is the most common type of data stored, and text itself is made up of ambiguous, messy ideas and concepts. When we go to a website for advice on retirement investing, to learn about restaurants in Mendocino County, or to find out what's happening with the Manchester United football team, we are essentially looking for ideas and concepts that inform us and help us make decisions. The answer, if there is one, is an ambiguous moving target.

So back to the question: what do people want? Let's use the metaphor of fishing to get at the answer:

The perfect catch
> Sometimes users really are looking for the right answer. Let's think of that as fishing with a pole, hoping to hook that ideal fish. What is the population of San Marino? You go to Wikipedia or some other useful site that's jam-packed with data, and you hook in that number (it's 32,576, by the way, according to the latest estimate). And you're done, just as the "too-simple" model would have it.

Lobster trapping
> What about the times you're looking for more than just a single answer? Let's say you're hoping to find out about good bed-and-breakfast inns in Stratford, Ontario. Or you want to learn something about Lewis and Clark's journey of exploration. Or you need to get a sense of what sort of financial plans can help you save for retirement. You don't really know much about what you're looking for, and aren't ready to commit to retrieving anything more than just a few useful items, or suggestions of where to learn more. You're not hoping to hook the perfect fish, because you wouldn't know it if you caught it. Instead, you're setting out the equivalent of a lobster trap—you hope that whatever ambles in will be useful, and if it is, that's good enough. Perhaps it's a few candidate restaurants that you'll investigate further by calling and checking their availability and features. Or maybe it's a motley assemblage of Lewis and Clark stuff,

ranging from book reviews to a digital version of Clark's diary to information about Lewis & Clark College in Oregon. You might be happy with a few of these items, and toss out the rest.

Indiscriminate driftnetting

Then there are times when you want to leave no stone unturned in your search for information on a topic. You may be doing research for a doctoral thesis, or performing competitive intelligence analysis, or learning about the medical condition affecting a close friend, or, heck, ego surfing. In these cases, you want to catch every fish in the sea, so you cast your driftnets and drag up everything you can.

I've seen you before, Moby Dick...

There's some information that you'd prefer to never lose track of, so you'll tag it so you can find it again. Thanks to social bookmarking and collection services like Pinterest, it's possible to toss a fish back in the sea with the expectation of finding it again.

This fishing metaphor is helpful because it illustrates four common information needs. When you're hoping to make the perfect catch, you usually know what you're looking for, what to call it, and where you'll find it—this is called *known-item* seeking. An example is when you search the staff directory to find a colleague's phone number.

When you're hoping to find a few useful items in your traps, you're doing something called *exploratory seeking*. In this case, you're not exactly sure what you're looking for. In fact, whether you realize it or not, you're looking to learn something from the process of searching and browsing. For example, a user may go to his employer's human resources site to learn something about retirement plans that the company offers. In the process, he may encounter some basic information on specific types of plans, and then change his search to learning more about such plans. As he learns more about these plans, he shifts his search again to learning whether a simple or more complex plan is best for him. Exploratory seeking is typically open ended; there is no clear expectation of a "right" answer, nor does the user necessarily know how to articulate what exactly he is looking for. He is happy to retrieve a few good results, and use them as a springboard for the next iteration of the search. It's not always possible to definitively determine when exploratory searching is finished.

When you want everything, you're performing *exhaustive research*. You're looking for everything available on a particular topic, hoping to leave no stone unturned. In this case, the user often has many ways to express what she's looking for, and may have the patience to construct her search using all those varied terms. For example, someone who is trying to learn more about a friend's medical condition might execute multiple searches for "AIDS," "HIV," "acquired immuno-deficiency syndrome," and so forth. Again, there isn't necessarily a "right" answer. And in this case, the user must be patient enough to wade through more results than are typical with other information needs.

Finally, our failing memories and busy schedules continually force us to engage in *refinding* pieces of useful information that we've happened upon before. For example, while you're at work, you might surf for a few minutes and stumble on a great but long explanation of Django Reinhardt's guitar technique. Naturally, you won't read it now and risk losing your job. You'll refind it later instead, or use a "read later" service such as Instapaper to return to it at a more convenient time.

Figure 3-2 illustrates these four different types of information needs. They are by no means the only ones, but many of your users' needs will fall into these categories.

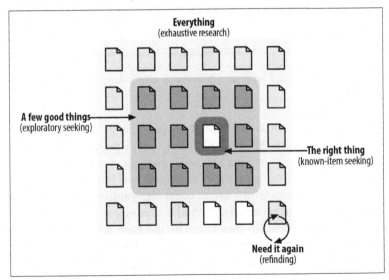

Figure 3-2. Four common information needs

Information-Seeking Behaviors

How do website users find information? They enter queries in search systems, browse from link to link, and ask humans for help (through email, chat interfaces, etc.). *Searching*, *browsing*, and *asking* are all methods for finding, and these are the basic building blocks of information-seeking behavior.

There are two other major aspects to seeking behaviors: *integration* and *iteration*. We often integrate searching, browsing, and asking in the same finding session. Figure 3-3 shows how you might search your corporate intranet for guidelines on traveling abroad. You might first browse your way through the intranet portal to the HR site, browse the policies area, and then search for the policy that includes the string "international travel." If you still didn't get your question answered, you might send an email to Biff, the person responsible for that policy, to ask exactly what your per diem will be while spending the week in Timbuktu. Let's hope your intranet's information architecture was designed to support such integration!

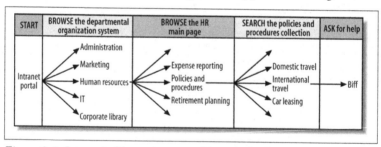

Figure 3-3. Integrated browsing, searching, and asking over many iterations

Figure 3-3 also illustrates the iteration you may go through during one finding session. After all, we don't always get things right the first time. And our information needs may change along the way, causing us to try new approaches with each new iteration. So, while you may have begun with a broad quest for "guidelines on traveling abroad," you might be satisfied to find something as specific as "recommended per diem in Timbuktu" by the time you're done. Each iteration of searching, browsing, asking, and interacting with content can greatly impact what it is we're seeking.

These different components of information-seeking behaviors come together in complex models, such as the "berry-picking" model developed by Marcia Bates of the University of Southern California. [1] In this model (shown in Figure 3-4), users start with an information need, formulate an information request (a query), and then move iteratively through an information system along potentially complex paths, picking bits of information ("berries") along the way. In the process, they modify their information requests as they learn more about what they need and what information is available from the system.

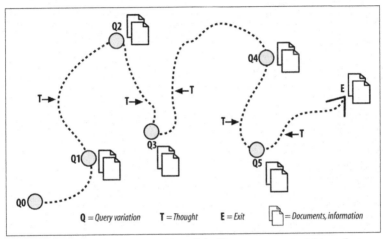

Figure 3-4. The "berry-picking" model of how users move through an information system

The berry-picking diagram looks messy—much more so than the "too-simple" model. It should; that's the way our minds often work. After all, we're not automatons.

If the berry-picking model is common to your users, you'll want to look for ways to support moving easily from search to browse and back again. Amazon.com provides one such integrated approach to consider: you can search within the categories you find through browsing, and you can browse through categories that you find by searching, as shown in Figure 3-5.

---

1 Bates's seminal paper, *"The Design of Browsing and Berrypicking Techniques for the Online Search Interface"* (*http://bit.ly/berrypicking*) (*Online Review* 13:5, 1989, 407–425), is required reading for every information architect. She later expanded these ideas into a more comprehensive framework: see "Toward an Integrated Model of Information Seeking and Searching" (*New Review of Information Behaviour Research* 3, 2002, 1–15).

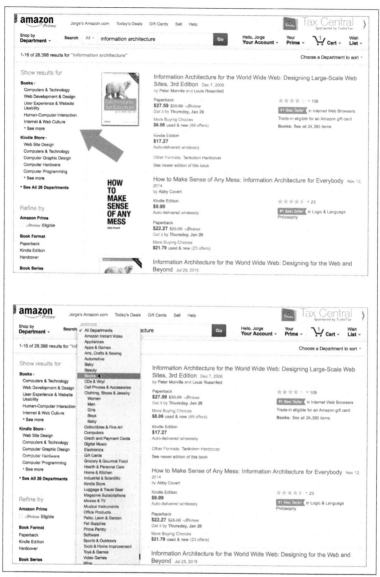

Figure 3-5. Browsing and searching are tightly integrated on Amazon.com

Another useful model is the "pearl-growing" approach. Users start with one or a few good documents that are exactly what they need. They want to get "more like this one." To meet this need, Google and many other search engines allow users to do just that: Google provides a command called "Similar pages" next to each search result. A similar approach is to allow users to link from a "good" document to documents indexed with the same keywords. In sites that contain scientific papers and other documents that are heavy with citations, you can find other papers that share many of the same citations as yours or that have been co-cited with the one you like. Delicious and Flickr are examples of sites that allow users to navigate to items that share something in common—in this case, the same user-supplied tags. All of these architectural approaches help us find "more like this one."

Corporate websites and intranets often utilize a "two-step" model. Confronted with a site consisting of links to perhaps hundreds of departmental subsites, users first need to know where to look for the information they need. They might search or browse through a directory until they find a good candidate or two, and then perform the second step: looking for information within those subsites. Their seeking behaviors may be radically different for each of these two steps; certainly, the information architectures typical of portals are usually nothing like those of departmental subsites.

Learning About Information Needs and Information-Seeking Behaviors

How can we learn about users' information needs and seeking behaviors? There are a variety of user research methods to consider—too many to cover in detail here—so we'll recommend a pair of our favorites: search analytics and contextual inquiry. Search analytics[2] involves reviewing the most common search queries on your site (usually stored in your search engine's logfiles) as a way to diagnose problems with search performance, metadata, navigation, and content. Search analytics provides a sense of what users commonly seek, and can help inform your understanding of their information needs and seeking behaviors (and it's handy in other ways, too, such as developing task-analysis exercises).

While search analytics is based on a high volume of real user data, it doesn't provide an opportunity to interact with users and learn more

---

2 For more on search analytics, read Lou's *Search Analytics for Your Site: Conversations with Your Customers* (Brooklyn, NY: Rosenfeld Media, 2011).

about their needs directly. Contextual inquiry,[3] a user research method with roots in ethnography, is a great complement to search analytics because it allows you to observe how users interact with information in their "natural" settings and, in that context, ask them why they're doing what they're doing.

Other user research methods you might look to are task analysis, surveys, and, with great care, focus groups. Ultimately, you should consider any method that might expose you to users' direct statements of their own needs, and when you can, use a combination of methods to cover as many bases as possible.

Finally, remember that your goal is to do your best to learn about your users' major information needs and likely information-seeking behaviors. A better understanding of what users actually want from your system will, naturally, help you determine and prioritize which architectural components to build, which makes your job much simpler (especially considering how many ways a particular information architecture could be designed). You'll also have great user data to help counterbalance the other drivers that too often influence design, such as budget, time, politics, entrenched technologies, and designers' personal preferences.

Recap

Let's recap what we've learned in this chapter:

- IA starts with people and the reason they use your product or service: they have an information need.
- There are different models of what happens when people look for information.
- The most simple of these is problematic, because it doesn't accurately represent what actually happens when people have an information need.
- Information needs are like fishing: sometimes people know exactly what they're looking for, but often they're casting a wider net.

---

3 For more on contextual inquiry, read Hugh Beyer and Karen Holtzblatt's *Contextual Design: Defining Customer-Centered Systems* (Burlington, MA: Morgan Kaufmann, 1997).

- People act on these information needs through various information-seeking behaviors.
- There are various research methods that allow us to learn about these behaviors.

Now that we've learned about how people find information, let's move on to IA's second big goal: helping people *understand* information.

CHAPTER 4

Design for Understanding

A frame is a way of creating a little world round something...Is there anything in a work that is not frame, actually?
—Brian Eno

In this chapter, we'll cover:

- How people make sense of where they are and what they can do there
- Placemaking in the physical world and in information environments
- Basic organizing principles to make information environments more understandable

We only understand things in relationship to something else. The frame around a painting changes how we perceive it, and the place the frame is hanging in changes it even more: we understand an image displayed in New York's Museum of Modern Art differently than one hanging in a shared bathroom in a ratty hotel. Context matters.

When designing an information architecture, we are engaging in a new type of placemaking: one that alters how we perceive and understand information. As with (building) architects, information architects are concerned with creating environments that are understandable and usable by human beings, and which can grow and adapt over time to meet the needs of users and their organizations.

In Chapter 3, we saw how the lens of information architecture can help designers make stuff easier to find by setting it in structures made of information. Now we'll explore how these structures can make stuff more understandable by shaping the context that we perceive it in.

A Sense of Place

You get out of bed. You stumble clumsily to the bathroom, use the toilet, then walk to the kitchen to brew a cup of coffee and toast some bread. It's not even 6:00 a.m. yet, and you have already traversed three distinct places with different uses and configurations: bedroom, bathroom, and kitchen.

Humans—perceptive, self-ambulatory organisms that we are—have a complex, symbiotic relationship with our surroundings. We have senses that allow us to detect where we are at any given moment, and to move around from place to place. We can also change these places to suit our needs. The differences between places play a critical role in how we understand one another and the things we can (or can't) do in each of those places: this is where we get food, this is where we sleep, this is where we defecate. As a result, our ability to perceive and make places has been very important in our evolution as a species, and is deeply ingrained in who we are. Over time, our ability to set apart and reconfigure places for special use has evolved along with us: we have gone from "this is the clearing where we worship" to building Chartres Cathedral in a relatively short amount of time (Figure 4-1).

We bring this awareness of place—and the placemaking drive—to information environments as well. When we talk about digital media, we use metaphors that betray a sense of place: we "go" online, "visit" a website, "browse" Amazon.com. Increasingly, these environments are also taking over many of the functions we've traditionally associated with physical places: we meet with our friends in WhatsApp, pay our bills in our bank's website, learn in Khan Academy. As with physical places, we experience them as contexts that differ from one another, supporting different needs.

Figure 4-1. Chartres Cathedral is a place that communicates at more than one level: at a base level, it appeals to our animal nature: "here is shelter from the elements"; at a higher level, it communicates "place of worship"; at an even higher level, it tells stories about the Christian religion (images: Wikipedia, http://bit.ly/chartres_cathedral and http://bit.ly/Chartres_central_tympanum)

The Architecture of (Real-World) Places

We go from one place to another in our day-to-day lives without paying too much attention to where we are: we subconsciously know when we're in the bedroom, and that it is a place for resting, and we know when we're in the kitchen, and that it is a place for nourishing. The kitchen has a refrigerator, sink, stovetop, and counter, set in a particular configuration,[1] while the bedroom has a bed and dresser in a configuration specific to it. Our senses and nervous systems pick up environmental cues that let us know the difference between one and the other.[2]

The world outside our home is also made up of a variety of different places, with configurations and signs of their own that give us clues to their use. Churches are different from banks, which are different from police stations, which are different from fast food restaurants, and so on. Over time, cultural convention and patterns of use have led to the evolution of these spaces, objects, and forms into the structures we recognize today. The differences between them make it possible for us to navigate and make sense of the world around us;

---

1 See "Language + Meaning + User Experience Architecture" (*http://bit.ly/lang_mean ing_ux*) by Andy Fitzgerald.

2 To become more aware of these differences, try serving your family dinner in the bathroom one evening.

we learn them when we are very young, and they become second nature.

In the "real" world, the discipline of (building) architecture has advanced and guided this cultural evolution of placemaking forms. Working from historical models, architects—both trained and untrained—adapt building and urban models that work well to new contexts and uses as required by the needs of society at a particular moment in time. Architects must make sure that a bank's building functions well as a bank. This means they must accommodate both the things that all buildings must have in common to make them usable by human beings (e.g., ceilings with enough height clearance to allow people to walk around) and those that are specific to banks and which make them different from other building types (e.g., having a large, secure vault in the middle of the space).[3]

Places Made of Information

We also experience information environments as types of places. When you visit a bank's website and peruse its navigation structures, headlines, section headings, images, and other information elements, your senses and nervous system are picking up semantic cues that tell you that you are now "in a bank." You would be hard-pressed to confuse the bank's site with that of a teaching hospital; just as you can tell the difference between a bank and a hospital in the real world by picking up on features of their respective physical environments, you can tell the difference between a bank's website and a hospital's website by picking up on semantic elements of their user interfaces (Figure 4-2). You understand the information presented in the site differently because you perceive it as "a bank."

---

3 It's worth noting that architects design for both the reality and the perception of security. The structure of a bank physically protects the safe, but there are additional elements (e.g., video cameras) that protect against theft. There's a language of security that maps across physical and digital places.

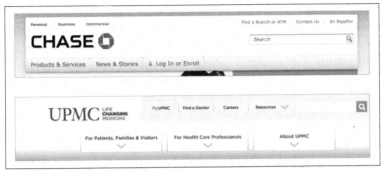

Figure 4-2. Banks and hospitals serve different information needs; their website navigation structures highlight the differences between them, and you understand the information they present in the context of the roles and functions these organizations serve in society

It's worth noting that because banks are also places in the real world, and because their information needs tend to be transactional, we think of their information environments as more place-like than we would a collection of recipes, as shown in Figure 4-3, which we perceive as being more analogous to a book or magazine.

Figure 4-3. The content-centric "How to Cook Everything" iPad app feels more like a recipe book than like a place

Some information environments exist primarily to allow people to interact and socialize with one another. Facebook, for example, serves to bring together people who already know one another in an information environment where they can share pictures/videos/stories, play games, chat in real time, and more. We perceive these social information environments as places as well. Like their real-world counterparts, they also offer places within places—subenvironments—for groups of people to congregate around shared interests that may not be of interest to everyone else. For example, there is a Facebook group for people who are interested in information architecture (Figure 4-4).

Figure 4-4. The Information Architects Facebook group

Building architecture aims to produce physical environments that can serve and communicate their social functions effectively, and information architecture aims to do the same for information environments. The main difference is that instead of defining compositions of forms, spaces, and objects such as walls, roofs, and furniture, information architecture defines compositions of semantic elements such as navigation labels, section headings, and keywords, and produces the design principles, goals, and guidelines that capture the intended feeling of the place (e.g., is this a serious, solitary place, or a fun, social space?).

Organizing Principles

Architects employ a variety of time-tested organizing principles to give physical environments structure and narrative. Information environments, too, have organizing principles that help bring coherence and structure to the whole.

One important difference between information architecture and building architecture is that the products of the latter are exclusive instances of a particular design in space and time. There is only one Guggenheim Museum like the one Frank Gehry designed for Bilbao, and although it is experienced quite differently by different people (e.g., children, people in wheelchairs, blind people), its structure and other formal elements are unique to it, as is its relationship with its context.

Information environments, on the other hand, can be manifested in various different ways. For example, a website can look and feel very differently when accessed using a desktop browser with a mouse and a large screen than when it is accessed on the four-inch touchscreen of a mobile phone. However, navigation and structural elements such as section headers tend to use the same terminology in both cases.

As a result, the semantic structures that information architecture produces are more abstract than the products of other design disciplines. Coherence between different instances of the architecture is achieved by consistent use of language, and by establishing a particular relationship, or order, between the linguistic elements that comprise it.

Structure and Order

The hierarchy and order of elements in an information architecture infuse the resulting products with meaning and a sense of place. It is an important part of what makes them different from other products or services in the same industry.

In buildings, hierarchy and order are conveyed using various compositional and structural patterns that have evolved over time. For example, building entrances are often highlighted with porticos that serve as visual indicators pointing to the way in (Figure 4-5). Changes in the roof, as well as the deep shadows and colonnades that characterize porticos, serve as signs that say to people, "this opening is more important than others in the skin of this building."

Figure 4-5. Buildings using common patterns to let users know where their entrances are (images: http://bit.ly/greek_nat_archaeological, http://bit.ly/building_front, http://bit.ly/walker_art_gallery, http:// bit.ly/capitol_high_court)

The semantic structures in an information architecture also have hierarchies that indicate the relative importance of individual components within the whole. For example, navigation structures for large-scale websites or content-rich apps usually have "top-level" links that are limited to the highest-level elements in a hierarchical structure. (When discussing these structures conceptually, we often render them in diagrams such as sitemaps.) This first-level order plays a large role in defining the conceptual boundaries and overall perceived "form" of the information environment, much as the primary structural supports of a building tend to define its physical form, use, and adaptability over time.

Another common ordering principle in buildings is *rhythm*, usually the result of patterns evident in the structural grid, skin ornamentation, or both. These patterns can add interest, dynamism, and scale, and help smooth the transition between the street and the interior of the building. Rhythms and patterns are also important ordering principles in information environments, which change the way we perceive information. For example, how search results are presented can suggest different "beats," with some environments requiring denser patterns than others (Figure 4-6).

We also experience a strong sense of rhythm in information environments that show a constant feed or stream of similar information nuggets, such as Twitter and Flipboard (shown in Figure 4-7). This sense of rhythm is not just the result of the interaction design of these products, but a manifestation of architectural decisions that affect how they are experienced across various different platforms.

Figure 4-6. When you "choose a department to sort," the rhythm of Amazon's search results changes

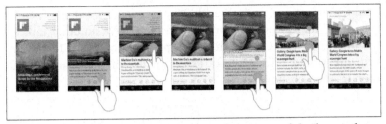

Figure 4-7. Flipboard users experience a clear sense of rhythm as they flip through stories with their finger, one at a time; in this example, we show the iPhone app, but this is true in the other systems in which Flipboard is available as well

Typologies

Earlier in this chapter, we talked about how different building types have evolved in order to serve the needs of the institutions that erect them. For example, today most bank branches—even those from competing firms—are more similar to than different from one another.

These building types have changed and adapted over time. Consider a classic building type called the *basilica*, shown in Figure 4-8. This type, which consists of a rectangular building with a central nave and two aisles on its sides, was initially used for conducting legal matters during the Roman era. Over time, the basilica form was adopted for use in Christian religious buildings, and many churches are still based on it today. As a result, when they encounter a building with the form of a basilica, many Westerners think of it as a place of worship. They know how they are supposed to interact with the place, given that they have done so in similar places many times in the past.

Digital information environments are much newer than buildings, but they, too, have started to evolve typologies. The information structures that underlie bank websites, for example, tend to be similar to those of competing banks. The same is true for airlines, universities, hospitals, newspapers, online stores, and more.

Having abstract, generalized types of information environments is useful for various reasons. First, it serves as shorthand to communicate to users what type of place they are in. Much like when we enter a basilica-type building we think, "church," when we enter a site that has navigation elements with labels like "Banking," "Loans and

Credit," "Investing," and "Wealth Management," we think "bank." Even if we didn't know the brand, and there were no other indicators that this was a bank, the mere presence of this information structure would offer clues as to the nature of the business that operates the website (Figure 4-9).

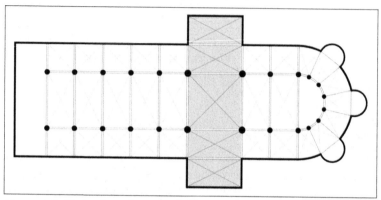

Figure 4-8. Floor plan of a typical Christian basilica form, with a transept added (image: Wikipedia, http://bit.ly/transept_arm)

Second, it makes it easier for users to understand and navigate the environment. If you're designing a bank's website today, it will probably not be the first such site your users will have encountered. They will bring to the interaction learned behaviors and expectations of how such an information environment should work, and where they can find the information they are looking for. For organizations operating in a space characterized by common types, such as banks, the understandability and ease of use of your final product will be greatly affected by how closely it hews to the norm.

Finally, having a standard structure to work against makes it easier to differentiate an information environment from those of competitors, as shown in Figure 4-10. This may sound contradictory, but when the overall structure is similar for many organizations in the space, small differences—such as the use of particular words or a different tone—help them stand out. These differences can help define the brand of the organization (as long as they don't go too far afield and "lose" the user).

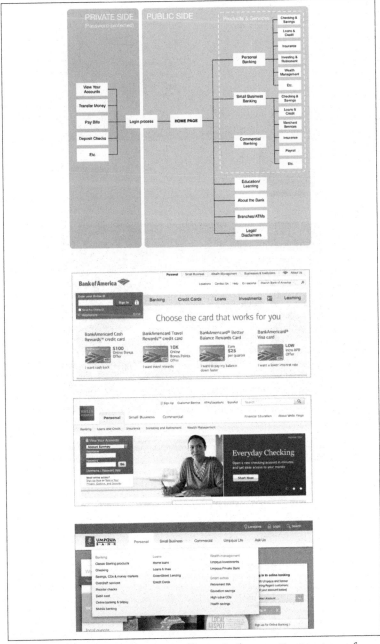

Figure 4-9. A sitemap illustrating the typical semantic structure of bank websites, along with screenshots from three banks that show variants of the typology

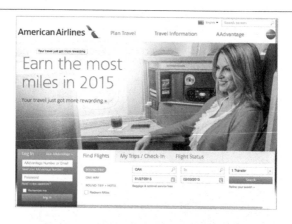

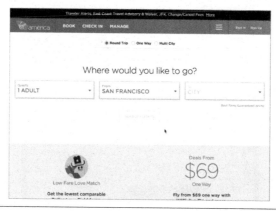

Figure 4-10. Three airline websites with slight structural differences that help set them apart; all three keep enough of the "airline" typology to avoid confusing users

Modularity and Extensibility

Most information environments are dynamic and ephemeral. Driven by changing business needs, popular taste, and new technologies and techniques, they are subject to constant change. However, not all parts of an information environment change at the same rate. For example, a website's visual design may change considerably over a span of five years, while its underlying information structures remain relatively stable.

In his book *How Buildings Learn: What Happens After They're Built*, Stewart Brand explains that buildings are composed of six layers (the "six S's"), which change at different rates over time (Figure 4-11). In order of slowest to fastest, they are:

Site
> The geographical setting of the building; it changes the slowest ("Site is eternal," says Frank Duffy, who originated this concept of shearing layers)

Structure
> The skeleton that holds up the building, including the foundation, columns, slabs, and other support elements

Skin
> The exterior surface of the building

Services
> The "working guts" of the building (electrical systems, heating, ventilation, air conditioning, plumbing, etc.)

Space plan
> The internal layout of the building, including partitions and doors between spaces

Stuff
> Furnishings, appliances, day-to-day objects, and the like; these change the fastest, sometimes on a month-to-month basis

So, while the furniture and internal partitions of a building may change relatively frequently, depending on its use, the slower-changing layers such as structure and skin tend to stick around for much longer. A well-designed building can accommodate many different uses over a long span of time. Often, the possible new uses of a building are dictated by the relatively unchanging layers in the system, such as the support structure.

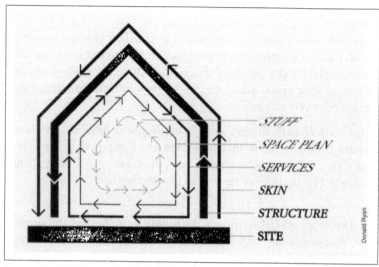

Figure 4-11. Stewart Brand's "shearing layers of change"

Information environments, too, are composed of different layers that change at different rates over time. While the page layouts, visual design, and interaction mechanisms of websites can change to reflect popular styles, their semantic structures tend to remain relatively stable. Information architecture is primarily focused on defining these semantic structures, which tend to be relatively long lived (Figure 4-12). Users of these systems become used to their semantic structures, and can become disoriented if they change too abruptly.

Figure 4-12. The primary navigation structure of FedEx's website in 2005 and 2015—the newer version is greatly simplified and more user friendly, but the fundamental structure is still recognizable

Given the dynamism of digital information environments, graceful adaptability and extensibility are even more important for information architecture than for building architecture. Any one information architecture can be placed in a continuum that ranges from "very flexible" to "very brittle." While you would expect that "very flexible" would be the ideal, this is not often the case: suppleness in information architecture usually invites the use of ambiguous language, which is not conducive to clear communication. The ideal is somewhere in the middle, where the environment can accommodate change but is also clear and crisp in its objectives and affordances.

One way to achieve this balance is by setting off parts of the environment that have different rates of change, and making them obviously separate, but related, parts of the whole. If the overall structure can accommodate many of these subenvironments in an obvious way, the whole becomes more flexible and open to change (Figure 4-13).

Figure 4-13. Google has a variety of subsites, each with its own subdomain and identity—this allows it the flexibility to create new products and services with little obvious impact on the whole

The Happiest Place(s) on Earth

As with the design of physical places, information architecture aims to bring into balance the needs of the user (who wants to be able to find and understand information in a comfortable, familiar setting)

with those of the organization that owns the environment (which usually has business objectives to meet, such as a certain sales target) and those of society as a whole. When the right balance is struck, the result is coherence and understandability in products and services across the organization, from websites to the wayfinding systems of physical environments.

A carefully designed organizational structure can help users understand new and unfamiliar environments. A good illustration of this principle is Disneyland, the first theme park (a new concept in 1955, when Disneyland opened). In its earliest incarnations, the design for the park consisted of a few attractions in a small lot across the street from Disney's Burbank studio. As Walt Disney's ideas and ambitions for the park grew, it became evident that an organizing principle was needed.

The eventual solution that emerged was a design with a central hub, with spokes leading to five distinct thematic "lands": Adventureland, Frontierland, Fantasyland, Tomorrowland, and Main Street, U.S.A. Each "land" contains attractions (rides, shows, exhibits), restaurants, shops, and services such as restrooms, as shown in Figure 4-14. All of them are carefully—and obsessively—themed to make guests feel like they are in the South Pacific, a remote Western town, or Alice's Wonderland.

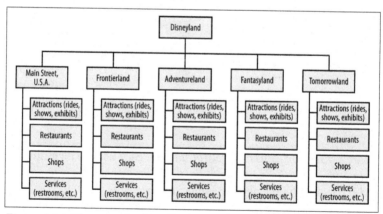

Figure 4-14. The organizational structure of Disneyland made a new, unfamiliar concept—the theme park—easily understandable to mid-1950s Americans by appealing to their emotions and fantasies

The "lands" also introduced structural narrative to the whole. It is no coincidence that the initial set reflects themes that were popular in mid-1950s America: the space race was revving up, Westerns were all the rage, and adults were feeling nostalgic for the Main Streets of their youth (which automobile culture had started to displace). The new, unfamiliar idea of the theme park was made understandable and enticing by giving it a clear organization, based on concepts that the target audience understood and was emotionally engaged with.

This conceptual structure was also reflected in other products of the Disney Company. For example, this division into "lands" was also used to organize Disney's first television show: one week, it would feature an Adventureland story; the next, viewers would see a tale from Tomorrowland. Disney movies of the period also reflected (and influenced) the themes of the park: *Sleeping Beauty* manifested the Fantasyland theme, while the *True-Life Adventures* documentaries manifested the Adventureland theme. (Disney is widely regarded as one of the first and best practitioners of end-to-end corporate synergy.)

The semantic structures that define the Disneyland experience go beyond setting the context for the place itself: they also extend to the people who participate in it. In Disney parks, customers are referred to as "guests" (an innovation introduced to the hospitality industry by Disney) and park employees are referred to as "cast members." These carefully chosen terms help to define and differentiate how these people act in the environment.

The themed-lands-around-a-hub structure has also served Disney well over time, as it accommodates organic growth and change within a coherent structure. New attractions are added to individual lands to cater to changing tastes (a spate of thrill rides were added in the 1970s) while reinforcing the themes of their respective lands. Although less frequently, whole new lands have been added as well, increasing the variety of experiences available to guests. Because the park is organized around distinct "lands," guests can more easily accept and understand these (sometimes jarring) changes: there is an overall method to the madness.

Since the early 1970s, Disney has been building a new Disneyland-style park somewhere in the world every 10 years or so, and these new parks follow the original's organizing scheme with variations to make them contextually relevant to their time and location (Figure 4-15).

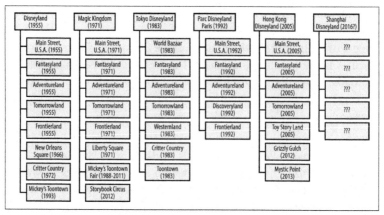

Disneyland (1955)	Magic Kingdom (1971)	Tokyo Disneyland (1983)	Parc Disneyland Paris (1992)	Hong Kong Disneyland (2005)	Shanghai Disneyland (2016?)
Main Street, U.S.A. (1955)	Main Street, U.S.A. (1971)	World Bazaar (1983)	Main Street, U.S.A. (1992)	Main Street, U.S.A. (2005)	???
Fantasyland (1955)	Fantasyland (1971)	Fantasyland (1983)	Fantasyland (1992)	Fantasyland (2005)	???
Adventureland (1955)	Adventureland (1971)	Adventureland (1983)	Adventureland (1992)	Adventureland (2005)	???
Tomorrowland (1955)	Tomorrowland (1971)	Tomorrowland (1983)	Discoveryland (1992)	Tomorrowland (2005)	???
Frontierland (1955)	Frontierland (1971)	Westernland (1983)	Frontierland (1992)	Toy Story Land (2005)	???
New Orleans Square (1966)	Liberty Square (1971)	Critter Country (1983)		Grizzly Gulch (2012)	
Critter Country (1972)	Mickey's Toontown Fair (1988-2011)	Toontown (1983)		Mystic Point (2013)	
Mickey's Toontown (1993)	Storybook Circus (2012)				

Figure 4-15. The conceptual structure of Disneyland parks allows coherence, extensibility, and adaptability to cultural and temporal context (note that Tokyo Disneyland's Frontierland is called Westernland, and that Hong Kong Disneyland doesn't have one at all)

The information architecture of digital products and services functions in a similar placemaking role. An example of an information environment that shows a structure akin to Disneyland's is eBay. Instead of themed "lands," eBay has categories that focus the user's attention on a particular set of goods. Some, such as eBay Motors, are effectively subsites with highly specialized navigation structures (Figure 4-16). eBay also employs carefully chosen labels to define user roles: at any given moment, you can act either as a "buyer" or "seller," nouns that constrain your expected range of behaviors to a predefined set.

While consistency between channels is important, the information architecture must be tailored to serve the specific information needs of the current users of each channel. It's important to note that the Disneyland website doesn't employ the "lands" structure as its primary organizing principle (Figure 4-17). Visitors to the website have different information needs from guests in the park: most of them are not there to experience Disneyland itself, but to book a vacation in the park. As a result, the information architecture of the Disneyland website reflects the typical travel-and-hospitality type, such as that of a hotel. The "lands" structure is still visible—at a much lower level of importance—in the section of the site that describes the attractions in the park.

Figure 4-16. eBay's categories serve a similar role to Disneyland's "lands": they help set the context for the user's experience of the place—search terms are shown alongside suggested categories, attempting to guess the user's meaning in context

Figure 4-17. The information architecture used on Disneyland's website is the "travel and hospitality" type; the "lands" structure, which so dominates the parks, plays a minor supporting role in the site

Recap

So, let's recap what we learned in this chapter:

- The structure of information environments influences more than how we find stuff: it also changes how we understand it.
- We experience information environments as places where we go to transact, learn, and connect with other people, among many other activities.
- When designing information environments, we can learn from the design of physical environments.
- Some organizing principles that carry over to information environments from physical environments include structure and order, rhythm, typologies, and modularity and extensibility.

As you may have surmised at this point, finding and understanding are not really separate goals: they are flip sides of the same coin. The way we understand an information environment—the context it sets information in—influences how we find information in it, and vice versa. The organizational structure of the environment is a critical factor in influencing how people make sense of what they can do there, and the information they hope to find and produce when participating in the environment.

In any case, we hope we've done a good job of setting the stage. We'll now move on to Part II of the book, in which we explore the basic principles by which information architecture achieves these aims.

PART II

Basic Principles of Information Architecture

Thus far, we've discussed information architecture from a conceptual perspective: what its goals are, and how it can improve information-rich products and services. You should now have a good high-level understanding of what IA is.

In Part II, we'll examine IA at a lower level, looking at four systems that are shared by most interactive information environments: organization systems, labeling systems, navigation systems, and search systems. We'll also discuss thesauri, controlled vocabularies, and metadata—"invisible" systems that help shape the information environment behind the scenes.

These are the components that make up an information architecture. We'll start by giving you an overview of these components and how they affect the overall experience of interacting with your information environment. Onward!

CHAPTER 5

The Anatomy of an Information Architecture

We are searching for some kind of harmony between
two intangibles: a form which we have not yet designed
and a context which we cannot properly describe.
—*Christopher Alexander*

In this chapter, we'll cover:

- Why it's important (and difficult) to make an information architecture as tangible as possible
- Examples that help you visualize an information architecture from both the top down and the bottom up
- Ways of categorizing the components of an information architecture so you can better understand and explain IA

In Part I, we discussed information architecture from a conceptual perspective. This chapter presents a more concrete view of what information architecture actually is to help you recognize it when you see it. We also introduce the components of an architecture; these are important to understand because they make up our palette. We'll cover them in greater detail in Chapters 6–10.

Visualizing Information Architecture

Why is it important to be able to visualize information architecture? As we mentioned in Chapter 2, the field is abstract, and many who might conceptually understand the basic premise of information architecture won't really "get it" until they see it and experience it. Also, a well-designed information architecture is invisible to users (which, paradoxically, is quite an unfair reward for IA success).

Because it's highly probable that you'll need to explain information architecture to several important people, including colleagues, managers, prospects, clients, and perhaps your significant other, it's in your interest to be able to help them visualize what an information architecture actually is.

Let's start by looking at something many of us are familiar with: a website's main page. Figure 5-1 shows the main page for Gustavus Adolphus College in Saint Peter, Minnesota.

What's obvious here? Most immediately, you see that the site's visual design stands out. You can't help but notice the site's colors, typeface choices, and photographs. You also notice aspects of the site's information design; for example, the number of columns—and their widths—change throughout the page.

What else? With a careful eye, you can detect aspects of the site's interaction design, such as the use of mouseovers over main menu choices. Although the college's logo and logotype are prominent, the site relies on textual content (e.g., "Make your life count," "Where Gustavus can take you," etc.) to convey its message and brand. And although this particular site functions well, you'd learn something about its supporting technology (and related expertise) just from the main page—for example, if it didn't reflow properly when rendered in small browser windows, you might guess that the designers weren't aware of or concerned with responsive web design techniques for display in mobile browsers (Figure 5-2).

Figure 5-1. Gustavus Adolphus College's main page

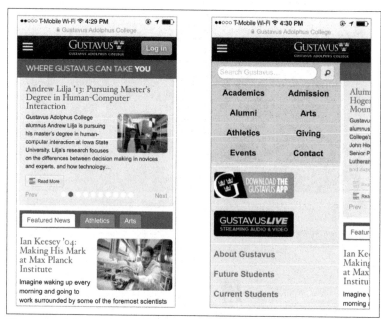

Figure 5-2. The Gustavus Adolphus site employs responsive web design techniques so that it can be viewed properly in smartphone browsers— the "hamburger" menu icon provides access to the site's navigation and search systems

Thus far, we've noticed all sorts of things that aren't information architecture. So what is recognizable as information architecture? You might be surprised by how much information architecture you can see if you know how to look. For example, the information has been structured in some basic ways, which we'll explain further in later chapters:

- *Organization systems* present the site's information to us in a variety of ways, such as content categories that pertain to the entire campus (e.g., the top bar and its "Academics" and "Admission" choices), or to specific audiences (the block on the middle left, with such choices as "Future Students" and "Staff").

- *Navigation systems* help users move through the content, such as with the custom organization of the individual drop-down menus in the main navigation bar.

- *Search systems* allow users to search the content; when the user starts typing in the site's search bar, a list of suggestions is shown with possible matches for the user's search term.
- *Labeling systems* describe categories, options, and links in language that (hopefully) is meaningful to users; you'll see examples throughout the page (e.g., "Admission," "Alumni," "Events").

Top-Down Information Architecture

Categories are used to group pages and applications throughout the site; labels systematically represent the site's content; navigation systems and a search system can be used to move through the site. In effect, the Gustavus main page tries to anticipate users' major information needs, such as "How do I find out about admissions?" or "What's going on this week on campus?" The site's designers have worked hard to determine the most common questions, and have designed the site to meet those needs. We refer to this as *top-down information architecture* (Figure 5-3), and the Gustavus main page addresses many common "top-down" questions that users have when they land on a site, including:

- Where am I? (1)
- I know what I'm looking for; how do I search for it? (2)
- How do I get around this site? (3)
- What's important and unique about this organization? (4)
- What's available on this site? (5)
- What's happening there? (6)
- How do I engage with them via various other popular digital channels? (7)
- How can I contact a human? (8)
- What's their address? (9)
- How can I access my account? (10)

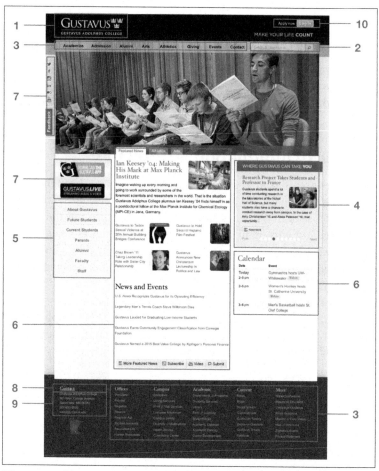

Figure 5-3. The Gustavus site's main page is crammed with answers to users' questions

In top-down information architecture, the environment's designers posit a structure that aims to answer users' questions such as these. The form that the environment takes—its content, page layout, etc. —is designed and produced to support this structure that has been centrally defined "from above." This was the main way information architecture was done when we wrote the first edition of this book— not surprisingly, given many of that era's readers were designing new sites from scratch. Over time, as information environments have become more dynamic and search engines have become more powerful and widespread, a different modality—bottom-up information architecture—has gained prominence.

Bottom-Up Information Architecture

Content itself can have information architecture embedded within it. For example, the recipe in Figure 5-4 shows a refreshing drink in the Epicurious Android app.

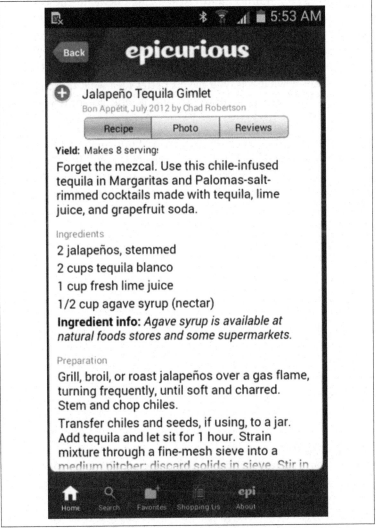

Figure 5-4. A recipe for the thirsty from the Epicurious Android app

Beyond the navigational options at the bottom of the screen, there's not much information architecture here. Or is there?

The recipe itself has a clear, strong structure: a title at the top, a list of ingredients, then preparation directions and serving information. This information is "chunked" so you know what's what. The recipe's native chunking could also support searching and browsing; for example, users might be able to search on the chunks known as "recipe titles" for "gimlet" and retrieve this one. And these chunks are sequenced in a logical manner; after all, you'll want to know the ingredients ("Do I have agave syrup?") before you start mixing the drink. The definition and sequential placement of chunks helps you to recognize that this content is a recipe before you even read it. And once you know what it is, you have a better idea what this content is about and how to use it, move around it, and go somewhere else from it.

So, if you look closely enough, you can see information architecture even when it's embedded in the guts of your content. In fact, by supporting searching and browsing, the structure inherent in content enables the answers to users' questions to "rise" to the surface. This is *bottom-up information architecture*; content structure, sequencing, and tagging help you answer such questions as:

- Where am I?
- What's here?
- Where can I go from here?

Instead of being dictated "from above," bottom-up information architecture is suggested by and inherent in the system's content. It's important because users are increasingly likely to bypass your system's top-down information architecture; instead, they're using web-wide search tools like Google Search, clicking through ads, and clicking links while reading your content via social networks such as Facebook or Twitter to find themselves deep in your site. Once there, they'll want to jump to other relevant content on your site without learning how to use its top-down structure. A good information architecture is designed to anticipate this type of use; Keith Instone's simple and practical *"navigation stress test"* (*http:// instone.org/navstress*) is a great way to evaluate a site's bottom-up information architecture.

Figure 5-5 shows a slightly different example of a bottom-up information architecture: images stored in one of this book's authors' iCloud account, as displayed in the iOS Photos app.

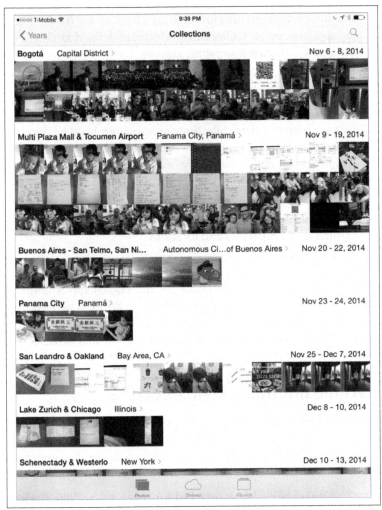

Figure 5-5. Image collections in the iOS Photos app

There is little to see here besides the information architecture and the content itself. In fact, as the content is just collections of thumbnails pointing to individual images, the information architecture is what dominates the display. It provides context for the content, and tells us what we can do while we're here:

- The information architecture tells us where we are (in the Photos app, looking at "Collections," which are defined as ranges of dates in a particular geographic region).
- It helps us move to other closely related views (e.g., by switching to "Albums," collections of photos we've defined).
- It helps us move through the information hierarchically (e.g., we can choose to view collections of images grouped by the year they were saved, instead of by more granular ranges of dates and locations) and contextually (e.g., by clicking on the city in which they were shot, we can see them arranged spatially over a map).
- It allows us to search the content based on various criteria, such as different time periods and locations.
- It allows us to share the content with others.

In many respects, the user interface for the Photos app is nothing but information architecture. Its bottom-up structure is defined primarily by the metadata and deep contextual links embedded in the content (the photos) it contains, presented in a way that makes sense given how people are used to organizing photographs.

Invisible Information Architecture

You now know that information architecture is something that can be seen, if you know what to look for. But it's important to understand that information architecture is often invisible. For example, Figure 5-6 shows some search results from the BBC's website.

What's going on here? We've searched for "ukraine," and the site has presented us with a couple of different things, most interestingly three results labeled "Editor's Choice." As you'd imagine, all the search results were retrieved by a piece of software—a search engine—that the user never sees. The search engine has been configured to index and search certain parts of the site, to display certain kinds of information in each search result (i.e., page title, extract, and date), and to handle search queries in certain ways, such as removing "stop words" (e.g., "a," "the," and "of"). All of these decisions regarding search system configuration are unknown to users, and are integral aspects of information architecture design.

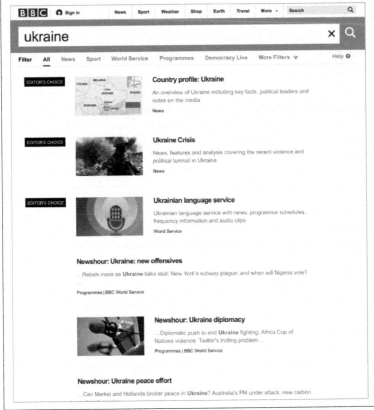

Figure 5-6. BBC search results include three "Editor's Choice" links

What's different is that the "Editor's Choice" results are manually created: some people at the BBC decided that "ukraine" is an important term and that some of the BBC's best content is not news stories, which normally come up at the top of most retrieval sets. So they applied some editorial expertise to identify three highly relevant pages and associated them with the term "ukraine," thereby ensuring that these three items are displayed when someone searches for "ukraine." Users might assume these search results are automatically generated, but humans are manually modifying the information architecture in the background;[1] this is another example of invisible information architecture.

---

1 This effort is often guided by search logs that allow editors to identify which search terms would benefit most from editorial intervention.

Information architecture is much more than just blueprints that portray navigational routes and wireframes that inform visual design. Information architecture involves more than meets the eye, and both its visible and invisible aspects help define what we do and illustrate how challenging it really is.

Information Architecture Components

It can be difficult to know exactly what components make up an information architecture. People interact directly with some, while (as we just saw) others are so behind the scenes that users are unaware of their existence.

In the next four chapters, we'll present and discuss information architecture components by breaking them up into the following four categories, which were introduced earlier:

Organization systems
> How we categorize information (e.g., by subject or chronology); see Chapter 6

Labeling systems
> How we represent information—for example, using scientific terminology ("Acer") or lay terminology ("maple"); see Chapter 7

Navigation systems
> How we browse or move through information (e.g., clicking through a hierarchy); see Chapter 8

Searching systems
> How we search information (e.g., executing a search query against an index); see Chapter 9

Like any categorization scheme, this one has challenges. For example, it can be difficult to distinguish organization systems from labeling systems (hint: you organize content into groups, and then label those groups; each group can be labeled in different ways). As in other situations that involve categorization, it can be useful to group objects in new ways to examine them from different perspectives. So, before we delve into these systems, we'll present an alternative method of categorizing information architecture components. This method is comprised of browsing aids, search aids, content and tasks, and "invisible" components.

Browsing Aids

These components present users with a predetermined set of paths to help them navigate the information environment. They also help create a sense of place, as we explained in Chapter 4. When browsing, users don't articulate their queries through search fields, but instead find their way through menus and links. Types of browsing aids include:

Organization systems
> Also known as taxonomies and hierarchies, these are the main way of categorizing or grouping content (e.g., by topic, by task, by audiences, or by chronology); user-generated tags are also a form of organization system

General navigation systems
> Primary navigation systems that help users understand where they are and where they can go within an information environment

Local navigation systems
> Primary navigation systems that help users understand where they are and where they can go within a portion of an information environment (e.g., a subsite)

Sitemaps/tables of contents
> Navigation systems that supplement primary navigation systems; provide a condensed overview of and links to major content areas within the environment, usually in outline form

Indices
> Supplementary navigation systems that provide an alphabetized list of links to the contents of the environment

Guides
> Supplementary navigation systems that provide specialized information on specific topics, as well as links to related subsets of content

Walkthroughs and wizards
> Supplementary navigation systems that lead users through sequential sets of steps; may also link to related subsets of content

Contextual navigation systems
> Consistently presented links to related content; often embedded in text and generally used to connect highly specialized content within an information environment

Search Aids

These components allow the entry of user-defined queries (e.g., searcheses) and automatically present users with customized sets of results that match their queries. Think of these as dynamic and mostly automated counterparts to browsing aids. Types of search components include:

Search interface
> The means of entering and revising a search query, typically with information on how to improve your query, as well as other ways to configure your search (e.g., selecting from specific search zones)

Query language
> The grammar of a search query; query languages might include Boolean operators (e.g., AND, OR, NOT), proximity operators (e.g., ADJACENT, NEAR), or ways of specifying which field to search (e.g., AUTHOR="Shakespeare")

Query builders
> Ways of enhancing a query's performance; common examples include spell checkers, stemming, concept searching, and drawing in synonyms from a thesaurus

Retrieval algorithms
> The part of a search engine that determines which content matches a user's query; Google's PageRank is perhaps the best-known example

Search zones
> Subsets of site content that have been separately indexed to support narrower searching (e.g., searching the tech support area within a software vendor's site)

Search results
> Presentation of content that matches the user's search query; involves decisions about what types of content should make up

each individual result, how many results to display, and how sets of results should be ranked, sorted, and clustered

Content and Tasks

These are the users' ultimate destinations, as opposed to separate components that get users to their destinations. However, it's difficult to separate content and tasks from an information architecture, as there are components embedded in them that help us find our way. Examples of information architecture components embedded in content and tasks include:

Headings
> Labels for the content that follows them

Embedded links
> Links within text; these label (i.e., represent) the content they link to

Embedded metadata
> Information that can be used as metadata but must first be extracted (e.g., in a recipe, if an ingredient is mentioned, this information can be indexed to support searching by ingredient)

Chunks
> Logical units of content; these can vary in granularity (e.g., sections and chapters are both chunks) and can be nested (e.g., a section is part of a book)

Lists
> Groups of chunks or links to chunks; these are important because they've been grouped together (e.g., they share some trait in common) and have been presented in a particular order (e.g., chronologically)

Sequential aids
> Clues that suggest where the user is in a process or task, and how far he has to go before completing it (e.g., "step 3 of 8")

Identifiers
> Clues that suggest where the user is in an information system (e.g., a logo specifying what site she is using, or a breadcrumb explaining where she is)

"Invisible" Components

Certain key architectural components are manifest completely in the background; users rarely (if ever) interact with them. These components often "feed" other components, such as a thesaurus that's used to enhance a search query. Some examples of invisible information architecture components include:

Controlled vocabularies and thesauri
> Predetermined vocabularies of preferred terms that describe a specific domain (e.g., auto racing or orthopedic surgery); typically include variant terms (e.g., "brewski" is a variant term for "beer"). Thesauri are controlled vocabularies that generally include links to broader and narrower terms, related terms, and descriptions of preferred terms (aka "scope notes"). Search systems can enhance queries by extracting a query's synonyms from a controlled vocabulary.

Retrieval algorithms
> Used to rank search results by relevance; retrieval algorithms reflect their programmers' judgments on how to determine relevance.

Best bets
> Preferred search results that are manually coupled with a search query; editors and subject matter experts determine which queries should retrieve best bets and which documents merit best bet status.

Whichever method you use for categorizing architectural components, it's useful to drill down beyond the abstract concept of information architecture and become familiar with its more tangible and, when possible, visual aspects. In the following chapters, we'll take an even deeper look at the nuts and bolts of an information architecture.

Recap

Let's recap what we learned in this chapter:

- You'll probably need to explain information architecture to others, so it's important that you help them visualize it.
- You can visualize information architecture from the top down, or from the bottom up.
- There are various ways of categorizing IA components, but here we'll be looking at four categories: organization systems, labeling systems, navigation systems, and searching systems.

And now that we've given you the overview of the basic systems we'll be discussing, we'll dive into the first of them: organization systems.

CHAPTER 6

Organization Systems

The beginning of all understanding is classification.
—Hayden White

In this chapter, we'll cover:

- Subjectivity, politics, and other reasons why organizing information is so difficult
- Exact and ambiguous organization schemes
- Hierarchy, hypertext, and relational database structures
- Tagging and social classification

Our understanding of the world is largely determined by our ability to organize information. Where do you live? What do you do? Who are you? Our answers reveal the systems of classification that form the very foundations of our understanding. We live in towns within states within countries. We work in departments in companies in industries. We are parents, children, and siblings, each an integral part of a family tree.

We organize to understand, to explain, and to control. Our classification systems inherently reflect social and political perspectives and objectives. We live in the first world. They live in the third world. She is a freedom fighter. He is a terrorist. The way we organize, label, and relate information influences the way people comprehend that information.

We organize information so that people can find the right answers to their questions, and to give them context to understand those answers. We strive to support casual browsing and directed searching. Our aim is to design organization and labeling systems that make sense to users.

Digital media provide us with wonderfully flexible environments in which to organize. We can apply multiple organization systems to the same content and escape the physical limitations of the analog world. So why are many digital products so difficult to navigate? Why can't the people who design these products make it easy to find information? These common questions focus attention on the very real problem of organizing information.

Challenges of Organizing Information

In recent years, increasing attention has been focused on the challenge of organizing information. Yet this challenge is not new. People have struggled with the difficulties of information organization for centuries. The field of librarianship has been largely devoted to the task of organizing and providing access to information. So why all the fuss now?

Believe it or not, we're all becoming librarians. This quiet yet powerful revolution is driven by the decentralizing force of the global Internet. Not long ago, the responsibility for labeling, organizing, and providing access to information fell squarely in the laps of librarians. These librarians spoke in strange languages about Dewey Decimal Classification and the Anglo-American Cataloguing Rules. They classified, cataloged, and helped you find the information you needed.

As the Internet provides users with the freedom to publish information, it quietly burdens them with the responsibility to organize that information. New information technologies open the floodgates for exponential content growth, which creates a need for innovation in content organization (see Figure 6-1).

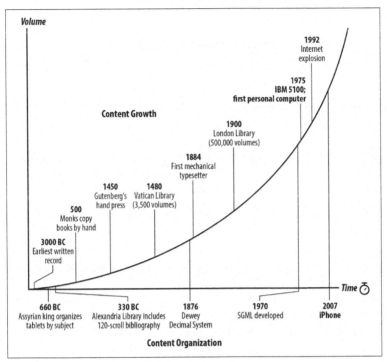

Figure 6-1. Content growth drives innovation

As we struggle to meet these challenges, we unknowingly adopt the language of librarians. How should we *label* that content? Is there an existing *classification scheme* we can borrow? Who's going to *catalog* all of that information?

We're living in a world in which tremendous numbers of people publish and organize their own information. As we do so, the challenges inherent in organizing that information become more recognized and more important. Let's explore some of the reasons why organizing information in useful ways is so difficult.

Ambiguity

Classification systems are made of language, and language is ambiguous: words are capable of being understood in more than one way. Think about the word *pitch*. When I say "pitch," what do you hear? There are more than 15 definitions, including:

- A throw, fling, or toss
- A black, sticky substance used for waterproofing
- The rising and falling of the bow and stern of a ship in a rough sea
- A salesman's persuasive line of talk
- An element of sound determined by the frequency of vibration

This ambiguity results in a shaky foundation for our classification systems. When we use words as labels for our categories, we run the risk that users will miss our meaning. This is a serious problem. (See Chapter 7 to learn more about labeling.)

It gets worse. Not only do we need to agree on the labels and their definitions, but we also need to agree on which documents to place in which categories. Consider the common tomato. According to Webster's dictionary, a tomato is "a red or yellowish fruit with a juicy pulp, used as a vegetable: botanically it is a berry." Now I'm confused. Is it a fruit, a vegetable, or a berry?[1] And of course, this assumes that the user reads English to begin with—an unrealistic assumption in our increasingly multicultural digital media.

If we have such problems classifying the common tomato, consider the challenges involved in classifying website content. Classification is particularly difficult when you're organizing abstract concepts such as subjects, topics, or functions. For example, what is meant by "alternative healing," and should it be cataloged under "philosophy," "religion," "health and medicine," or all of the above? The organization of words and phrases, taking into account their inherent ambiguity, presents a very real and substantial challenge.

Heterogeneity

Heterogeneity refers to an object or collection of objects composed of unrelated or unlike parts. You might refer to grandma's homemade

---

1 The tomato is technically a berry and thus a fruit, despite a 1893 US Court decision that declared it a vegetable. (John Nix, an importer of West Indies tomatoes, had brought suit to lift a 10% tariff, mandated by Congress, on imported vegetables. Nix argued that the tomato is a fruit. The Court held that because a tomato was consumed as a vegetable rather than as a dessert-like fruit, it was a vegetable.) Source: Denise Grady, "Best Bite of Summer" (Self 19:7, 1997, 124–125).

broth with its assortment of vegetables, meats, and other mysterious leftovers as "heterogeneous." At the other end of the scale, "homogeneous" refers to something composed of similar or identical elements. For example, Ritz crackers are homogeneous. Every cracker looks and tastes the same.

An old-fashioned library card catalog is relatively homogeneous. It organizes and provides access to books. It does not provide access to chapters in books or collections of books. It may not provide access to magazines or videos. This homogeneity allows for a structured classification system. Each book has a record in the catalog. Each record contains the same fields: author, title, and subject. It is a high-level, single-medium system, and it works fairly well.

Most digital information environments, on the other hand, are highly heterogeneous in many respects. For example, websites often provide access to documents and their components at varying levels of *granularity*. A site might present articles and journals and journal databases side by side. Links might lead to pages, sections of pages, or other websites. And websites typically provide access to documents in multiple formats. You might find financial news, product descriptions, employee home pages, image archives, and software files. Dynamic news content shares space with static human-resources information. Textual information shares space with video, audio, and interactive applications. The website is a great multimedia melting pot, where you are challenged to reconcile the cataloging of the broad and the detailed across many mediums.

The heterogeneous nature of information environments makes it difficult to impose any single structured organization system on the content. It usually doesn't make sense to classify documents at varying levels of granularity side by side. An article and a magazine should be treated differently. Similarly, it may not make sense to handle varying formats the same way. Each format will have uniquely important characteristics. For example, we need to know certain things about images, such as file format (JPG, PNG, etc.) and resolution (1024 × 768, 1280 × 800, etc.). It is difficult and often misguided to attempt a one-size-fits-all approach to the organization of heterogeneous content. This is a fundamental flaw of many enterprise taxonomy initiatives.

Differences in Perspectives

Have you ever tried to find a file on a coworker's computer? Perhaps you had permission. Perhaps you were engaged in low-grade corporate espionage. In either case, you needed that file. In some instances, you may have found the file immediately. In others, you may have searched for hours. The ways people organize and name files and directories on their computers can be maddeningly illogical. When questioned, they will often claim that their organization system makes perfect sense. "But it's obvious! I put current proposals in the folder labeled */office/clients/green* and old proposals in */office/clients/red*. I don't understand why you couldn't find them!"[2]

The fact is that labeling and organization systems are intensely affected by their creators' perspectives.[3] We see this at the corporate level with websites organized according to internal divisions or org charts, with groupings such as *marketing, sales, customer support, human resources,* and *information systems*. How does a customer visiting this website know where to go for technical information about a product she just purchased? To design usable organization systems, we need to escape from our own mental models of content labeling and organization.

We employ a mix of user research and analysis methods to gain real insight. How do users group the information? What types of labels do they use? How do they navigate? This challenge is complicated by the fact that most information environments are designed for multiple users, and all users will have different ways of understanding the information. Their levels of familiarity with your company and your content will vary. For these reasons, even with a massive barrage of user tests, it is impossible to create a perfect organization system. One system does not fit all! However, by recognizing the importance of perspective, by striving to understand the intended audiences

---

2 It actually gets even more complicated, because an individual's needs, perspectives, and behaviors change over time. A significant body of research within the field of library and information science explores the complex nature of information models. For an example, see N.J. Belkin, "Anomalous States of Knowledge as a Basis for Information Retrieval" (*Canadian Journal of Information Science* 5, 1980, 133–143).

3 For a fascinating study on the idiosyncratic methods people use to organize their physical desktops and office spaces, see T.W. Malone, "How Do People Organize Their Desks? Implications for the Design of Office Information Systems" (*ACM Transactions on Office Information Systems* 1, 1983, 99–112).

through user research and testing, and by providing multiple navigation pathways, you can do a better job of organizing information for public consumption than your coworker does on his desktop computer.

Internal Politics

Politics exist in every organization. Individuals and departments constantly position for influence or respect. Because of the inherent power of information organization in forming understanding and opinion, the process of designing information architectures can involve a strong undercurrent of politics. The choice of organization and labeling systems can have a big impact on how users of the system perceive the company, its departments, and its products. For example, should we include a link to the library site on the main page of the corporate intranet? Should we call it "The Library," "Information Services," or "Knowledge Management"? Should information resources provided by other departments be included in this area? If the library gets a link on the main page, why not corporate communications? What about daily news?

As a designer, you must be sensitive to your organization's political environment. In certain cases, you must remind your colleagues to focus on creating an architecture that works for the users. In others, you may need to make compromises to avoid serious political conflict. Politics raise the complexity and difficulty of creating usable information architectures. However, if you are sensitive to the political issues at hand, you can manage their impact upon the architecture.

Organizing Information Environments

The organization of information environments is a major factor in determining their success, and yet many teams lack the understanding necessary to do the job well. Our goal in this chapter is to provide a foundation for tackling even the most challenging information organization projects.

Organization systems are composed of *organization schemes* and *organization structures*. An organization scheme defines the shared characteristics of content items and influences the logical grouping of those items. An organization structure defines the types of relationships between content items and groups. Both organization schemes and structures have an important impact on the ways information is found and understood.

Before diving in, it's important to understand information organization in the context of system development. Organization is closely related to navigation, labeling, and indexing. The organization structures of information environments often play the part of the primary navigation system. The labels of categories play a significant role in defining the contents of those categories. Manual indexing or *metadata tagging* is ultimately a tool for organizing content items into groups at a very detailed level. Despite these closely knit relationships, it is both possible and useful to isolate the design of organization systems, which will form the foundation for navigation and labeling systems. By focusing solely on the grouping of information, you avoid the distractions inherent in implementation details (such as the design of the navigation user interface) and can design a better product.

Organization Schemes

We navigate through organization schemes every day. Contact directories, supermarkets, and libraries all use organization schemes to facilitate access. Some schemes are easy to use. We rarely have difficulty finding a particular word's definition in the alphabetical organization scheme of a dictionary. Some schemes are intensely frustrating. Trying to find marshmallows or popcorn in a large and unfamiliar supermarket can drive us crazy. Are marshmallows in the snack aisle, the baking ingredients section, both, or neither?

In fact, the organization schemes of the dictionary and the supermarket are fundamentally different. The dictionary's alphabetical organization scheme is exact. The hybrid topical/task-oriented organization scheme of the supermarket is ambiguous.

Exact Organization Schemes

Let's start with the easy ones. Exact or "objective" organization schemes divide information into well-defined and mutually exclusive sections. For example, country names are usually listed in alphabetical order. If you know the name of the country you are looking for, navigating the scheme is easy. "Chile" is in the Cs, which are after the Bs but before the Ds. This is called *known-item* searching. You know what you're looking for, and it's obvious where to find it. No ambiguity is involved. The problem with exact organization schemes is that they require users to know the specific name of the resource they are looking for ("What's the name of that country that borders Guyana and French Guiana?").

Exact organization schemes are relatively easy to design and maintain because there is little intellectual work involved in assigning items to categories. They are also easy to use. The following sections explore three frequently used exact organization schemes.

Alphabetical schemes

An alphabetical organization scheme is the primary organization scheme for encyclopedias and dictionaries. Almost all nonfiction books, including this one, provide an alphabetical index. Phone books, department-store directories, bookstores, and libraries all make use of our 26-letter alphabet for organizing their contents.

Alphabetical organization often serves as an umbrella for other organization schemes. We see information organized alphabetically by last name, by product or service, by department, and by format. Most address book applications organize contacts alphabetically by last name, as shown in Figure 6-2.

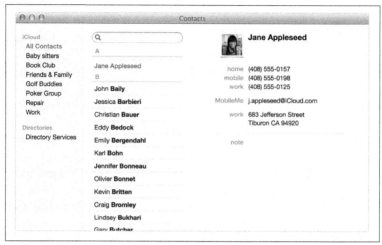

Figure 6-2. The OS X Contacts application (image: https:// www.apple.com/osx/apps/#contacts)

Chronological schemes

Certain types of information lend themselves to chronological organization. For example, an archive of press releases might be organized by the date of release. Press release archives are obvious candidates for chronological organization schemes (see Figure 6-3). The date of announcement provides important context for the release. However, keep in mind that users may also want to browse the releases by title, product category, or geography, or to search by keyword. A complementary combination of organization schemes is often necessary. History books, magazine archives, diaries, and television guides tend to be organized chronologically. As long as there is agreement on when a particular event occurred, chronological schemes are easy to design and use.

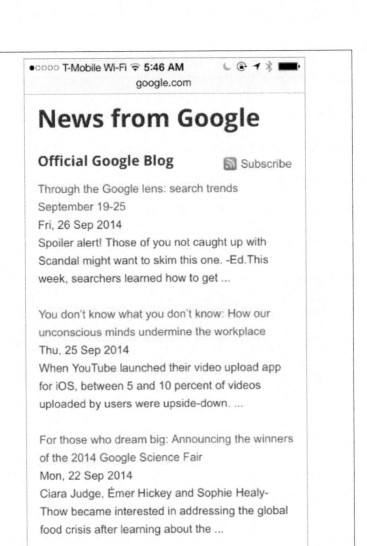

Figure 6-3. Press releases in reverse chronological order

Geographical schemes

Place is often an important characteristic of information. We travel from one place to another. We care about the news and weather that affect us in our location. Political, social, and economic issues are frequently location dependent. And in a world where location-aware mobile devices have become the main way in which many people interact with information, companies like Google and Apple are investing heavily in local search and directory services, with the map as the main interface to this information.

Border disputes aside, geographical organization schemes are fairly straightforward to design and use. Figure 6-4 shows an example of a geographical organization scheme from Craigslist. The user can select her nearest local directory. If her browser supports geolocation, the site navigates directly to it.

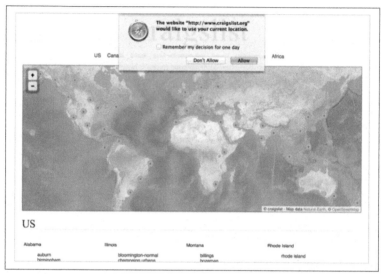

Figure 6-4. A geographical organization scheme with geolocation

Ambiguous Organization Schemes

Now for the tough ones. Ambiguous or "subjective" organization schemes divide information into categories that defy exact definition. They are mired in the ambiguity of language and organization, not to mention human subjectivity. They are difficult to design and maintain. They can be difficult to use. Remember the tomato? Do we classify it under fruit, berry, or vegetable?

However, these schemes are often more important and useful than exact organization schemes. Consider the typical library catalog. There are three primary organization schemes: you can search for books by author, by title, or by subject. The author and title organization schemes are exact and thereby easier to create, maintain, and use. However, extensive research shows that library patrons use ambiguous subject-based schemes such as the Dewey Decimal and Library of Congress classification systems much more frequently.

There's a simple reason why people find ambiguous organization schemes so useful: we don't always know what we're looking for. In some cases, you simply don't know the correct label. In others, you may have only a vague information need that you can't quite articulate. As we mentioned in Chapter 3, information seeking is often iterative and interactive. What you find at the beginning of your search may influence what you look for and find later in your search. This information-seeking process can involve a wonderful element of associative learning. Seek and ye shall find, but if the system is well designed, you also might learn along the way.

Ambiguous organization supports this serendipitous mode of information seeking by grouping items in intellectually meaningful ways. In an alphabetical scheme, closely grouped items may have nothing in common beyond the fact that their names begin with the same letter. In an ambiguous organization scheme, someone other than the user has made an intellectual decision to group items together. This grouping of related items supports an associative learning process that may enable the user to make new connections and reach better conclusions. While ambiguous organization schemes require more work and introduce a messy element of subjectivity, they often prove more valuable to the user than exact schemes.

The success of an ambiguous organization scheme depends upon the quality of the scheme and the careful placement of individual items within that scheme. Rigorous user testing is essential. In most situations, there is an ongoing need for classifying new items and for modifying the organization scheme to reflect changes in the industry. Maintaining these schemes may require dedicated staff with subject matter expertise. Let's review a few of the most common and valuable ambiguous organization schemes.

Topical organization schemes

Organizing information by subject or topic is one of the most useful and challenging approaches. Newspapers are organized topically, so if you want to see the scores from yesterday's game, you know to turn to the sports section. Academic courses and departments, and the chapters of most nonfiction books, are all organized along topical lines. Many people assume that these topical groupings are fixed, when in fact they are cultural constructs that can vary over time.

While few information environments are organized solely by topic, most should provide some sort of topical access to content. In designing a topical organization scheme, it is important to define the breadth of coverage. Some schemes, such as those found in an encyclopedia, cover the entire breadth of human knowledge. Research-oriented websites such as Consumer Reports (shown in Figure 6-5) rely heavily on their topical organization schemes. Others, such as corporate websites, are limited in breadth, covering only those topics directly related to that company's products and services. In designing a topical organization scheme, keep in mind that you are defining the universe of content (both present and future) that users will expect to find within that area of the system.

Figure 6-5. A topical taxonomy showing categories and subcategories

Task-oriented schemes

Task-oriented schemes organize content and applications into collections of processes, functions, or tasks. These schemes are appropriate when it's possible to anticipate a limited number of high-priority tasks that users will want to perform. Task-oriented organization schemes are common in desktop and mobile apps, especially those that support the creation and management of content (such as word processors and spreadsheets; see Figure 6-6).

Figure 6-6. Like many apps, Microsoft Word on iOS features a task-oriented organization scheme

On the Web, task-oriented organization schemes are most common in the context of websites where customer interaction takes center stage. Intranets and extranets also lend themselves well to a task orientation, because they tend to integrate powerful applications as well as content. You will rarely find a website organized solely by task. Instead, task-oriented schemes are usually embedded within specific subsites or integrated into hybrid task/topic navigation systems, as we see in Figure 6-7.

Figure 6-7. Task, topic, and audience coexist on the Smithsonian home page

Audience-specific schemes

In cases where there are two or more clearly definable audiences for a product or service, an audience-specific organization scheme may make sense. This type of scheme works well if there is value in customizing the content for each audience. Audience-oriented schemes break a site into smaller, audience-specific mini-sites, thereby allowing for clutter-free pages that present only the options of interest to that particular audience. CERN, shown in Figure 6-8, presents an audience-oriented organization scheme that invites users to self-identify.

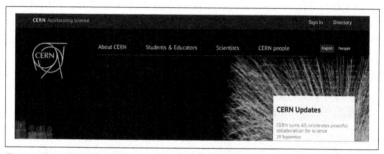

Figure 6-8. CERN invites users to self-identify

Organizing by audience brings all the promise and peril associated with any form of personalization. For example, CERN understands its audience segments and brings this knowledge to bear on its website. If I visit the site and identify myself as a member of the "Scientist" audience, CERN will present me with research results, papers from CERN researchers, and other information of interest to the scientific community. This information is not readily available in the "Students & Educators" section of the site. But what if I'm a science student doing research, and need access to research papers? All ambiguous schemes require us to make these educated guesses and revisit them over time.

Audience-specific schemes can be open or closed. An open scheme will allow members of one audience to access the content intended for other audiences. A closed scheme will prevent members from moving between audience-specific sections. This may be appropriate if subscription fees or security issues are involved.

Metaphor-driven schemes

Metaphors are commonly used to help users understand the new by relating it to the familiar. You need not look further than your *desktop* computer with its *folders, files,* and *trash can* or *recycle bin* for an example. Applied to an interface in this way, metaphors can help users understand content and function intuitively. In addition, the process of exploring possible metaphor-driven organization schemes can generate new and exciting ideas about the design, organization, and function of a website.

While metaphor exploration can be useful while brainstorming, you should use caution when considering a metaphor-driven global organization scheme. First, metaphors, if they are to succeed, must be familiar to users. Organizing the website of a computer-hardware vendor according to the internal architecture of a computer will not help users who don't understand the layout of a motherboard.

Second, metaphors can introduce unwanted baggage or be limiting. For example, users might expect a digital library to be staffed by a librarian that will answer reference questions. Most digital libraries do not provide this service. Additionally, you may wish to provide services in your digital library that have no clear corollary in the real world. Creating your own customized version of the library is one such example. This will force you to break out of the metaphor, introducing inconsistency into your organization scheme.

Another, perhaps less obvious, example: when you first log into Facebook, you are greeted by a "news feed" of content published by your Facebook friends. Initially, the news feed metaphor was apt, because the stream of posts consisted of the latest (chronologically) published friend content. However, as the frequency of posts grew, Facebook eventually introduced a different algorithm for choosing which posts to show first. The result is a news feed that can show posts that are several days old above more recent posts, breaking the chronological order that is expected in a news feed and potentially causing confusion. As shown in Figure 6-9, Facebook allows users to choose between "top stories" and "most recent" to determine which algorithm to use when ordering posts shown in the feed—an awkward solution at best.

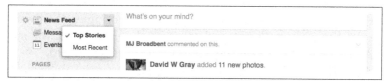

Figure 6-9. Facebook allows users to select which algorithm controls the sequence of posts in their news feed

Hybrid schemes

The power of a pure organization scheme derives from its ability to suggest a simple mental model that users can quickly understand. Users easily recognize an audience-specific or topical organization. And fairly small, pure organization schemes can be applied to large amounts of content without sacrificing their integrity or diminishing their usability.

However, when you start blending elements of multiple schemes, confusion often follows, and solutions are rarely scalable. Consider the example in Figure 6-10. This hybrid scheme includes elements of audience-specific, topical, metaphor-based, task-oriented, and alphabetical organization schemes. Because they are all mixed together, we can't form a mental model. Instead, we need to skim through each menu item to find the option we're looking for.

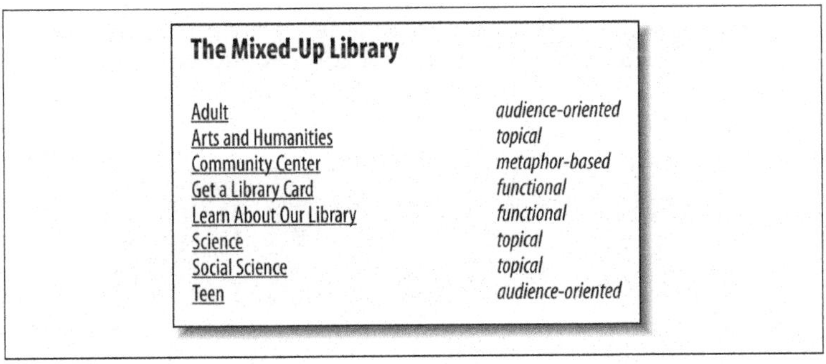

```
The Mixed-Up Library

Adult                       audience-oriented
Arts and Humanities         topical
Community Center            metaphor-based
Get a Library Card          functional
Learn About Our Library     functional
Science                     topical
Social Science              topical
Teen                        audience-oriented
```

Figure 6-10. A hybrid organization scheme

The exception to these cautions against hybrid schemes exists within the surface layer of navigation. As illustrated by the Smithsonian example (Figure 6-7), many websites successfully combine topics and tasks on their main page and within their global navigation. This reflects the reality that both the organization and its users typically identify finding content and completing key tasks at the top of their priority lists. Because only the highest-priority tasks are included, the solution does not need to be scalable. It's only when such schemes are used to organize a large volume of content and tasks that the problems arise. In other words, shallow hybrid schemes are fine, but deep hybrid schemes are not.

Unfortunately, deep hybrid schemes are still fairly common. This is because it is often difficult to agree upon any one scheme, so people throw the elements of multiple schemes together in a confusing mix. There is a better alternative. In cases where multiple schemes must be presented on one page, you should communicate to designers the importance of preserving the integrity of each scheme. As long as the schemes are presented separately on the page, they will retain the powerful ability to suggest a mental model for users. For example, a look at the main menu in the Stanford University website in Figure 6-11 reveals a topical scheme, an audience-oriented scheme, and a search function. By presenting them separately, Stanford provides flexibility without causing confusion.

Figure 6-11. Stanford provides multiple organization schemes

Organization Structures

Organization structure plays an intangible yet very important role in the design of information environments. Although we interact with organization structures every day, we rarely think about them. Movies are linear in their physical structure. We experience them frame by frame, from beginning to end. However, the plots themselves may be nonlinear, employing flashbacks and parallel subplots. Maps have a spatial structure. Items are placed according to physical proximity, although the most useful maps cheat, sacrificing accuracy for clarity.

The structure of information defines the primary ways in which users can navigate. Major organization structures that apply to information architectures include the hierarchy, the database-oriented model, and hypertext. Each organization structure possesses unique strengths and weaknesses. In some cases, it makes sense to use one or the other. In many cases, it makes sense to use all three in a complementary manner.

The Hierarchy: A Top-Down Approach

The foundation of many good information architectures is a well-designed hierarchy. In this hypertextual, free-ranging world of nets and webs, such a statement may seem blasphemous, but it's true. The mutually exclusive subdivisions and parent–child relationships of hierarchies are simple and familiar. We have organized information into hierarchies since the beginning of time. Family trees are hierarchical. Our division of life on earth into kingdoms, classes, and species is hierarchical. Organization charts are usually hierarchical. We divide books into chapters into sections into paragraphs into sentences into words into letters. Hierarchy is ubiquitous in our lives and informs our understanding of the world in a profound and meaningful way. Because of this pervasiveness of hierarchy, users can easily and quickly understand information environments that use hierarchical organization models. They are able to develop a mental model of the environment's structure and their location within that structure. This provides context that helps users feel comfortable. Figure 6-12 shows an example of a simple hierarchical model.

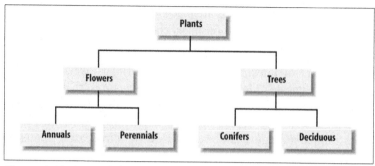

Figure 6-12. A simple hierarchical model

Because hierarchies provide a simple and familiar way to organize information, they are usually a good place to start the information architecture process. The top-down approach allows you to quickly get a handle on the scope of the information environment without going through an extensive content-inventory process. You can begin identifying the major content areas and exploring possible organization schemes that will provide access to that content.

Designing hierarchies

When designing hierarchies, you should remember a few rules of thumb. First, you should be aware of, but not bound by, the idea that hierarchical categories should be mutually exclusive. Within a single organization scheme, you will need to balance the tension between exclusivity and inclusivity. Hierarchies that allow cross-listing are known as *polyhierarchical*. Ambiguous organization schemes in particular make it challenging to divide content into mutually exclusive categories. Do tomatoes belong in the fruit, vegetable, or berry category? In many cases, you might place the more ambiguous items into two or more categories so that users are sure to find them. However, if too many items are cross-listed, the hierarchy loses its value. This tension between exclusivity and inclusivity does not exist across different organization schemes. You would expect a listing of products organized by format to include the same items as a companion listing of products organized by topic. Topic and format are simply two different ways of looking at the same information. Or, to use a technical term, they're two independent *facets*. (See Chapter 10 for more about metadata, facets, and polyhierarchy.)

Second, it is important to consider the balance between breadth and depth in your hierarchy. *Breadth* refers to the number of options at each level of the hierarchy. *Depth* refers to the number of levels in the hierarchy. If a hierarchy is too narrow and deep, users have to click or tap through an inordinate number of levels to find what they are looking for. The top of Figure 6-13 illustrates a narrow-and-deep hierarchy in which users are faced with six clicks to reach the deepest content. The bottom shows a broad-and-shallow hierarchy, where users must choose from 10 categories to reach 10 content items. If a hierarchy is too broad and shallow, as in this case users are faced with too many options on the main menu and are unpleasantly surprised by the lack of content once they select an option.

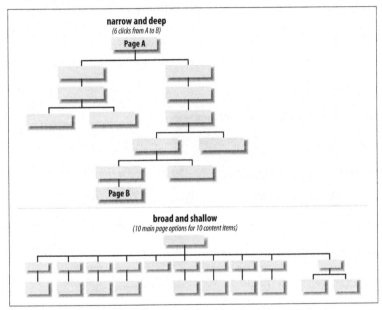

Figure 6-13. Balancing depth and breadth

When considering breadth, you should be sensitive to people's visual scanning abilities and to the cognitive limits of the human mind. Now, we're not going to tell you to follow the infamous seven plus or minus two rule.[4] There is general consensus that the number of links you can safely include is constrained by users' abilities to visually scan the page rather than by their short-term memories.

---

4 G. Miller, "The Magical Number Seven, Plus or Minus Two: Some Limits on Our Capacity for Processing Information" (*Psychological Review* 63:2, 1956, 81–97).

Instead, when dealing with issues of breadth versus depth we suggest that you:

- Recognize the danger of overloading users with too many options.
- Group and structure information at the page level.
- Subject your designs to rigorous user testing.

Consider the National Cancer Institute's award-winning main page, shown in Figure 6-14.[5] It's one of the US government's most visited (and tested) pages on the Web, and the portal into a large information system. Presenting information hierarchically at the page level, as NCI has done, can make a major positive impact on usability.

Figure 6-14. The National Cancer Institute groups items within the page

---

5 Just before this book went to press, the National Cancer Institute (*http://www.cancer.gov/*) launched a new, improved version of this page—which we like quite a bit!

There are roughly 85 links on NCI's main page, and they're organized into several key groupings (Table 6-1).

Table 6-1. Links on NCI's main page

Group	Notes
Global navigation	Global navigation (e.g., Cancer Topics, Clinical Trials, Cancer Statistics) has seven links plus Search.
Highlighted stories	Includes 9 links.
Types of Cancer	Includes 12 Common Cancer Types and 4 alternate ways to explore All Cancer Types.
Clinical Trials	Includes 4 links.
Cancer Topics	Includes 9 links.
Cancer Statistics	Includes 3 links.
Research & Funding	Includes 5 links.
NCI Vision & Priorities	Includes 4 links.
News	There are 3 headlines plus a link to the archive.
Resources	Includes 7 links.
Footer navigation	Includes 20 links.

These 80-odd links are subdivided into 10 discrete categories, with a limited number of links per category.

In contrast to breadth, when considering depth, you should be even more conservative. If users are forced to click through more than two or three levels, they may simply give up and leave your website. At the very least, they'll become frustrated. An excellent study conducted by Microsoft Research suggests that a balance of breadth and depth may provide the best results.[6]

For new information environments that are expected to grow, you should lean toward a broad-and-shallow rather than a narrow-and-deep hierarchy. This allows for the addition of content without major restructuring. It is less problematic to add items to secondary levels of the hierarchy than to the main page, for a couple of reasons. First, in many systems, the main page or screen serves as the most prominent and important navigation interface for users, helping set

---

6 Kevin Larson and Mary Czerwinski, Microsoft Research, "Web Page Design: Implications of Memory, Structure and Scent for Information Retrieval" (*http://bit.ly/larson_czerwinski*).

their expectations of what they can do in the system. Second, because of the main page's prominence and importance, companies tend to put lots of care (and money) into its graphic design and layout. Changes to the main page can be more time consuming and expensive than changes to secondary pages.

Finally, when designing organization structures, you should not become trapped by the hierarchical model. Certain content areas will invite a database or hypertext-based approach. The hierarchy is a good place to begin, but it is only one component in a cohesive organization system.

The Database Model: A Bottom-Up Approach

A database is defined as "a collection of data arranged for ease and speed of search and retrieval." A Rolodex provides a simple example of a flat-file database (see Figure 6-15). Before computers became commonplace, Rolodexes were a common tool to store people's contact information. They consisted of rolls of physical cards, with each card representing an individual contact: a *record* in the system. Each record contains several *fields*, such as name, address, and telephone number. Each field may contain data specific to that contact. The collection of records is a database.

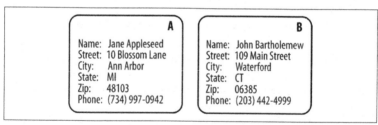

	A		B
	Name: Jane Appleseed		Name: John Bartholemew
	Street: 10 Blossom Lane		Street: 109 Main Street
	City: Ann Arbor		City: Waterford
	State: MI		State: CT
	Zip: 48103		Zip: 06385
	Phone: (734) 997-0942		Phone: (203) 442-4999

Figure 6-15. The printed card Rolodex is a simple database

In an old-fashioned Rolodex, users are limited to searching for a particular individual by last name. In a digital contact-management system, we can also search and sort using other fields. For example, we can ask for a list of all contacts who live in Connecticut, sorted alphabetically by city.

Most of the heavy-duty databases we use are built upon the relational database model. In relational database structures, data is stored within a set of relations or tables. Rows in the tables represent records, and columns represent fields. Data in different tables may be linked through a series of keys. For example, in Figure 6-16, the au_id and title_id fields within the AUTHOR_TITLE table act as keys linking the data stored separately in the AUTHOR and TITLE tables.

A Relational Data Base

AUTHOR

au_id	au_lname	au_fname	address	city	state
172-32-1176	White	Johnson	10932 Bigge Rd.	Menlo Park	CA
213-46-8915	Green	Marjorie	309 63rd St. #411	Oakland	CA
238-95-7766	Carson	Cheryl	589 Darwin Ln.	Berkeley	CA
267-41-2394	O'Leary	Michael	22 Cleveland Av. #14	San Jose	CA
274-80-9391	Straight	Dean	5420 College Av.	Oakland	CA
341-22-1782	Smith	Meander	10 Mississippi Dr.	Lawrence	KS
409-56-7008	Bennet	Abraham	6223 Bateman St.	Berkeley	CA
427-17-2319	Dull	Ann	3410 Blonde St.	Palo Alto	CA
472-27-2349	Gringlesby	Burt	PO Box 792	Covelo	CA
486-29-1786	Locksley	Charlene	18 Broadway Av.	San Francisco	CA

TITLE

title_id	title	type	price	pub_id
BU1032	The Busy Executive's Database Guide	business	19.99	1389
BU1111	Cooking with Computers	business	11.95	1389
BU2075	You Can Combat Computer Stress!	business	2.99	736
BU7832	Straight Talk About Computers	business	19.99	1389
MC2222	Silicon Valley Gastronomic Treats	mod_cook	19.99	877
MC3021	The Gourmet Microwave	mod_cook	2.99	877
MC3026	The Psychology of Computer Cooking	UNDECIDED		877
PC1035	But Is It User Friendly?	popular_comp	22.95	1389
PC8888	Secrets of Silicon Valley	popular_comp	20	1389
PC9999	Net Etiquette	popular_comp		1389
PS2091	Is Anger the Enemy?	psychology	10.95	736

PUBLISHER

pub_id	pub_name	city
736	New Moon Books	Boston
877	Binnet & Hardley	Washington
1389	Algodata Infosystems	Berkeley
1622	Five Lakes Publishing	Chicago
1756	Ramona Publishers	Dallas
9901	GGG&G	München
9952	Scootney Books	New York
9999	Lucerne Publishing	Paris

AUTHOR_TITLE

au_id	title_id
172-32-1176	PS3333
213-46-8915	BU1032
213-46-8915	BU2075
238-95-7766	PC1035
267-41-2394	BU1111
267-41-2394	TC7777
274-80-9391	BU7832
409-56-7008	BU1032
427-17-2319	PC8888
472-27-2349	TC7777

Figure 6-16. A relational database schema (image: http://bit.ly/rela-tional_model).

So why are database structures important to information architects? In a word, *metadata*. Metadata is the primary key that links information architecture to the design of database schemas. It allows us to apply the structure and power of relational databases to the heterogeneous, unstructured environments of websites and intranets. By tagging documents and other information objects with metadata, we enable powerful searching, browsing, filtering, and dynamic linking. (We'll discuss metadata and controlled vocabularies in more detail in Chapter 9.)

The relationships between metadata elements can become quite complex. Defining and mapping these formal relationships requires significant skill and technical understanding. For example, the entity relationship diagram (ERD) in Figure 6-17 illustrates a structured approach to defining a metadata schema. Each entity (e.g., Resource) has attributes (e.g., Name, URL). These entities and attributes become records and fields. The ERD is used to visualize and refine the data model before design and population of the database.

We're not suggesting that you must become an expert in SQL, XML schema definition, the creation of entity relationship diagrams, and the design of relational databases—though these are all extremely valuable skills. In many cases, you'll be better off working with a professional programmer or database designer who really knows how to do this stuff. And for large websites, you will hopefully be able to rely on content management system (CMS) software to manage your metadata and controlled vocabularies.

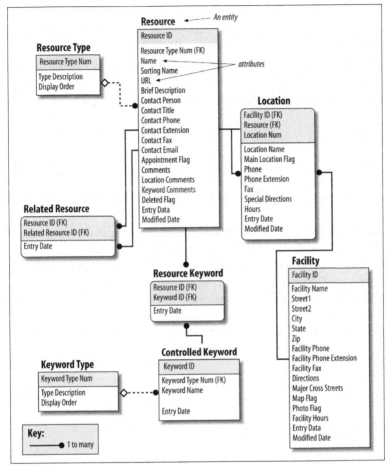

Figure 6-17. An entity relationship diagram showing a structured approach to defining a metadata schema (courtesy of Peter Wyngaard of Interconnect of Ann Arbor)

Instead, you need to understand how metadata, controlled vocabularies, and database structures can be used to enable:

- Automatic generation of alphabetical indexes (e.g., a product index)
- Dynamic presentation of associative "see also" links and content
- Fielded searching
- Advanced filtering and sorting of search results

The database model is particularly useful when applied within relatively homogeneous subsites such as product catalogs and staff directories. However, enterprise controlled vocabularies can often provide a thin horizontal layer of structure across the full breadth of a site. Deeper vertical vocabularies can then be created for particular departments, subjects, or audiences.

Hypertext

Hypertext is a highly nonlinear way of structuring information. A hypertext system involves two primary types of components: the items or chunks of information that will be linked, and the links between those chunks.

These components can form hypermedia systems that connect text, data, image, video, and audio chunks. Hypertext chunks can be connected hierarchically, nonhierarchically, or both, as shown in Figure 6-18. In hypertext systems, content chunks are connected via links in a loose web of relationships.

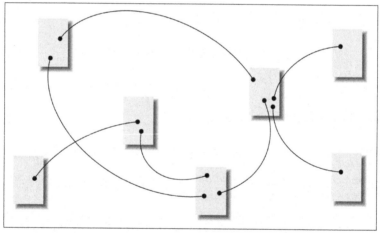

Figure 6-18. A network of hypertextual connections

Although this organization structure provides you with great flexibility, it presents substantial potential for complexity and user confusion. Why? Because hypertext links reflect highly personal associations. The relationships that one person sees between content items may not be apparent to others. Additionally, as users navigate through highly hypertextual websites, it is easy for them to get lost. It's as if they are thrown into a forest and are bouncing from tree to tree, trying to understand the lay of the land. They simply can't create a mental model of the environment's organization. Without context, users can quickly become overwhelmed and frustrated.

For these reasons, hypertext is rarely a good candidate for the primary organization structure. Rather, it can be used to complement structures based upon the hierarchical or database models.

Hypertext allows for useful and creative relationships between items and areas in the hierarchy. It usually makes sense to first design the information hierarchy and then identify ways in which hypertext can complement the hierarchy.

Social Classification

Social media has become a mainstay of the digital experience. Platforms like Facebook and Twitter have enabled hundreds of millions of people to share their interests, photos, videos, and more with one another and with all of us. As a result, social classification—primarily driven by user-generated content tagging—has emerged as an important tool for organizing information in shared information environments.

Free tagging, also known as collaborative categorization, mob indexing, and ethnoclassification, is a simple yet powerful tool. Users tag objects with one or more keywords. These tags can be informally supported in text fields, or they can be provided for with bespoke fields in the formal structure of content objects. The tags are public and serve as pivots for social navigation. Users can move fluidly between objects, authors, tags, and indexers. And when large numbers of people get involved, interesting opportunities arise to transform user behavior and tagging patterns into new organization and navigation systems.

For example, in Twitter, words with a prepended hash (#) have a special meaning: the system picks them up as tags. When you include one of these tagged words in a tweet, the system marks that post as belonging to a group of posts that has been informally defined by the users of Twitter (Figure 6-19). No single person or centralized team created a taxonomy to define these relationships.

Rather, they emerged (and continue to emerge) through the tagging efforts of many individuals.[7]

Figure 6-19. The "Discover" and "Trending" features in Twitter, which allow you to discover new and potentially interesting content, are driven by user-generated tags

Similarly, LinkedIn allows users to "endorse" their professional contacts as possessing certain individual professional skills (Figure 6-20). These endorsements are in effect tags: they allow users to describe their business contacts in a granular way that informs how the system groups them with similar people. Though users can suggest new endorsement labels, these are not free-form, unstructured tags like the ones that Twitter employs; they have been built as bespoke, dedicated structures within the architecture of LinkedIn.

In the early days of information architecture, an impassioned debate raged over whether or not free-form tag structures (or "folksonomies," as information architect Thomas Vander Wal cleverly christened them) would eliminate the need for top-down, centrally defined information structures. The passage of time has proven the value of top-down structures: high-profile experiments in tag-driven systems—such as the bookmarking service Delicious.com—fizzled in the marketplace, and most of these systems employed tags within centrally defined structures anyway. Still, free-form tagging has pro-

---

7 Twitter tags weren't originally included in the system: they emerged informally, included by the users of the platform in unstructured text fields.

ven its usefulness in specific situations, and it remains a valuable tool in the information architect's toolset.

Figure 6-20. LinkedIn allows you to "endorse" your contacts as having certain professional skills, from a set of predefined tags

Creating Cohesive Organization Systems

User experience designer Nathan Shedroff suggests that the first step in transforming data into information is exploring its organization. As you've seen in this chapter, organization systems are fairly complex. You need to consider a variety of exact and ambiguous organization schemes. Should you organize by topic, by task, or by audience? How about a chronological or geographical scheme? What about using multiple organization schemes?

You also need to think about the organization structures that influence how users can navigate through these schemes. Should you use a hierarchy, or would a more structured database model work best? Perhaps a loose hypertextual web would allow the most flexibility? Taken together in the context of a large website development project, these questions can be overwhelming. That's why it's important to break down the information enviornment into its components, so you can tackle one question at a time. Also, keep in mind that all information-retrieval systems work best when applied to narrow domains of homogeneous content. By decomposing the content collection into these narrow domains, you can identify opportunities for highly effective organization systems.

However, it's also important not to lose sight of the big picture. As with cooking, you need to mix the right ingredients in the right way to get the desired results. Just because you like mushrooms and pancakes doesn't mean they will go well together. The recipe for cohesive organization systems varies from one information environment to another. However, there are a few guidelines to keep in mind.

When considering which organization schemes to use, remember the distinction between exact and ambiguous schemes. Exact schemes are best for known-item searching, when users know precisely what they are looking for. Ambiguous schemes are best for browsing and associative learning, when users have a vaguely defined information need. Whenever possible, use both types of schemes. Also, be aware of the challenges of organizing information on the Web. Language is ambiguous, content is heterogeneous, people have different perspectives, and politics can rear their ugly head. Providing multiple ways to access the same information can help to deal with all of these challenges.

When thinking about which organization structures to use, keep in mind that large systems typically require several types of structures. The top-level, umbrella architecture for the environment will almost certainly be hierarchical. As you are designing this hierarchy, keep a look out for collections of structured, homogeneous information. These potential subenvironments are excellent candidates for the database model. Finally, remember that less structured, more creative relationships between content items can be handled through author-supplied hypertext or user-contributed tagging. In this way, myriad organization structures together can create a cohesive organization system.

Recap

Let's recap what we've learned in this chapter:

- Our understanding of the world is informed by how we classify things.
- Classifying things is not easy; we have to deal with ambiguity, heterogeneity, differences in perspective, and internal politics, among other challenges.

- We can organize things using exact organization schemes or ambiguous organization schemes.

- Exact organization schemes include alphabetical, chronological, and geographical groupings.

- Ambiguous organization schemes include topical, task-based, audience-based, metaphorical, and hybrid groupings.

- The structure of organization schemes also plays an important role in the design of information environments.

- Social classification has emerged as an important tool for organizing information in shared digital environments.

Now let's move on to cover another critical component of an information architecture: labeling systems.

CHAPTER 7

Labeling Systems

*Now the LORD God had formed out of the ground all the
wild animals and all the birds in the sky. He brought them
to the man to see what he would name them; and whatever
the man called each living creature, that was its name.*

—*Genesis 2:19*

In this chapter, we'll cover:

- What labeling is and why it's important
- Common types of labels
- Guidelines for developing labels
- Sources of inspiration for your labeling system

Labeling is a form of representation. Just as we use spoken words to represent concepts and thoughts, we use labels to represent larger chunks of information in our information environments. For example, "Contact Us" is a label that represents a chunk of content, often including a contact name, an address, and telephone, fax, and email information. You cannot present all this information quickly and effectively on an already crowded web page without overwhelming impatient people who might not actually need that information. Instead, a label like "Contact Us" works as a shortcut that triggers the right association in someone's mind without presenting all that stuff prominently. The person can then decide whether to click through or read on to get more contact information. So, the goal of a label is to communicate information efficiently—that is, to convey meaning without taking up too much of a page's physical space or the user's cognitive space.

Unlike the weather, hardly anyone ever talks about labeling (aside from a few deranged librarians, linguists, journalists, and information architects), but everyone can do something about it. In fact, we are doing something about it, albeit unconsciously: anyone developing content or an architecture for a website or app is creating labels without even realizing it. And our label creation goes far beyond our information products; ever since Adam named the animals, labeling has been one of the things that make us human. Spoken language is essentially a labeling system for concepts and things. Perhaps because we constantly label, we take the act of labeling for granted. That's why labeling can often be confusing, and users suffer the consequences. This chapter provides some advice on how to think through an information environment's labeling before diving into implementation.

How does labeling fit with the other systems we've discussed? Well, labels are often the most obvious way to clearly show the user your organization and navigation schemes across multiple systems and contexts. For example, a single screen layout might contain different groups of labels, with each group representing a different organization or navigation system. Examples include labels that match the environment's organization system (e.g., Home/Home Office, Small Business, Medium & Large Business, Government, Health Care), a global navigation system (e.g., Main, Search, Feedback), a subsite navigation system (e.g., Add to Cart, Enter Billing Information, Confirm Purchase), and systems specific to other channels such as interactive voice response (IVR) phone services and printed catalogs.

Why You Should Care About Labeling

Prerecorded or canned communications, including print, the Web, scripted radio, and TV, are very different from interactive real-time communications. When we talk with another person, we rely on constant user feedback to help us hone the way we get our message across. We subconsciously notice our conversation partner zoning out, getting ready to make her own point, or beginning to clench her fingers into an angry fist, and we react by shifting our own style of communication, perhaps by raising our speaking volume, increasing our use of body language, changing a rhetorical tack, or fleeing.

Unfortunately, when we "converse" with users through the systems we design, the feedback isn't quite so immediate, if it exists at all. There are certainly exceptions—social media such as Twitter, for example—but in most cases an information environment serves as an intermediary that slowly translates messages from the system's owners and authors to users, and back again. This "telephone game"[1] muddies the message. So in such a disintermediated medium with few visual cues, communicating is harder, and labeling is therefore more important.

To minimize this disconnect, we must try our best to design labels that speak the same language as our environment's users while reflecting its content. And, just as in a dialogue, when there is a question or confusion over a label, there should be clarification and explanation. Labels should educate people about new concepts and help them quickly identify familiar ones.

The conversation between a user and the environment's owner often begins on a website's main page. To get a sense of how successful this conversation might be, look at a site's main page, do your best to ignore the other aspects of its design, and ask yourself a few questions: Do the prominent labels on this page stand out to you? If they do, why? (Often, successful labels are invisible; they don't get in your way.) If a label is new, unanticipated, or confusing, is there an explanation? Or are you required to click through to learn more? Although unscientific, this label testing exercise will help you get a sense of how the conversation might go with actual users.

Let's try it with an average corporate information environment: Starbucks's public website, which is shown in Figure 7-1.[2]

---

1 A popular game that goes by different names around the world. Players pass a message in secret from one person to another. When it reaches the last player, they compare the (often unrecognizable) final message to the one they started with.

2 Thanks to information architect Andrew Hinton, who brought this example to our attention. You can read more about Andrew's take on Starbucks's labels in his book *Understanding Context* (Sebastopol, CA: O'Reilly, 2014).

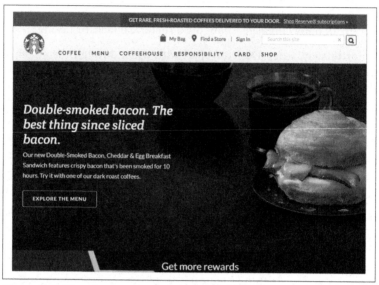

Figure 7-1. How do you respond to these labels?

Starbucks's labels don't seem terribly out of the ordinary. However, mediocrity isn't an indicator of value or success; in fact, trouble spots arise from an informal cruise through the site's labels. Let's have a look:

My Bag | Find a Store | Sign In | Search this site
> So far so good: these are fairly standard labels on websites for companies that sell goods in physical and online stores. The location pin icon next to the "Find a Store" link implies that this will lead to the geographic locations of Starbucks's stores, and the "My Bag" label, while not as common, is accompanied by a fairly standard bag icon that implies "shopping cart."

Coffee
> Again, not bad—Starbucks sells coffee, so we'd expect something like this here. It's also good that it's the first label next to the Starbucks logo, because it reinforces the association of the company logo with its primary product.

Menu
> This is where we start spotting trouble. What do we mean by "Menu" in the context of a website? Does this refer to the navigation menu of the site? A list of coffee drinks? Or is it a menu in the sense of a restaurant? (It turns out to be the latter.) While

this label doesn't seem to be that ambiguous in a desktop browser—after all, the rest of the site menu items are laid out next to it—it becomes more problematic when rendered in a mobile browser, because the label "Menu" is more often experienced in those browsers as a way of accessing the system's main navigation menu (Figure 7-2).

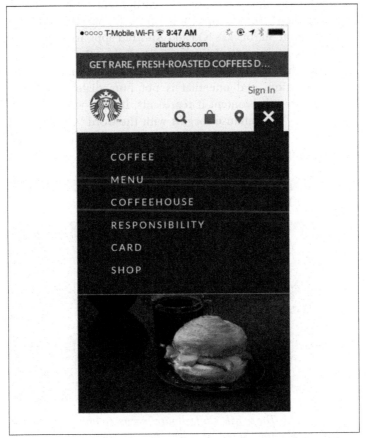

Figure 7-2. When accessed in a mobile browser, the labels used on the Starbucks website are experienced in a different context, which can change their meaning

It's worth noting here that while clicking the global menu links in the desktop version of the Starbucks website reveals megamenus for each label, mobile users can't derive additional contextual clues; all they have to go by are the labels of the global navigation menu.

Coffeehouse

You've probably seen this word before. What does it mean to you? According to the OS X dictionary, it means "a cafe or other place where coffee is served, sometimes also offering informal entertainment"—in other words, a physical place where you can buy coffee. So you'd think that this is where you will find a list of Starbucks's stores, and you'd be partly right... But there is much more there! For example, this is also where you find information about Starbucks's iOS and Android apps and the company's "Online Community" (Figure 7-3). It gives the impression that "Coffeehouse" has a particular meaning within the Starbucks Corporation, and one that is not immediately evident from examining the content it represents. It's also worth noting that because "Coffeehouse" begins with the word "Coffee" (and sits close to it in the navigation menu), this label may cause users to do a double-take when looking for coffee.

Figure 7-3. The word "Coffeehouse" seems to have a particular meaning in the context of Starbucks

Responsibility

Again, we don't have too many issues with this label; it's fairly common for large corporations to have social responsibility programs, and we'd expect to find that type of information here.

Card

"Card" seems like a very broad term. Does it refer to your Starbucks Card, the Starbucks eGift Card you received for your birthday, or the credit card that is registered as a valid payment method in your Starbucks account?

Shop

"Shop" can be a verb or a noun. Here it is meant as a verb: it's where you shop online in the "Starbucks Store" (which is not the same type of physical Starbucks "store" referred to in the "Find a Store" link). This is the only verb in the global navigation, a potential source of confusion for users who may read it as leading to information about a physical "shop."

The results of this quick exercise can be summarized by these categories:

The labels aren't representative and don't differentiate

Many of Starbucks's labels don't represent the content they link to or precede. Other than clicking through, users have no way to learn what "Menu" means, or what the difference is between "Coffeehouse," "Coffee," and "Shop." Groupings of dissimilar items (e.g., "Wi-Fi," "Starbucks Mobile Apps," and "Online Community") don't provide any context for what those items' labels really represent. There is too much potential for confusion to consider these labels effective.

Some labels are jargony, not user-centric

Labels like "Coffeehouse" and "Starbucks Store" can expose an organization that, despite its best intentions, does not consider the importance of its customers' needs as important as its own goals, politics, and culture. This is often the case when websites use organizational jargon for their labels. You've probably seen such sites; their labels are crystal clear, obvious, and enlightening, as long as you're one of the .01% of users who actually work for the sponsoring organization. A sure way to lose a sale is to label your site's product-ordering system as an "Order Processing and Fulfillment Facility."

The labels waste money

There are too many chances for a user to step into one of the many confusing cognitive traps presented by Starbucks's labels. And any time an architecture intrudes on a user's experience and forces him to pause and say "huh?" there is a reasonable chance that he will give up on a site and go somewhere else, especially given the competitive nature of this medium. In other words, confusing labels can negate the investment made to design and build a useful site and to market that site to intended audiences.

The labels don't make a good impression

The way you communicate or represent information on your site says a lot about you, your organization, and its brand. If you've ever read an airline magazine, you're familiar with those ads for some educational series that develops your vocabulary. "The words you use can make or break your business deals," or something like that. The same is true with an information environment's labeling—poor labeling can destroy a user's confidence in an organization. While it may have spent heavily on traditional branding, Starbucks doesn't seem to have given much thought to the labels on the most important piece of its virtual real estate—its main page.

Like writing or any other form of professional communication, labels do matter. It's fair to say that they're as integral to an effective web presence as any other aspect of your website, be it brand, visual design, functionality, content, or navigability.

Varieties of Labels

In information environments, we regularly encounter labels in two formats: textual and iconic. In this chapter, we'll spend most of our time addressing textual labels (as they remain the most common, despite the Web's highly visual nature), including:

Contextual links

Hyperlinks to chunks of information on other pages or to other locations on the same page

Headings

Labels that simply describe the content that follows them, just as print headings do

Navigation system choices

Labels representing the options in navigation systems

Index terms

Keywords, tags, and subject headings that represent content for searching or browsing

These categories are by no means perfect or mutually exclusive. A single label can do double duty; for example, the contextual link "Naked Bungee Jumping" could lead to a page that uses the heading label "Naked Bungee Jumping" and has been indexed as being about (you guessed it) naked bungee jumping. And some of these labels could be iconic rather than textual, although we'd rather not imagine a visual representation of naked bungee jumping!

In the following section, we'll explore the varieties of labels in greater detail and provide you with some examples.

Labels as Contextual Links

Labels describe the hypertext links within the body of a document or chunk of information, and naturally occur within the descriptive context of their surrounding text. Contextual links are easy to create and are the basis for the exciting interconnectedness that drives much of the Web's success.

However, just because contextual links are relatively easy to create doesn't mean they necessarily work well. In fact, ease of creation introduces problems. Contextual links are generally not developed systematically; instead, they are developed in an ad hoc manner when the author makes a connection between her text and something else, and encodes that association in her document. These hypertext connections are therefore more heterogeneous and personal than, say, the connections between items in a hierarchy, where links are understood to be connecting parent items and child items. The result is that contextual link labels mean different things to different people. You see the link "Shakespeare" and, upon clicking it, expect to be taken to the Bard's biography. I, on the other hand, expect to be taken to his Wikipedia entry. In fact, the link actually takes us to a page for the village of Shakespeare, New Mexico. Go figure...

To be more representational of the content they connect to, contextual links rely instead upon, naturally, context. If the content's author succeeds at establishing that context in his writing, then the label draws meaning from its surrounding text. If he doesn't, the label loses its representational value, and users are more likely to experience occasionally rude surprises.

Because GOV.UK (Figure 7-4) is a site dedicated to providing information to the entire population of the UK, contextual links need to be straightforward and meaningful. GOV.UK's contextual link labels, such as "Benefits," "Money and tax," and "Disabled people," are representational, and draw on surrounding text and headings to make it clear what type of help you'll receive if you click through. These highly representational labels are made even clearer by their context: explanatory text, clear headings, and a site that itself has a few straightforward uses.

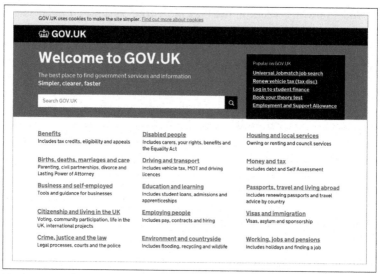

Figure 7-4. The contextual links on the GOV.UK home page are straightforward and meaningful

On the other hand, contextual links on a blog aren't necessarily so clear. The author is among friends and can assume that her regular readers possess a certain level of background (or, really, contextual) knowledge. Or she knows that keeping her link labels less representational creates some mystery around what they'll lead to. So the author may choose to design contextual link labels that aren't so representational.

In Figure 7-5, the author expects us to know who "Dr. Drang" is— perhaps s/he's been mentioned in this blog before. Or the author knows that we'll recognize the label "Dr. Drang" as a person, and provides some mysterious context—"Your favorite snowman and mine"—to entice the user to click through. "Brent Simmons' observation" is equally obscure; we have no idea what this label represents, but the blog author summarizes it by stating that "software engineers don't *really* have a code of ethics." Nonrepresentational labels have their place; as it's likely that we already trust the author's opinion, we'll probably want to click through and learn more. In a case like the blog illustrated here, they can even convey the feeling that you are dropping in on a discussion among friends. But without that degree of trust already in place, nonrepresentational links could be damaging.

Liss is More
By Casey Liss

ABOUT · CONTACT · CREEP · RSS

True Development is Boring
Friday, 27 February 2015

Your favorite snowman and mine, Dr. Drang, has responded to Brent Simmons' observation that software engineers don't *really* have a code of ethics. Certainly not like traditional professional engineers from old and boring tangible disciplines like civil engineering.

In his post, Dr. Drang makes an observation:

> Not that long ago, Daniel [Jalkut] couldn't be a licensed engineer, because there was no licensure procedure for software engineers, but that changed a couple of years ago. Now there's a licensing exam for software engineering, although I don't know how many states currently accept it.

Figure 7-5. These contextual links aren't very representational, but that's acceptable when there is a high degree of trust in the author

As we'll see, other varieties of labels derive context, and therefore meaning, from being part of larger sets of labels or labeling systems. But systematic consistency isn't quite so possible with link labels. These labels are glued together by the copy and context rather than membership in a peer group. However, consistency among these labels and the chunks of information to which they link remains an issue to keep in mind.

We can ensure that contextual link labels are representational by asking, "What kind of information will the person expect to be taken to?" before creating and labeling a contextual link. Contextual links are created in such an ad hoc manner that simply asking this question will improve the quality of representation. (An easy way to study people's interpretations of labels is to provide a printout of a page with the labels clearly identified, and have participants jot down what they'd expect each to link to.)

On the other hand, it's important to acknowledge that contextual links are often not within our control. Usually, content authors are responsible for contextual links. They are the ones who know the meaning of their content and how to best link it to other content. So while you may want to enforce rules for contextual link labels (such as what an employee's name should always link to), you may be better off suggesting guidelines to content authors (such as suggesting that employees' names link to corresponding directory listings when possible).

Labels as Headings

Labels are often used as headings that describe the chunks of information that follow. Headings, as shown in Figure 7-6, are often used to establish a hierarchy within content. Just as in a book, where headings help us distinguish chapters from sections, they also help us determine a site's subsites, or differentiate categories from subcategories.

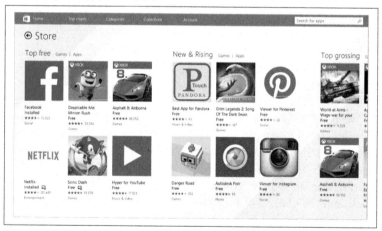

Figure 7-6. Layout, typographic treatment, and whitespace help the reader distinguish labels and hierarchy in the Windows Store

The hierarchical relationships between headings—whether parent, child, or sibling—are usually established visually through consistent use of numbering, font sizes, colors and styles, whitespace and indentation, or combinations thereof. A visually clear hierarchy, often the work of information or graphic designers, can take some pressure off information architects by reducing the need to create labels that convey that hierarchy. So, a set of labels that don't mean much can suddenly take on meaning when presented in a hierarchy. For example, this set of inconsistent headings may be quite confusing:

```
Our Furniture Selection
Office Chairs
Our buyer's picks
Chairs from Steelcase
Hon products
Herman Miller
Aerons
Lateral Files
```

However, they are much more meaningful when presented in a hierarchy:

```
Our Furniture Selection
    Office Chairs
        Our buyer's picks
            Chairs from Steelcase
                Hon products
                Herman Miller
                    Aerons
    Lateral Files
```

It's also important not to be too rigidly bound to showcasing hierarchical relationships. In Figure 7-7, heading labels such as "Leaders" and "Southeastern Standings" represent the content that follows them. Yet the game schedule closer to the top of the page doesn't merit the same treatment, because most readers could visually distinguish these without actually reading them. In other words, inserting the heading "Game Schedule" before the table and applying to it the same typographic style as that used for "Leaders" and "Southeastern Standings" wouldn't greatly benefit users, who would likely recognize the schedule already.

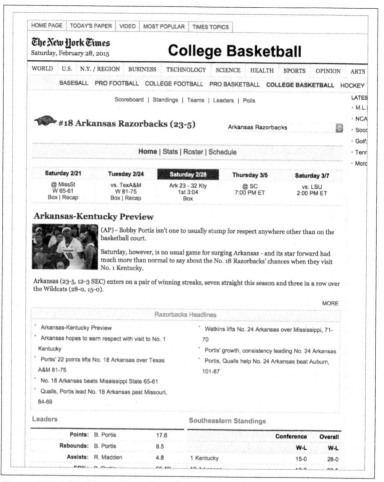

Figure 7-7. This hierarchy of heading labels is inconsistent, but that's OK

It is interesting to note, however, that it'd be impossible to correctly read the schedule if each column in the table didn't have its own heading label.

We can be a bit more flexible when designing hierarchical headings, but it's especially important to maintain consistency when labeling steps in a process. To successfully navigate a process, it's typically necessary for users to complete each step along the way, so heading labels have to be obvious and must also convey sequence. Using numbers is an obvious way to communicate progression, and consistently framing the labels as actions—utilizing verbs—also helps tie together the sequence of steps. In effect, the labels should tell users where to start, where to go next, and what action will be involved in each step along the way. Figure 7-8 shows a page in the process to sign up to become a Google Play Developer, which clearly describes the actions required in each step.

Figure 7-8. Clear sequential labeling in the Google Play Developer signup process

Heading labels, whether hierarchical or sequenced, come in multiples, and should be more systematically designed than contextual link labels.

Labels Within Navigation Systems

Because navigation systems typically have a small number of options, their labels demand consistent application more than any other type of label. A single inconsistent option can introduce an "apples and oranges" effect more quickly in a navigation system, which usually has fewer than 10 choices, than in a set of index terms, which might have thousands. Additionally, a navigation system is typically experienced repeatedly throughout the environment, so navigation labeling problems are magnified through repeated exposure.

Users rely on a navigation system to behave "rationally" through a consistent location and look; labels should be no different.

Effectively applied labels are integral to building a sense of familiarity, so they'd better not change from page to page. Using the label "Main" on one page, "Main Page" on another, and "Home" elsewhere could destroy the familiarity that the user needs when navigating a site. In Figure 7-9, the horizontal navigation system's four labels—"The Janus Advantage," "Our Funds," "Planning," and "My Account"—are applied consistently throughout the website, and would be even more effective if their colors and locations were also consistent.

There are no standards, but some common variants exist for many navigation system labels. You should consider selecting one from each of these categories and applying it consistently, as these labels are already familiar to most web users. Here is a nonexhaustive list:

- Main, Main Page, Home
- Search, Find, Browse, Search/Browse
- Site Map, Contents, Table of Contents, Index
- Contact, Contact Us
- Help, FAQ, Frequently Asked Questions
- News, News & Events, News & Announcements, Announcements
- About, About Us, About <company name>, Who We Are

Of course, the same label can often represent different kinds of information. For example, in one system, "News" may link to an area that includes announcements of new additions to the website. In another site, "News" may link to an area of news stories describing national and world events. Obviously, if you use the same labels in different ways within your own system, your users will be very confused. One alternative in such cases is to include brief descriptions under navigational labels, with the obvious trade-off being that these descriptions consume valuable screen real estate.

Figure 7-9. Janus's navigation system labels remain consistent through-out the website

Labels as Index Terms

Often referred to as keywords, tags, descriptive metadata, taxono-mies, controlled vocabularies, and thesauri, sets of index term labels can be used to describe any type of content: sites, subsites, pages, content chunks, and so on. By representing the meaning of a piece of content, index terms support more precise searching than simply searching the full text—someone has assessed the content's meaning and described it using index terms, and searching those terms ought to be more effective than having a search engine match a query against the content's full text.

Index terms are also used to make browsing easier: the metadata from a collection of documents can serve as the source of browsable lists or menus. This can be highly beneficial to users, as index terms provide an alternative to a primary organization system, such as an information architecture organized by business unit. Index terms in the form of indexes and other lists provide a valuable alternative view by "cutting across the grain" of organizational silos.

The index of the SFGate website shown in Figure 7-10 is generated from index term labels, which in turn are used to identify content from many different sections of the site. Much of the content already accessible through the site's primary organization system is also accessible by browsing these index terms (i.e., keywords).

Figure 7-10. The SFGate site index

Frequently, index terms are completely invisible to users. The records we use to represent documents in content management systems and other databases typically include fields for index terms, which are often heard but not seen: they come into play only when you search. Similarly, index terms may be hidden as embedded metadata in an HTML document's `<meta>` or `<title>` tags. For example, a furniture manufacturer's website might list the following index terms in the `<meta>` tags of records for its upholstered items:

```
<meta name="keywords" CONTENT="upholstery, upholstered, sofa,
    couch, loveseat, love seat, sectional, armchair, arm chair,
    easy chair, chaise lounge">
```

A search on "sofa" would then retrieve the page with these index terms even if the term "sofa" doesn't appear anywhere in the page's text. Figure 7-11 shows a similar, more delectable example from the *Bon Appétit* website. A search for "snack" retrieves this recipe, though there is no mention of the term in the recipe itself. "Snack" is likely stored separately as an index term in a database record for this recipe.

Figure 7-11. A search for "snack" retrieves this recipe, even though the term doesn't appear within the text

Web search engines such as Google have become the primary way in which people find and access websites. Using index terms to describe a main page is an effective way for getting that page, and the site as a whole, indexed and "known" so that users who search the Web are more likely to find it.[3]

Getting your pages to stand out from one another is a different and much more daunting challenge. That's where a more systematic approach to labeling—using index terms from controlled vocabularies or thesauri—has more value. These sets of labels are designed to describe delineated domains—such as products and services, or oncology—and to do so in a consistent, predictable manner. We'll describe these vocabularies in great detail in Chapter 10.

Iconic Labels

It's true that a picture is worth a thousand words. But which thousand?

Icons can represent information in much the same way as text can. We see them most frequently used as navigation system labels, especially in mobile apps where screen space is constrained. Additionally, icons occasionally serve as heading labels and have even been known to show up as link labels, although this is rare.

The problem with iconic labels is that they constitute a much more limited language than text. That's why they're more typically used for navigation system or small organization system labels, where the list of options is small, than for larger sets of labels such as index terms, where iconic "vocabularies" are quickly outstripped. They also can work well for less text-oriented audiences, such as children.

Even so, iconic labels are still a risky proposition in terms of whether or not they can represent meaning. Figure 7-12 shows navigation tiles on the Microsoft Band fitness tracker. What do the icons mean to you?

---

3 Search Engine Watch (*http://www.searchenginewatch.com*) is the most useful resource for learning how web-wide search engines and directories work, and how you can index your site's main and other major pages so they "rise to the top" of retrieval results.

Figure 7-12. Icons from the Microsoft Band's navigation system (image: https://www.microsoft.com/microsoft-band/en-us)

(They are, respectively: Mail, Run, Calendar, Exercise, Sleep, Messaging, and Finance.)

Even given the fairly specific context of a fitness band, most users probably won't understand this language immediately, although they might correctly guess the meaning of one or two of these labels.

Iconic labels like these add aesthetic appeal to an information environment, and as long as they don't compromise the system's usability, there's no reason not to use them. In fact, the iconic "language" might get established in your users' minds through repeated exposure. In such situations, icons are especially useful shorthand, both representational and easy to visually recognize—a double bonus. Unless your system has a patient, loyal audience of users who are willing to learn your visual language, however, we suggest using iconic labels only for environments with a limited set of options, being careful not to place form ahead of function.

Designing Labels

Designing effective labels is perhaps the most difficult aspect of information architecture. Language is simply too ambiguous for you to ever feel confident that you've perfected a label. There are always synonyms and homonyms to worry about, and different contexts influence our understanding of what a particular term means. And of course, the challenge is much more complicated if your system deals with more than one language. But even labeling conventions are questionable: you absolutely cannot assume that the label "main page" will be correctly interpreted by 100% of your system's users. Your labels will never be perfect, and you can only hope that your efforts make a difference, as measuring label effectiveness is an extremely difficult undertaking.

If it sounds to you like labeling is an art rather than a science, you're absolutely correct. And, as in all such cases, you can forget about finding incontrovertible rules, and hope for guidelines instead. Following are some guidelines and related issues that will help you as you delve into the mysterious art of label design.

General Guidelines

Remember that *content*, *users*, and *context* affect all aspects of an information architecture, and this is particularly true with labels. Any of the variables attached to users, content, and context can drag a label into the land of ambiguity.

Let's revisit the term "pitch." From baseball (what's thrown) to football (the field where it's played in the United Kingdom), from business (what's sometimes made while riding in an elevator) to sailing (the angle of the boat in the water), there are at least 15 different definitions, and it's hard to make sure that your site's users, content, and context will converge upon the same definition. This ambiguity makes it difficult to assign labels to describe content, and difficult for users to rely on their assumptions about what specific labels actually mean.

So what can we do to make sure our labels are less ambiguous and more representational? The following two guidelines may help.

Narrow the scope whenever possible

If we focus our information environments on a more defined audience, we reduce the number of possible perspectives on what a label means. Sticking to fewer subject domains achieves more obvious and effective representation. A narrower business context means clearer goals for the system, its architecture, and therefore its labels.

Labeling is easier if your content, users, and context are kept simple and focused. Too many environments have tried to take on too much, achieving broad mediocrity rather than nailing a few choice tasks. Accordingly, labeling systems often cover too much ground to truly be effective. If you are planning any aspect of your environment's scope—who will use it, what content it will contain, and how, when, and why it should be used—erring toward simplicity will make your labels more effective.

If your environment must be a jack of all trades, avoid using labels that address the entire system's content. The obvious exceptions are the labels for global navigation systems, which do cover the entire system. But in the other areas of labeling, modularizing and simplifying content into subsections that meet the needs of specific audiences will enable you to design more modular, simpler collections of labels to address those specific areas.

This modular approach may result in separate labeling systems for different areas of your environment. For example, records in your staff directory might benefit from a specialized labeling system that wouldn't make sense for other parts of the site, while your site-wide navigation system's labels wouldn't really apply to entries in the staff directory.

Develop consistent labeling systems, not labels

It's also important to remember that labels, like organization and navigation systems, are systems in their own right. Some are planned systems; some aren't. A successful system is designed with one or more characteristics that unify its members. In successful labeling systems, one characteristic is typically consistency.

Why is consistency important? Because consistency means predictability, and systems that are predictable are simply easier to learn. You see one or two labels, and then you know what to expect from the rest—if the system is consistent. This is especially important for first-time users, but consistency benefits all users by making labeling easy to learn, easy to use, and therefore invisible.

Consistency is affected by many issues:

Style
> Haphazard usage of punctuation and case is a common problem within labeling systems, and can be addressed, if not eliminated, by using style guides. Consider hiring a proofreader and purchasing a copy of Strunk & White.

Presentation
> Similarly, consistent application of fonts, font sizes, colors, whitespace, and grouping can help visually reinforce the systematic nature of a group of labels.

Syntax
> It's not uncommon to find verb-based labels (e.g., "Grooming Your Dog"), noun-based labels (e.g., "Diets for Dogs"), and question-based labels (e.g., "How Do You Paper Train Your Dog?") all mixed together. Within a specific labeling system,

consider choosing a single syntactical approach and sticking with it.

Granularity

Within a labeling system, it can be helpful to present labels that are roughly equal in their specificity. Exceptions (such as site indexes) aside, it's confusing to encounter a set of labels that cover differing levels of granularity—for example, "Chinese restaurants," "Restaurants," "Taquerias," "Fast Food Franchises," "Burger Kings."

Comprehensiveness

People can be tripped up by noticeable gaps in a labeling system. For example, if a clothing retailer's website lists "trousers," "ties," and "shoes," while somehow omitting "shirts," we may feel like something's wrong. Do they really not carry shirts? Or did they make a mistake? Aside from improving consistency, a comprehensive scope also helps people do a better job of quickly scanning and inferring the environment's content.

Audience

Mixing terms like "lymphoma" and "tummy ache" in a single labeling system can also throw people off, even if only temporarily. Consider the languages of your environment's major audiences. If each audience uses a very different terminology, you may have to develop a separate labeling system for each audience, even if these systems are describing exactly the same content.

There are other potential roadblocks to consistency. None is particularly difficult to address, but you can certainly save a lot of labor and heartache if you consider these issues before you dive into creating labeling systems.

Sources of Labeling Systems

Now that you're ready to design your labeling systems, where do you start? Believe it or not, this is the easy part. Unless you're dealing with ideas, concepts, and topics that until now were unknown to humanity, you'll probably have something to start with. And already having a few labels generally beats starting from scratch, which can be prohibitively expensive, especially with large vocabularies.

Existing labeling systems might include the labels currently on your website, or comparable or competitors' sites. Ask yourself who might have taken this on before. Study, learn, and "borrow" from what you find in other environments. And keep in mind that a major benefit of examining existing labeling systems is that they're *systems*—they're more than groups of odd, miscellaneous labels that don't necessarily fit together.

As you look for existing labeling systems to draw upon, consider what works and what doesn't. Which systems can you learn from, and, perhaps more importantly, which of those labels can you keep? There are a variety of sources for labels that you should examine.

Your current information environment

Your current website or app probably already has labeling systems by default. At least some reasonable decisions had to have been made during the course of its creation, so you probably won't want to throw all those labels out completely. Instead, use them as a starting point for developing a complete labeling system, taking into consideration the decisions made while creating the original system.

A useful approach is to capture the existing labels in a single document. To do so, walk through the entire system, either manually or automatically, and gather the labels. You might consider assembling them in a simple table containing a list or outline of each label and the documents it represents. Creating a labeling table is often a natural extension of the content inventory process. It's a valuable exercise, though we don't recommend it for indexing term vocabularies, which are simply too large to table-ize unless you focus on small, focused segments of those vocabularies.

Table 7-1 provides a breakdown of the navigation system labels on Budget Rent A Car's main page.[4]

---

4 Like many information environments, Budget.com is evolving. Prior to going to press, the site implemented changes to its design and labeling that fixed many of the issues presented here.

Table 7-1. Budget Rent A Car's navigation labels

Label	Destination's heading label	Destination's <TITLE> label
Top-of-page navigation system labels		
car rental	-	Automobile Rental from Budget
specials	Daily, Weekly, Weekend Day & Monthly Specials	Budget coupons and car rental deals U.S. | Budget.com
car types	Rental car, SUV, and truck fleet	Rental Car, SUV & Truck Fleet
locations	find your location in USA	United States Car Rentals and car rental deals at Budget.com
services	Smart Car Rental Services	Smart Car Rental Services - Perks & Products - Budget.com
customer care	Customer Care	contact us | customer care | Budget
car sales	-	Great Prices on Used Rental Cars - Budget Car Sales
country / language	Renting outside of the U.S.?	-
Sign in	Sign In Authentication	sign in | frequent renter | Budget
Reserve with customer ID	-	rent your car today | Budget
Create customer ID	Frequent Renter Account Services	Car Rental Deals
Body navigation system labels		
Rent a car in 60 seconds	-	rent your car today | Budget
Make a Car Reservation	-	rent your car today | Budget
Already Have a Reservation?	View, Change or Cancel an Existing Reservation	rent your car today | Budget
Common Questions	Just the FAQs	Common Questions - Car Rental FAQs - Budget.com
Find a Location	find your location in USA	United States Car Rentals and car rental deals at Budget.com
Bottom-of-page navigation system labels		
About Budget	About Us	About Us - Car Rentals - Budget.com
Privacy	U.S. Privacy	US Privacy Policy - Customer Care - Budget.com
Site map	Budget.com car rental site map	Site Map - Car Rental, Reservations & Discounts - Budget.com

Label	Destination's heading label	Destination's <TITLE> label
Contact Us	Customer Care	contact us | customer care | Budget
Employment	avis budget group	Avis Budget Group
Car Rental Locations	find your location in USA	United States Car Rentals and car rental deals at Budget.com
Budget Worldwide	Budget Rental Car Locations: Worldwide	Budget Car Rentals Locations Worldwide - Budget
US & Canada	Budget Rental Car Locations: World	Budget Car Rentals Locations - Budget
Major Airports	Popular Airport Car Rental Locations	Airport Car Rental Locations from Budget.com
Orlando Car Rental	Orlando Car Rental	Orlando Car Rental - Rent a Car in Orlando, Florida at Budget.com
Featured Rentals	Popular Available Car Types	Available Car Types from Budget.com
Van Rentals	Van Car Rental	Van Rental - Passenger Van rental from Budget
Car Rental Deals	Budget Coupons at Budget.com	Budget Rental Car Coupons - Save On a Budget Car Rental
One Way Car Rental	One Way Car Rental	One Way Car Rental - Budget offers special deals on one way car rentals
Monthly Car Rental	Long Term Car Rental	Monthly Car Rental - Save more with long term car rental
Featured Products	Smart Car Rental Services	Smart Car Rental Services - Perks & Products - Budget.com
Small Business Rentals	Budget Business Program	company account | frequent renters | Budget
Car in the shop?	Reservations	Budget Reservations - Vehicle Replacement
Budget Mobile Apps	The Budget Mobile App	Budget Rent A Car - Budget Mobile
Go Green - Rent Clean	Go Greener. Drive Cleaner.	Green Car Rental - Rent an Eco-Friendly Vehicle - Budget.com
Business accounts	U.S. Budget Business Program®	Budget Business Car Rental Program - Budget.com
Partners	Partners	Partners, Affiliates, Travel Agents - Budget.com
Affiliates	Travel Affiliate Program	affiliates | partners | about us | Budget
Travel agents	Car Rental Services for Travel Agents	Rent A Car at Budget - Travel Agents
Car sales	Love it. Buy it.	Car Sales - Buy Used Cars from Budget

Label	Destination's heading label	Destination's <TITLE> label
Budget is your earth friendly alternative	Go Greener. Drive Cleaner.	Green Car Rental - Rent an Eco-Friendly Vehicle - Budget.com

Arranging labels in a table provides a more condensed, complete, and accurate view of navigation labels as a *system*. Inconsistencies are easier to catch; in Budget's case, we encounter three variants of the company's name: "Budget," "Budget Rent A Car," and "Budget.com." We find inconsistencies for a single page's labels: the contact page is labeled "Contact Us" and "Customer Care." Some pages don't have main headings. We encounter various other style and capitalization inconsistencies that may confuse users. We may decide that, personally, we just don't like certain labels. We may also decide that some of the problems aren't worth changing. In any case, we now have a sense of the site's current labeling system and how it could be improved.

Comparable and competitive environments

If you don't have a website or app in place or are looking for new ideas, look elsewhere for labeling systems. The open nature of the Web allows us to learn from one another. So, just as you might view the source of a wonderfully designed page, you can learn from another site's great labeling system.

Determine beforehand what your audiences' needs are most likely to be, and then surf your competitors' sites, borrowing what works and noting what doesn't (you might consider creating a label table for this specific purpose). If you don't have competitors, visit comparable sites or sites that seem to be best in class.

As we mentioned in Chapter 4, the Web is already old enough to have produced various industry-specific typologies. If you explore multiple competitive or comparative environments, you may find that labeling patterns emerge. These patterns may not yet be industry standards, but they at least can inform your choice of labels. For example, in a competitive analysis of eight financial services sites "personal finance" was found to be more or less the de facto label choice, compared to its synonyms. Such data may discourage you from using a different label.

Figure 7-13 shows labeling systems from United, Delta, Virgin America, and American Airlines, all competing in the airline business. Do you notice trends and differences here? Just a glance shows how much variation there is in terms of the number of labels (from five to as many as nine). Some use the "My..." approach, and some use brand-specific labels (e.g., "AAdvantage"). Task-based labels (e.g., "Book a trip") are less common than one would expect, as is the use of a "Home" or "Main" option.

United		Delta	
	Home		My Trips
	Reservations		Book a Trip
	Travel Information		Flight Status
	Deals & Offers		Check In
	MileagePlus©		Vacations
	Products & Services		
	United		
Virgin America		**American Airlines**	
	Book		Find Flights
	Check In		My Trips / Check-In
	Manage		Flight Status
	Deals		Plan Travel
	Flying With Us		Travel Information
	Where We Fly		AAdvantage
	Fees		
	Flight Status		
	Flight Alerts		

Figure 7-13. Labeling systems from United, Delta, Virgin America, and American Airlines

Controlled vocabularies and thesauri

Another great source for labels is existing controlled vocabularies and thesauri (a topic we'll cover in depth in Chapter 10). These especially useful resources are created by professionals with library or subject-specific backgrounds, who have already done much of the work of ensuring accurate representation and consistency. These vocabularies are often publicly available and have been designed for broad usage. You'll find these to be most useful for populating labeling systems used for indexing content.

Seek out narrowly focused vocabularies that help specific audiences to access specific types of content. For example, if your system's users are computer scientists, a computer science thesaurus "thinks" and represents concepts in a way your users are likely to understand, more so than a general scheme like the Library of Congress subject headings would.

A good example of a specific controlled vocabulary is the Educational Resources Information Center (ERIC) Thesaurus. This thesaurus was designed, as you'd guess, to describe the domain of education. An entry in the ERIC Thesaurus for "scholarship" is shown in Figure 7-14.

Figure 7-14. Controlled vocabularies and thesauri are rich sources of labels

If your environment has to do with education or if your audience is comprised of educators, you might start with ERIC as the source for your system's labels. You can use a thesaurus like ERIC to help you with specific labeling challenges, like determining a better variant for a particularly knotty label. You might go as far as to license the entire vocabulary and use it as your system's labeling system.

Unfortunately, there aren't controlled vocabularies and thesauri for every domain. Sometimes you may find a matching vocabulary that emphasizes the needs of a different audience. Still, it's always worth seeing if a potentially useful controlled vocabulary or thesaurus exists before creating labeling systems from scratch. Try these excellent resources as you hunt for sources of labels:

- Taxonomy Warehouse (*http://taxonomywarehouse.com/*)
- American Online Thesauri and Authority Files (American Society for Indexing) (*http://bit.ly/online_thesauri*)

Creating New Labeling Systems

When there are no existing labeling systems that meet your needs, or when you need to do more customizing than you'd expected, you face the tougher challenge of creating labeling systems from scratch. Your most important sources are your content (and potentially its authors), and the people who will be using your environment.

Content analysis

Labels can come directly from your content. You might read a representative sample of your environment's content and jot down a few descriptive keywords for each document along the way. It's a slow and painful process, and it obviously won't work with a huge set of documents. If you go this route, look for ways to speed up the process by focusing on any existing content representations like titles, summaries, and abstracts. Analyzing content for candidate labels is certainly another area where art dominates science.

There are software tools available that can perform *auto-extraction* of meaningful terms from content. These tools—typically referred to as "entity extraction" applications—can save you quite a bit of time if you face a huge body of content; like many software-based solutions, auto-extraction tools may get you 80% of the way to the finish line. You'll be able to take the terms that are output by the software and use them as candidates for a controlled vocabulary, but you'll still need to do a bit of manual labor to make sure the output actually makes sense. (And it's worth noting that auto-extraction tools—and the training and tuning required to make them work well—can be quite expensive.)

Content authors

Another manual approach is to ask content authors to suggest labels for their own content. This might be useful if you have access to authors; for example, you could talk to your company's researchers who create technical reports and white papers, or to the PR people who write press releases.

However, even when authors select terms from a controlled vocabulary to label their content, they don't necessarily do it with the realization that their documents are only one of many in a broader collection. So, they might not use sufficiently specific labels. Also, few authors happen to be professional indexers.

So take their labels with a grain of salt, and don't rely upon them for accuracy. As with other sources, labels from authors should be considered useful candidates for labels, not final versions.

User advocates and subject matter experts

Another approach is to find advanced users or user advocates who can speak on the users' behalf. Such people may include librarians, switchboard operators, or subject matter experts (SMEs) who are familiar with the users' information needs in a larger context. Some of these people—reference librarians, for example—keep logs of what people want; all will have a good innate sense of people's needs by dint of constant interaction.

We found that talking to user advocates was quite helpful when working with a major healthcare system. Working with its library's staff and SMEs, we set out to create two labeling systems: one with medical terms to help medical professionals browse the services offered by the healthcare system, the other for the lay audience to access the same content. It wasn't difficult to come up with the medical terms because there are many thesauri and controlled vocabularies geared toward labeling medical content. It was much more difficult to come up with a scheme for the layperson's list of terms. There didn't seem to be an ideal controlled vocabulary, and we couldn't draw labels from the site's content because it hadn't been created yet. So we were truly starting from scratch.

We solved this dilemma by using a top-down approach: we worked with the librarians to determine what they thought users wanted out of the system. We considered their general needs, and came up with a few major ones:

- They need information about a problem, illness, or condition.
- The problem is with a particular organ or part of the body.
- They want to know about the diagnostics or tests that the healthcare professionals will perform to learn more about the problem.
- They need information on the treatment, drug, or solution that will be provided by the healthcare system.
- They want to know how they can pay for the service.
- They want to know how they can maintain their health.

We then came up with basic terms to cover the majority of these six categories, taking care to use terms appropriate to this audience of laypersons. Table 7-2 shows some examples.

Table 7-2. Sample laypersons' labels for identified categories

Category	Sample labels
Problem/illness/condition	HIV, fracture, arthritis, depression
Organ/body part	Heart, joints, brain
Diagnostics/tests	Blood pressure, X-ray
Treatment/drug/solution	Hospice, bifocals, joint replacement
Payment	Administrative services, health maintenance organization, medical records
Health maintenance	Exercise, vaccination

By starting with a few groupings, we were able to generate labels to support indexing. We knew a bit about the audience (laypersons), and so were able to generate the right kinds of terms to support their needs (e.g., *leg* instead of *femur*). The secret was working with people (in this case, staff librarians) who were knowledgeable about the kind of information people want.

Users (directly)

The actual users of a system may be able to tell you what the labels should be. This isn't the easiest information to get your hands on, but if you can, it's the best source of labeling there is.

Card sorting. *Card sort* exercises are one of the best ways to learn how your users would use information.[5] (Card sorting methodologies are covered more extensively in Chapter 11.) There are two basic varieties of card sorts: open and closed. *Open card sorts* allow participants to cluster labels for existing content into their own categories and then label those categories (and clearly, card sorting is useful when designing organization systems as well as labeling systems). *Closed card sorts* provide participants with existing categories and ask them to sort content into those categories. At the start of a closed card sort, you can ask users to explain what they think each category label represents and compare these definitions to your own. Both approaches are useful ways to determine labels, although they're more appropriate for smaller sets of labels such as those used for navigation systems.

In the following example, we asked participants to categorize cards from the owner's section of a website for a large automotive company (let's call it "Tucker"). After we combined the data from this open card sort, we found that participants labeled the combined categories in different ways. "Maintenance," "maintain," and "owner's" were often used in labels for the first cluster, indicating that these were good candidates for labels (see Table 7-3).

Table 7-3. Cluster 1

Participant	Identified categories
Participant 1	Ideas & maintenance
Participant 2	Owner's guide
Participant 3	Items to maintain car
Participant 4	Owner's manual
Participant 5	Personal information from dealer
Participant 6	[No response]
Participant 7	Maintenance upkeep & ideas
Participant 8	Owner's tip AND owner's guide and maintenance

But in other cases, no strong patterns emerged (see Table 7-4).

---

5 Donna Spencer's book *Card Sorting: Designing Usable Categories* (Brooklyn, NY: Rosenfeld Media, 2011) is quite helpful here.

Table 7-4. Cluster 2

Participant	Identified categories
Participant 1	Tucker features
Participant 2	[No response]
Participant 3	Shortcut for info on car
Participant 4	Auto info
Participant 5	Associate with dealer
Participant 6	Tucker website info
Participant 7	Manuals specific to each car
Participant 8	[No response]

In a corresponding closed card sort, we asked participants to describe each category label before they grouped content under each category. In effect, we were asking participants to define each of these labels, and we compared their answers to see if they were similar or not. The more similar the answers, the stronger the label.

Some labels, such as "Service & Maintenance," were commonly understood, and were in line with the content that you'd actually find listed under that category (see Table 7-5).

Table 7-5. Service & Maintenance

Participant	Identified content
Participant 1	When to change the fluids, rotate tires; a place to keep track when I had my vehicle in for service (sic)
Participant 2	How to maintain vehicle: proper maintenance, features of car, where to find fuse box, etc., owner's manual
Participant 3	Find service that might be open on Sunday sometimes
Participant 4	When I will need service and where to go to get it
Participant 5	Reminders on when services is recommended (sic)
Participant 6	Timeline for service and maintenance
Participant 7	Maintenance schedule and tips to get best performance out of car and longevity of car
Participant 8	Maintenance tips, best place to go to fix car problem, estimated price

Other category labels were more problematic. Some participants understood "Tucker Features & Events" in the way that was intended, representing announcements about automobile shows, discounts, and so on. Others interpreted this label to mean a vehicle's actual features, such as whether or not it had a CD player (see Table 7-6).

Table 7-6. Tucker Features & Events

Participant	Identified content
Participant 1	New items for my vehicle; upcoming new styles—new makes & models; financial news—like 0% financing
Participant 2	Local & national sponsorship; how to obtain Tucker sponsorship; community involvement
Participant 3	Mileage, CD or cassette, leg room, passengers, heat/AC control dull or not, removable seats, automatic door openers
Participant 4	All information regarding the Tucker automobile I'm looking for and any sale events going on regarding this auto
Participant 5	Looking for special pricing events
Participant 6	Site for outlining vehicles and options available. What automobile shows are available and where.
Participant 7	About Tucker, sales, discounts, special events
Participant 8	No interested (sic)

Card sort exercises are very informative, but it's important to recognize that they don't present labels in the context of an actual product. Without this natural context, the labels' ability to represent meaning is diminished. So, like all other techniques, card sorts have value but shouldn't be seen as the only method of investigating label quality.

Free-listing. While card sorting isn't necessarily an expensive and time-consuming method, free-listing is an even lower-cost way to get users to suggest labels.[6] Free-listing is quite simple: select an item and have participants brainstorm terms to describe it. You can do this in person (capturing data with pencil and paper will be fine) or remotely, using a free or low-cost online survey tool like Survey-Monkey, Zoomerang, or Google Forms. That's really all there is to it.

Well, not quite: you'll want to consider your participants: who (ideally representative of your overall audience) and how many (three to

---

6 The best summary of this method is Rashmi Sinha's short but highly useful article, "Beyond Cardsorting: Free-Listing Methods to Explore User Categorizations," *Boxes & Arrows*, February 2003 (*http://bit.ly/beyond_cardsorting*).

five may not yield scientifically significant results, but it is certainly better than nothing and may yield some interesting results). You might also consider asking participants to rank the terms they've suggested as a way to determine which are the most appropriate.

You'll also need to choose which items to brainstorm terms for. Obviously you can only do this with a subset of your content. You could choose some representative content, such as a handful of your company's products. But even then, it'll be tricky—do you choose the most popular products or the more esoteric ones? It's important to get the labeling right for your big sellers, but conventions for their labels are already fairly established. The esoteric items? Well, they're more challenging, but fewer people care about them. So you may end up with a balance among the few items you select for a free-listing exercise. This is one of those cases where the art of information architecture is at least as important as the science.

What do you do with the results? Look for patterns and frequency of usage; for example, perhaps most of your participants use the term "cell phone" while surprisingly few prefer "mobile phone." Patterns like these not only can provide you with a sense of how to label an individual item, but may also demonstrate the tone of users' language overall. You might note that they use jargon quite a bit, or the reverse; perhaps you find a surprising amount of acronyms in their labels, or some other pattern emerges from free listing. The result won't be a full-fledged labeling system, but it will give you a better sense of what tone and style you should take when developing a labeling system.

Users (indirectly)

Most organizations—especially those whose information environments include search engines—are sitting on top of reams of user data that describe users' needs. Analyzing those search queries can be a hugely valuable way to tune labeling systems, not to mention to diagnose a variety of other problems with your system. Additionally, the popularization of free-form tagging in social networks has created a valuable, if indirect, source of data on users' needs that can help in the creation of labeling systems.

Search log analysis. Search log analysis (also known as search analytics) is one of the least intrusive sources of data on the labels your site's audiences actually use. Analyzing search queries[7] is a great way to understand the types of labels your site's visitors typically use (see Table 7-7). After all, these are the labels that users utilize to describe their own information needs in their own language. You may notice the use of acronyms (or lack thereof), product names, and other jargon, which could impact your own willingness to use jargony labels. You might notice that users' queries use single or multiple terms, which could affect your own choice of short or long labels. And you might find that people simply aren't using the terms you thought they would for certain concepts. You may decide to change your labels accordingly, or use a thesaurus-style lookup to connect a user-supplied term (e.g., "pooch") to the preferred term (e.g., "dog").

Table 7-7. 40 common queries from Michigan State University's site; each query tells us something about what the majority of users seek most often and how they label their information needs

Rank	Count	Cumulative	Percent of total	Query
1	1184	1184	1.5330	capa
2	1030	2214	2.8665	lon+capa
3	840	3054	3.9541	study+abroad
4	823	3877	5.0197	angel
5	664	4541	5.8794	lon-capa
6	656	5197	6.7287	library
7	584	5781	7.4849	olin
8	543	6324	8.1879	campus+map
9	530	6854	8.8741	spartantrak
10	506	7360	9.5292	cata
11	477	7837	10.1468	housing
12	467	8304	10.7515	map
13	462	8766	11.3496	im+west
14	409	9175	11.8792	computer+store
15	399	9574	12.3958	state+news
16	395	9969	12.9072	wharton+center
17	382	10351	13.4018	chemistry
18	346	10697	13.8498	payroll

---

7 For more on search analytics, an excellent resource is Lou's book *Search Analytics for Your Site: Conversations with Your Customers* (Brooklyn, NY: Rosenfeld Media, 2011).

Rank	Count	Cumulative	Percent of total	Query
19	340	11037	14.2900	breslin+center
20	339	11376	14.7289	honors+college
21	339	11715	15.1678	calendar
22	334	12049	15.6002	human+resources
23	328	12377	16.0249	registrar
24	327	12704	16.4483	dpps
25	310	13014	16.8497	breslin
26	307	13321	17.2471	tuition
27	291	13612	17.6239	spartan+trak
28	289	13901	17.9981	menus
29	273	14174	18.3515	uab
30	267	14441	18.6972	academic+calendar
31	265	14706	19.0403	im+east
32	262	14968	19.3796	rha
33	262	15230	19.7188	basketball
34	255	15485	20.0489	spartan+cash
35	246	15731	20.3674	loncapa
36	239	15970	20.6769	sparty+cash
37	239	16209	20.9863	transcripts
38	224	16433	21.2763	psychology
39	214	16647	21.5534	olin+health+center
40	206	16853	21.8201	cse+101

Another—perhaps less obvious—way to obtain search terms is by using Google AdWords to see what terms people are searching for. These terms can then inform the labeling of your information environment.

Tuning and Tweaking

Your list of labels might be raw, coming straight from your content, another system, your environment's users, or your own ideas of what should work best. Or, it may come straight from a polished controlled vocabulary. In any case, it'll need some work to become an effective labeling system.

First, sort the list of terms alphabetically. If it's a long list (e.g., from a search log), you'll likely encounter some duplicates; remove these.

Then review the list for consistency of usage, punctuation, letter case, and so forth, considering some of the consistency issues discussed earlier in this chapter. This is a good time to resolve these inconsistencies and to establish conventions for punctuation and style.

Decisions about which terms to include in a labeling system need to be made in the context of how broad and how large a system is required. First, determine if the labeling system has obvious gaps. Does it encompass all the possibilities that your environment may eventually need to include?

If, for example, your online store currently allows users to search only a portion of your product database, ask yourself if eventually it might provide access to all products. If you're not certain, assume it will, and devise appropriate labels for the additional products.

If the environment's labeling system is topical, try to anticipate the topics not yet covered. You might be surprised to see that the addition of these "phantom" labels has a large impact on your labeling system, perhaps even requiring you to change its conventions. If you fail to perform this predictive exercise, you might learn the hard way that future content doesn't fit into your system because you're not sure how to label it, or it ends up in cop-out categories such as "Miscellaneous," "Other Info," and the classic "Stuff." Plan ahead so that labels you might add in the future don't throw off the current labeling system.

Of course, this planning should be balanced with an understanding of what your labeling system is there to accomplish today. If you try to create a labeling system that encompasses the whole of human knowledge (instead of the current and anticipated content of your website), don't plan on doing anything else for the rest of your life. Keep your scope narrow and focused enough so that it can clearly address the requirements of your environment's unique content, the special needs of its audiences, and the business objective at hand, but be comprehensive within that well-defined scope. This is a difficult pursuit, to be sure—all balancing acts are.

Finally, remember that the labeling system you launch will need to be tweaked and improved shortly thereafter. That's because labels represent a relationship between two things—people and content— that is constantly changing. Stuck between two moving targets, your labeling system will also have to change. So be prepared to perform usability tests, analyze search logs on a regular basis, and adjust your labeling system as necessary.

Recap

OK, let's recap what we learned in this chapter:

- We label things all the time.
- Labeling is the most obvious way to show our organization schemes across multiple systems and contexts.
- We must try to design labels that speak the same language as our environment's users, while also reflecting its content.
- Textual labels are the most common type we encounter in our work; they include contextual links, headings, navigation system options, and index terms.
- Iconic labels are less common, but the widespread adoption of devices with less screen real estate means that they are an important component of many information environments.
- Designing labels is one of the most difficult aspects of information architecture.
- That said, there are various sources of inspiration—such as your existing information environment and search log analysis—that can help inform your labeling choices.

Let's now move on to Chapter 8, where we'll dig into one of the mainstays of effective information architectures: navigation systems.

Navigation Systems

*Just wait, Gretel, until the moon rises, and
then we shall see the crumbs of bread which I have
strewn about; they will show us our way home again.*

—Hansel

In this chapter, we'll cover:

- Balancing context and flexibility in web navigation
- Integrating global, local, and contextual navigation
- Supplemental navigation tools such as sitemaps, indexes, guides, wizards, and configurators
- Personalization, visualization, tag clouds, collaborative filtering, and social navigation

As our fairy tales suggest, getting lost is a bad thing. It is associated with confusion, frustration, anger, and fear. In response to this danger, humans have developed navigation tools to prevent us from getting lost and to help us find our way home. From breadcrumbs to compasses and astrolabes, to maps, street signs, and global positioning systems, people have demonstrated great ingenuity in the design and use of navigation tools and wayfinding strategies.

We use these tools to chart our course, to determine our position, and to find our way back. They provide a sense of context and comfort as we explore new places. Anyone who has driven through an unfamiliar city as darkness falls understands the importance these tools and strategies play in our lives.

In digital information environments, navigation is rarely a life or death issue. However, getting lost in a large website can be confusing and frustrating. While a well-designed taxonomy may reduce the chances that users will become lost, complementary navigation tools are often needed to provide context and to allow for greater flexibility. Structure and organization are about building rooms. Navigation design is about adding doors and windows.

In this book, we have split navigation and searching into individual chapters. This chapter focuses on navigation systems that support browsing; the next chapter digs deep into searching systems that are clearly components of navigation. In fact, structure, organization, labeling, browsing, and searching systems all contribute to effective navigation.

Before we dig in, we need to mention that the surface layer of navigation—that which users interact with—is changing very fast. In recent years, the proliferation of different device form factors has led designers and developers to come up with various strategies to deal with the wildly varying screen sizes and interaction mechanisms. The most popular of these strategies, responsive web design, is a subject for a book unto itself (many books, actually), so we won't be covering it in depth here. Suffice it to say that we've striven to select examples that compare and contrast desktop and mobile navigation schemes, especially as they relate to IA.

Types of Navigation Systems

Navigation systems are composed of several basic elements, or subsystems. First, we have the global, local, and contextual navigation systems that are integrated within site pages or app screens. They may look and behave differently when rendered in desktop-class web browsers than in mobile apps, but in both cases they serve similar purposes: they provide both context and flexibility, helping users understand where they are and where they can go. These three major systems, shown in typical desktop layouts in Figure 8-1, are generally necessary but not sufficient by themselves. (The need for global, local, and contextual navigation still exists in mobile environments. However, layouts tend to take different forms given the compromises imposed by the limited screen real estate in most mobile devices.)

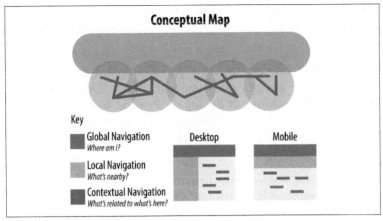

Figure 8-1. Global, local, and contextual embedded navigation systems

Second, we have *supplemental navigation systems* such as sitemaps, indexes, and guides that exist outside the content-bearing pages. These are shown in Figure 8-2.

Sitemap	Index	Guide
Category1 Subcat1, Subcat2, Subcat3	A	Step1
Category2 Subcat1, Subcat2, Subcat3	B	Step2
Category3 Subcat1, Subcat2, Subcat3	C	Step3

Figure 8-2. Supplemental navigation systems

Similar to search, these supplemental navigation systems provide different ways of accessing the same information. Sitemaps provide a bird's-eye view of the information environment. A-to-Z indexes allow direct access to content. And guides often feature linear navigation customized to a specific audience, task, or topic.

As we'll explain, each type of supplemental navigation system serves a unique purpose and is designed to fit within the broader framework of integrated searching and browsing systems.

Gray Matters

The design of navigation systems takes us deep into the gray area between information architecture, interaction design, information design, visual design, and usability engineering, all of which we might loosely classify under the umbrella of user experience design.

As soon as we start talking about global, local, and contextual navigation, we find ourselves on the slippery slope that connects strategy, structure, design, and implementation. Does the local navigation bar work best at the top of the page, or is it better running down the left side? Should we use mega-menus or fat footers to reduce the required number of clicks? Will users ever notice gray links?

For better or for worse, we're often drawn into these debates and are sometimes responsible for making these decisions. We could try to draw a clear line in the sand and argue that effective navigation is simply the manifestation of a well-organized system. Or we could abdicate responsibility and leave the interface to other designers.

But we won't. In the real world, the boundaries are fuzzy and the lines get crossed every day, and the best solutions often result from the biggest debates. While not always possible, interdisciplinary collaboration is the ideal, and collaboration works best when each of the experts understands something about the other areas of expertise.

So in this chapter, we roll up our sleeves, cross lines, step on toes, and get a little messy in the process. We tackle navigation design from the perspective of information architecture.

Browser Navigation Features

When designing a navigation system, it is important to consider the environment in which the system will exist. On the Web, people use web browsers such as Google Chrome and Microsoft Internet Explorer to move around and view websites. On mobile devices, browsers such as Safari feature different ways of interacting with sites, including various touch gestures. These browsers sport many built-in navigation features.

Open URL allows direct access to any page on a website. Back and Forward provide a bidirectional backtracking capability. The History menu allows access to pages visited in the past, and Bookmark or Favorites enables users to save the locations of specific pages for future reference. Although rarely used today, web browsers also support a "breadcrumbs" feature by color-coding hypertext links, a feature that can help users to retrace their steps through a website.

Although less constrained (due in part to not having to conform to a page-based model), non-browser applications have their own navigation conventions. Different operating systems provide standard mechanisms that define how people get around inside apps. For example, most Mac OS X applications feature a menu bar with a standard organization scheme that includes the application name as the first menu item, and "File" and "Edit" menus as the second and third items, respectively (Figure 8-3).[1]

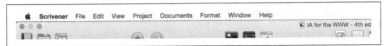

Figure 8-3. Most applications in Mac OS X feature a menu bar with a standard organization scheme

Much research, analysis, and testing has been invested in the design of these navigation features, and users expect them to work consistently. However, we are in a period of intense experimentation with regard to navigation mechanisms. Touch-based interfaces have made possible new ways of interacting with web content (e.g., pinching and swiping) and have obsoleted others (e.g., hovering to reveal multilevel menus). Because of the importance of navigation to the user's experience of interacting with information environments, designers must be judicious when experimenting with new and untested navigation schemes.[2]

Placemaking

As we mentioned in Chapter 4, transmitting a clear context—what the environment *is*, and what you can expect to find and do in it—makes information more easily understandable. Creating this sense of place through language and giving us clear paths to explore the environment are among the key roles navigation systems play.

---

1 Modern operating systems have good guidelines for designing standard navigation mechanisms. See *http://bit.ly/designing_for_ios, http://www.google.com/design/spec,* and *http://bit.ly/uwp_apps_guidelines.*

2 For more on navigation, see James Kalbach's *Designing Web Navigation* (Sebastopol, CA: O'Reilly, 2007).

With all navigation systems, before we can plot our course, we must locate our position. Whether we're visiting Yellowstone National Park or the Mall of America, the "You Are Here" mark on a fixed-location map is a familiar and valuable tool. Without it, we must struggle to triangulate our current position using less dependable features such as street signs or nearby stores. The "You Are Here" indicator can be the difference between knowing where you stand and feeling completely lost.

When designing complex information environments, it is particularly important to provide context within the greater whole. Many contextual clues available in the physical world do not exist online. There are no natural landmarks, no north and south. Unlike physical travel, hypertextual navigation allows users to be transported right into the middle of an unfamiliar system. For example, links from remote web pages and search engine results can allow users to completely bypass the main page of a website.

You should always follow a few rules of thumb to ensure that your design provides contextual clues. For example, users should always know which site or app they're in, even if they bypass the front door and enter through a search engine or a link to a subsidiary page. Extending the organization's name, logo, and graphic identity throughout is a fairly obvious way to accomplish this goal.

The navigation system should also present as much as possible of the structure of the information hierarchy in a clear and consistent manner, and indicate the user's current location, as shown in Figure 8-4. Sears's navigation system shows the user's location within the hierarchy with a variation of the "You Are Here" sign near the top of the page. This helps users to build a mental model of the organization scheme, which facilitates navigation and helps them feel comfortable.

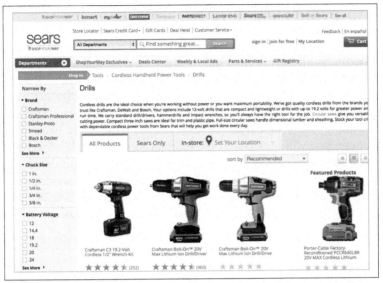

Figure 8-4. Sears's navigation system shows the user's location within the hierarchy

If you have an existing website, we suggest running a few users through a navigation stress test.[3] Here are the basic steps as outlined by Keith Instone:

1. Ignore the home page and jump directly into the middle of the site.

2. For each random page, can you figure out where you are in relation to the rest of the site? What major section are you in? What is the parent page?

3. Can you tell where the page will lead you next? Are the links descriptive enough to give you a clue what each is about? Are the links different enough to help you choose one over another, depending on what you want to do?

By parachuting deep into the middle of the site, you will be able to push the limits of the navigation system and identify any opportunities for improvement.

---

3 Keith Instone popularized the notion of a navigation stress test in his 1997 article, "Stress Test Your Site" (*http://instone.org/navstress*).

Improving Flexibility

As we explained in Chapter 6, hierarchy is a familiar and powerful way of organizing information. In many cases, it makes sense for a hierarchy to form the foundation for organizing content in a website. However, hierarchies can be limiting from a navigation perspective. If you have ever used the ancient information-browsing technology and precursor to the World Wide Web known as Gopher, you will understand the limitations of hierarchical navigation.[4] In Gopherspace, you were forced to move up and down the tree structures of content hierarchies (see Figure 8-5). It was impractical to encourage or even allow jumps across branches (lateral navigation) or between multiple levels (vertical navigation) of a hierarchy.

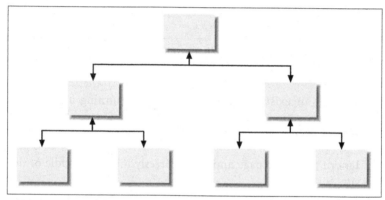

Figure 8-5. The pure hierarchy of Gopherspace

The Web's hypertextual capabilities removed these limitations, allowing tremendous freedom of navigation. Hypertext supports both lateral and vertical navigation. From any branch of the hierarchy, it is possible and often desirable to allow users to move laterally into other branches, to move vertically from one level to a higher or lower level in that same branch, or to move all the way back to the main page of the website. If the system is so enabled, users can get to anywhere from anywhere. However, as you can see in Figure 8-6, things can get confusing pretty quickly. It begins to look like an architecture designed by M.C. Escher.

---

4 If you're too young to remember Gopher, consider the category/subcategory navigation
  of the iOS Music app instead.

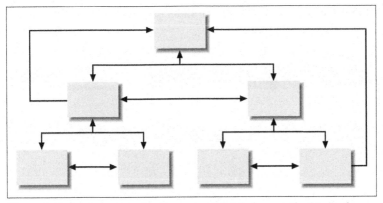

Figure 8-6. A hypertextual web can completely bypass the hierarchy

The trick to designing navigation systems is to balance the advantages of flexibility with the dangers of clutter. In a large, complex information environment, a complete lack of lateral and vertical navigation aids can be very limiting. On the other hand, too many navigation aids can bury the hierarchy and overwhelm the user. Navigation systems should be designed with care to complement and reinforce the hierarchy by providing added context and flexibility.

Embedded Navigation Systems

Most large information environments include all three of the major embedded navigation systems we saw back in Figure 8-1. Global, local, and contextual navigation are extremely common in desktop-oriented websites. They are also present in mobile sites, but take different forms than those shown here due to the constraints presented by smaller screens. Each system solves specific problems and presents unique challenges. To design a successful environment, it is essential to understand the nature of these systems and how they work together to provide context and flexibility.

Global Navigation Systems

By definition, a global navigation system is intended to be present on every page throughout a site. It is often implemented in the form of a navigation bar at the top of each page. These site-wide navigation systems allow direct access to key areas and functions, no matter where the user travels in the site's hierarchy.

Global navigation bars come in all shapes and sizes. Consider the examples shown in Figure 8-7.

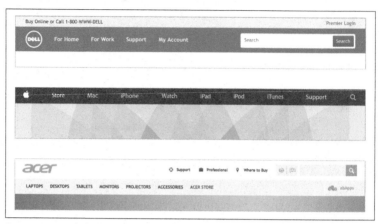

Figure 8-7. Global navigation bars from Dell, Apple, and Acer

Most global navigation bars provide a link to the home page, usually represented as the organization's logo. Many provide a link to the search function. Some, like Apple's and Acer's, reinforce the site's structure and provide contextual clues to identify the user's current location within the site. Others, like Dell's, have a simpler implementation and don't do either. This pushes the burden of providing context down to the local level and opens the door for inconsistency and disorientation. Global navigation system design forces difficult decisions that must be informed by user needs and by the organization's goals, content, technology, and culture. One size does not fit all.

Global navigation bars are constantly evolving. For example, in recent years mega-menus and fat footers have become common design patterns for rendering global navigation structures in websites. Mega-menus are like traditional drop-down menus: usually rendered at the top of a page, they provide access to second- and third-level elements when the user clicks on a first-level element. However, mega-menus are much richer than the simple lists of links of yesteryear; they often feature sophisticated typographic layouts, images, and other cues to give the user insight into the content and structure of the system (Figure 8-8).

Figure 8-8. Adidas's mega-menus give insights into the content and structure of the site

Fat footers are abridged sitemaps rendered at the bottom of web pages. They provide direct access to the most important sections of the site (Figure 8-9).

Figure 8-9. Microsoft.com is a large site, with multiple subsites and sub-brands; a fat footer on many of the site's pages gives users a consistent way to get around

Because global navigation bars are often the single consistent navigation element in the site, they have a huge impact on usability. Consequently, they should be subjected to intensive, iterative user-centered design and testing.

Local Navigation Systems

On many websites, the global navigation system is complemented by one or more local navigation systems that enable users to explore the immediate area. Some tightly controlled sites integrate global and local navigation into a consistent, unified system. For example, the *USA Today* website presents a global navigation bar that shows local navigation options for each category of news. A reader who selects "Money" sees different local navigation options than a reader who selects "Life," but both sets of options are presented within the same navigational framework (see Figure 8-10).

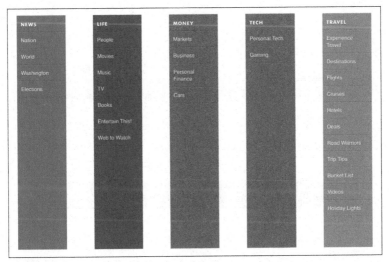

Figure 8-10. Local navigation at usatoday.com

In contrast, large sites like GE.com (Figure 8-11) often provide multiple local navigation systems that may have little in common with one another or with the global navigation system.

These local navigation systems and the content to which they provide access are often so different that these local areas are referred to as *subsites*, or sites within sites.[5] See Subsites exist for two primary reasons. First, certain areas of content and functionality really do merit a unique navigation approach. Second, due to the decentralized nature of large organizations, different groups of people are often responsible for different content areas, and each group may decide to handle navigation differently.

---

5 The term "subsite" was coined by Jakob Nielsen in his 1996 article "The Rise of the Subsite" (*http://www.useit.com/alertbox/9609.html*) to describe a collection of web pages within a larger site that invite a common style and shared navigation mechanism unique to those pages.

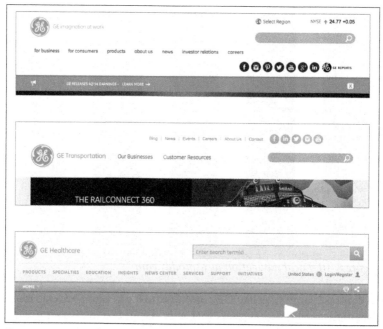

Figure 8-11. Local navigation at GE.com

In GE's case, the local navigation systems seem aligned with user needs and the local content. Unfortunately, there are many bad examples on the Web where the variation between local navigation systems is simply a result of multiple design groups choosing to run in different directions. Many organizations are still struggling with the question of how much central control to exercise over the look and feel of their local navigation systems. Grappling with these local navigation issues can make creaeting global navigation systems look easy.

Contextual Navigation

Some relationships don't fit neatly into the structured categories of global and local navigation. This demands the creation of *contextual* navigation links specific to a particular page, document, or object. In online stores, these "see also" links can point users to related products and services. On an educational site, they might point to similar articles or related topics.

In this way, contextual navigation supports associative learning. Users learn by exploring the relationships you define between items.

They might learn about useful products they didn't know about, or become interested in a subject they'd never considered before. Contextual navigation allows you to create a web of connective tissue that benefits users and the organization.

The actual definition of these links is often more editorial than architectural. Typically an author, editor, or subject matter expert will determine appropriate links once the content is placed into the architectural framework of the website. In practice, this usually involves representing words or phrases within sentences or paragraphs (i.e., prose) as embedded or "inline" hypertext links. A page from Stanford University's site, shown in Figure 8-12, provides an example of carefully chosen inline contextual navigation links.

Figure 8-12. Inline contextual navigation links

This approach can be problematic if these contextual links are critical to the content, because usability testing shows that users often tend to scan pages so quickly that they miss or ignore these less conspicuous links. For this reason, you may want to design a system that provides a specific area of the page or a visual convention for contextual links. As you can see in Figure 8-13, Adorama includes contextual navigation links to related products—in this case based on user views—in the layout of each page. Moderation is the primary rule of thumb for guiding the creation of these links. Used sparingly (as in this example), contextual links can complement the existing navigation systems by adding one more degree of flexibility. Used in excess, they can add clutter and confusion. Content authors have the option to replace or complement the embedded links with external links that are easier for the user to see.

Figure 8-13. External contextual navigation links

The approach used on each page should be determined by the nature and importance of the contextual links. For noncritical links provided as a point of interest, inline links can be a useful but unobtrusive solution.

When designing a contextual navigation system, imagine that every page on the site is a main page or portal in its own right. Once a user has identified a particular product or document, the rest of the site fades into the background. This page is now his interface. Where might he want to go from here? Consider the Adorama example. What additional information will the customer want before making a buying decision? What other products might he want to buy? Contextual navigation provides a real opportunity to cross-sell, up-sell, build brand, and provide customer value. In mobile environments, contextual navigation links can tap into device capabilities to take different actions (e.g., make a call, play a song.) Because these associative relationships are so important, we'll revisit this topic in Chapter 10.

Implementing Embedded Navigation

The constant challenge in navigation system design is to balance the flexibility of movement with the danger of overwhelming the user with too many options. One key to success is simply recognizing that global, local, and contextual navigation elements exist together on most pages in websites and in many content-driven apps as well. When integrated effectively, they can complement one another. But when designed independently, the three systems can combine to monopolize a great deal of screen real estate. Alone, they may each be manageable, but together on one page, the variety of options may overwhelm the user and drown out the content (consider the representation of a web page shown in Figure 8-14). In some cases, you may need to revisit the number of options within each navigation bar. In others, the problem may be minimized through careful design and layout.

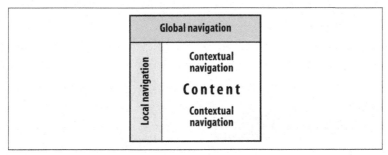

Figure 8-14. Navigation can drown out the content

In its simplest form, a navigation bar is a distinct collection of links that connect a series of sections in the system, enabling movement among them. They can support global, local, and contextual navigation. You can implement navigation in all sorts of ways, using text or graphics, pull-downs, pop-ups, rollovers, mega-menus, and so on. Many of these implementation decisions fall primarily within the realms of interaction design and technical performance rather than information architecture, but let's trespass briefly and hit a few highlights.

For example, is it better to create textual or graphical navigation bars? It is a matter of trade-offs: in desktop-class web browsers, which have the luxury of space, text labels are the norm because they tend to be clearer, easier to implement, and more easily accessible. However, in situations where screen real estate is at a premium, such as in mobile apps, iconic representations of navigation options may be a better choice.

And where do navigation bars belong on the page? Again, the answer depends on the context in which the bars will be rendered. In web pages targeting desktop browsers, the convention is to place global navigation bars somewhere at the top of pages, with local navigation structures arranged alongside the main content. In mobile web pages, navigation bars are often hidden offscreen on either the left or right side of the content; they are exposed using a menu button along the top of the screen. In mobile apps, primary navigation bars are often rendered at the bottom of the screen, within easy reach of the user's thumbs (Figure 8-15).

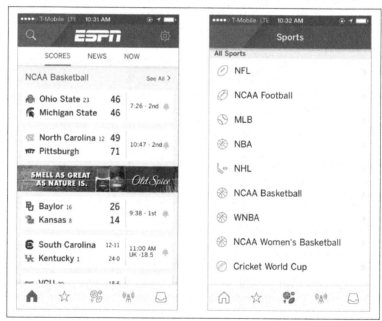

Figure 8-15. The global navigation bar on ESPN's iPhone app consists of a row of icons, aligned at the bottom of the screen; the app includes an extensive icon vocabulary to represent different sports leagues

In any case, you need to be aware of the conventions and limitations of the medium you are designing for. Any deviation from the norm should be tested with users before release.

Supplemental Navigation Systems

Supplemental navigation systems (shown back in Figure 8-2) include sitemaps, indexes, and guides. These are external to the basic hierarchy of a website and provide complementary ways of finding content and completing tasks. Search also belongs to the supplemental navigation family, but it's so important that we've dedicated all of Chapter 9 to it.

Supplemental navigation systems can be critical factors for ensuring usability and findability within large information systems. However, they're often not given the care and feeding they deserve. Some product owners still labor under the misconception that if they could only get the taxonomy right, all users and all user needs would be addressed. Usability pundits feed this fantasy by preaching the gospel of simplicity: users don't want to make choices, and they resort to sitemaps, indexes, guides, and search only when the taxonomy fails them.

Both statements are theoretically true but miss the point that the taxonomy and the embedded navigation systems will always fail for a significant percentage of users and tasks. You can count on this like death and taxes. Supplemental navigation systems give users an emergency backup. Do you really want to drive without a seatbelt?

Sitemaps

In a book or magazine, the table of contents presents the top few levels of the information hierarchy. It shows the organization structure for the printed work and supports random as well as linear access to the content through the use of chapter and page numbers. In contrast, a place map helps us navigate through physical space, whether we're driving through a network of streets and highways or trying to find our terminal in a busy airport.

In the early days of the Web, the terms "sitemap" and "table of contents" were used interchangeably. Of course, librarians thought the TOC was a better metaphor, but *sitemap* sounds sexier and less hierarchical, so it has become the de facto standard.

A typical sitemap (Figure 8-16) presents the top few levels of the information hierarchy. It provides a broad view of the content in the system and facilitates random access to segmented portions of that content via graphical or text-based links.

Figure 8-16. Apple's sitemap

A sitemap is most natural for large systems that lend themselves to hierarchical organization. If the architecture is not strongly hierarchical, an index or alternate visual representation may be better. You should also consider the system's size when deciding whether to employ a sitemap. For a small information environment with only two or three hierarchical levels, a sitemap may be unnecessary.

The design of a sitemap significantly affects its usability. When working with a graphic designer, make sure she understands the following rules of thumb:

- Reinforce the information hierarchy so the user becomes increasingly familiar with how the content is organized.

- Facilitate fast, direct access to the contents of the site for those users who know what they want.

- Avoid overwhelming the user with too much information. The goal is to help, not scare, the user.

Finally, it's worth noting that sitemaps are also useful from a search engine optimization perspective, because they point search engine spiders directly to important pages throughout the website.

Indexes

Similar to the back-of-book index found in many print materials, a digital index presents keywords or phrases alphabetically, without representing the hierarchy. Unlike a table of contents, indexes are relatively flat, presenting only one or two levels of depth. Therefore, indexes work well for users who already know the name of the item they are looking for. A quick scan of the alphabetical listing will get them where they want to go; there's no need for them to understand where you've placed that item within your hierarchy. In Figure 8-17, The United Nations website presents a comprehensive alphabetical index. Handcrafted links within the index lead directly to destination pages.

Figure 8-17. The UN's comprehensive alphabetical site index

Large, complex websites often require both a sitemap and a site index (and a search capability, for that matter). The sitemap reinforces the hierarchy and encourages exploration, while the site index bypasses the hierarchy and facilitates known-item finding. Comcast's XFINITY website presents a simple site index alongside a sitemap that mirrors the site's navigation structure (Figure 8-18).

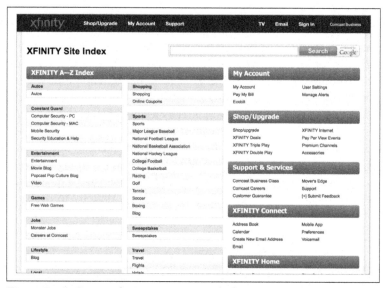

Figure 8-18. Comcast's XFINITY site index

A major challenge in indexing a website involves the level of granularity. Do you index web pages? Do you index individual paragraphs or concepts that are presented on web pages? Or do you index collections of web pages? In many cases, the answer may be all of the above. Perhaps a more valuable question is: what terms are users going to look for? The answers should guide the index design. To find those answers, you need to know your audience and understand their needs. You can learn more about the terms people will look for by analyzing search logs and conducting user research.

There are two very different ways to create an index. For small systems, you can simply create the index manually, using your knowledge of the full collection of content to inform decisions about which links to include. This centralized, manual approach results in a one-step index such as the one in Figure 8-18. Another example is shown in Figure 8-19, where the Centers for Disease Control and Prevention two-step site index features term rotation and see/see-also references. Yet another interesting example is Michigan State University's site index, shown in Figure 8-20, which takes hundreds of the site's best bet results and renders them as an alphabetical list.[6]

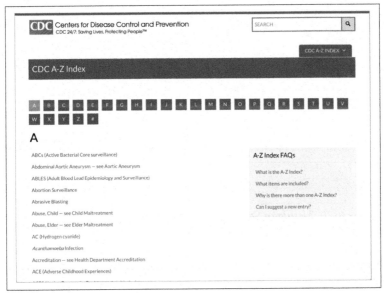

Figure 8-19. The Center for Disease Control and Prevention's site index

In contrast, on a large site with distributed content management, it may make sense to use controlled vocabulary indexing at the document level to drive automatic generation of the site index. Because many controlled vocabulary terms will be applied to more than one document, this type of index must allow for a two-step process: the user first selects the term from the index, and then selects from a list of documents indexed with that term.

---

6 This is clever work by the late, great Rich Wiggins, whose presence is felt in this book years after his passing.

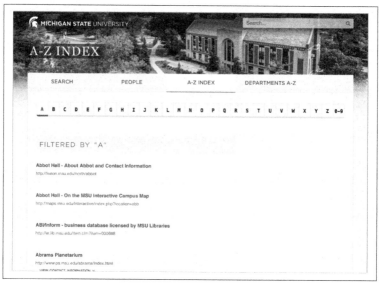

Figure 8-20. Michigan State University's site index

A useful trick in designing an index involves *term rotation*, also known as permutation. A permuted index rotates the words in a phrase so that users can find the phrase in two places in the alphabetical sequence. For example, in the CDC index, users will find listings for both "Abuse, Elder" and "Elder Maltreatment." This supports the varied ways in which people look for information. Term rotation should be applied selectively. You need to balance the probability of users seeking a particular term with the annoyance of cluttering the index with too many permutations. For example, it would probably not make sense in an event calendar to present "Sunday (Schedule)" as well as "Schedule (Sunday)." If you have the time and budget to conduct focus groups or user testing, that's great. If not, you'll have to fall back on common sense.

Guides

Guides can take several forms, including guided tours, tutorials, and walk-throughs focused around a specific audience, topic, or task. In each case, guides supplement the existing means of navigating and understanding the system's content and functionality.

Guides often serve as useful tools for introducing new users to the content and functionality of a website. They can also be valuable marketing tools for restricted-access systems (such as services that charge subscription fees), enabling you to show potential customers what they will get for their money. And, they can be valuable internally, providing an opportunity to showcase key features of a redesigned site to colleagues, managers, and venture capitalists.

Guides typically feature linear navigation (new users want to be guided, not thrown in), but hypertextual navigation should also be available to provide additional flexibility. Screenshots of major pages should be combined with narrative text that explains what can be found in each area.

The IRS Withholding Calculator, shown in Figure 8-21, provides an example: it consists of a highly editorialized selection of important links wrapped in helpful (and clearly structured) copy.

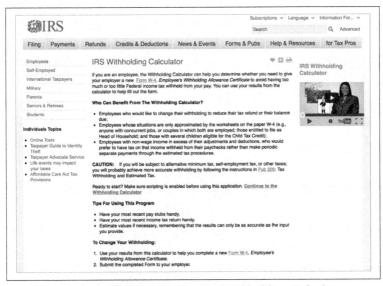

Figure 8-21. The introduction to the IRS Withholding Calculator

Rules of thumb for designing guides include:

- The guide should be short.
- At any point, the user should be able to exit the guide.
- Navigation (Previous, Home, Next, swiping gestures) should be consistent so that users can easily step back and forth through the guide.

- The guide should be designed to answer questions.

- Screenshots should be crisp, clear, and optimized, with enlarged details of key features.

- If the guide includes more than a few pages, it may need its own table of contents.

Remember that a guide is intended as an introduction for new users and as a marketing opportunity for the product or service. Many people may never use it, and few people will use it more than once. You should balance the inevitable big ideas about how to create an exciting, dynamic, interactive guide with the fact that it will not play a central role in the day-to-day use of the system.

Configurators

Though they could be considered a special class of guide, wizards that help users to configure products or navigate complex decision trees deserve separate highlighting. Sophisticated configurators, like Motorola's Moto Maker, shown in Figure 8-22, allow the user to easily traverse complicated decision-making processes.

Figure 8-22. The Moto Maker configurator

Moto Maker successfully combines a rich suite of navigation options without causing confusion. The user can move through a linear process or jump back and forth between steps, and the site's global navigation is always present, providing context and possible next steps.

Often, users don't have a clear understanding of the impact of the choices that affect the configuration process. It is desirable to provide them with contextual clues that help them make sense of the various options available. For example, the iOS Apple Store application (Figure 8-23) includes product images that show changes to the product based on the user's selected color finish, and includes text that explains the impact of more technical options on the product.

Figure 8-23. The iOS Apple Store application on the iPad

Search

As we noted earlier, the searching system is a central part of supplemental navigation. Search is a favorite tool of users because it puts them in the driver's seat, allowing them to use their own keyword terms to look for information. Search also enables a tremendous level of specificity. Users can search the content for a particular phrase (e.g., "socially translucent systems failure") that is unlikely to be represented in a sitemap or site index.

However, the ambiguity of language causes huge problems with most search experiences. Users, authors, and information architects all use different words for the same things. Because the design of effective search systems is so important and so complex, we've devoted an entire chapter to the topic (Chapter 9).

Advanced Navigation Approaches

So far, we've focused attention on the bread-and-butter components of navigation systems: the elements that form the foundation of useful, usable websites. Good navigation design is really important and really hard. Only after you've mastered the integration of these fundamental building blocks should you dare to wander into the minefield of advanced navigation.

Personalization and Customization

Personalization involves serving up information to the user based upon a model of the behavior, needs, or preferences of that individual. In contrast, *customization* involves giving the user direct control over some combination of presentation, navigation, and content options. In short, with personalization, we guess what the user wants, and with customization, the user tells us what he wants.

Both personalization and customization can be used to refine or supplement existing navigation systems. Unfortunately, however, both have been hyped by consultants and software vendors as the solution to all navigation problems. The reality is that personalization and customization:

- Typically play important but limited roles
- Require a solid foundation of structure and organization
- Are really difficult to do well
- Can make it more difficult to collect metrics and analyze user behavior

Amazon is the most cited example of successful personalization, and some of the things it's done are truly valuable. It's nice that Amazon remembers our names, and it's great that it remembers our address and credit card information. It's when Amazon starts trying to recommend products based on past purchases that the system breaks down (see Figure 8-24). In this example, Jorge already owns two of the top five recommended books, but the system doesn't know this because he purchased them elsewhere and (obviously) not as Kindle books. And this ignorance is not the exception, but the rule. Because we don't have time to teach our systems, or because we prefer to maintain our privacy, we often don't share enough information to drive effective personalization. In addition, in many cases, it's really hard to guess what people will want to do or learn or buy tomorrow. As they say in the financial world, past performance is no guarantee of future results. In short, personalization works really well in limited contexts, but fails when you try to expand it to drive the entire user experience.

Figure 8-24. Amazon's personalized recommendations

Customization introduces a similar set of promises and perils. The idea of giving users control and thereby alleviating some of the pressures on design is obviously very compelling. And customization can sometimes deliver great value. For example, Gmail allows the user to set the visibility and order of labels—a critical element in the structuring of the user's mail in the system—by dragging and dropping them within a global navigation structure (Figure 8-25).

The problem with customization is that most people don't want to spend much (if any) time customizing, and will do this work only on a small handful of sites that are most important to them. Because corporate intranets have a captive audience of repeat visitors, customization has a much better chance of being used there than it does on most public websites.

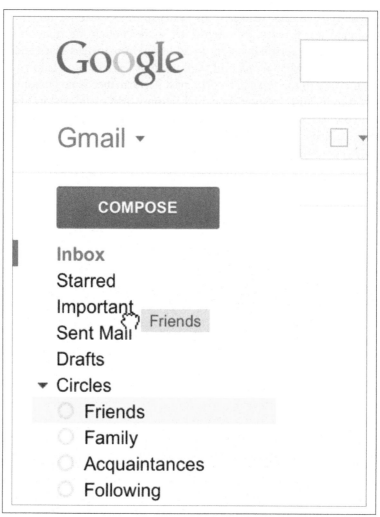

Figure 8-25. Customization in Gmail

However, there's another problem. Even users themselves don't always know what they will want to know or do tomorrow. Customization works great for tracking the sports scores of your favorite baseball team or monitoring the value of stocks you own, but not so well when it comes to broader news and research needs. One day you want to know the results of the French elections; the next day you want to know when dogs were first domesticated. Do you really know what you might need next month?

Visualization

Since the advent of the Web, people have struggled to create useful tools that enable users to navigate in a more visual way. First came the metaphor-driven attempts to display online museums, libraries, shopping malls, and other websites as physical places. Then came the dynamic, fly-through "sitemaps" that tried to show relationships between pages on a website. Both looked very cool and stretched our imaginations, but neither proved to be very useful. Visualization has proven most useful when the user must select among a result set of elements that she knows by their looks, as in the case of shopping for physical goods (Figure 8-26).

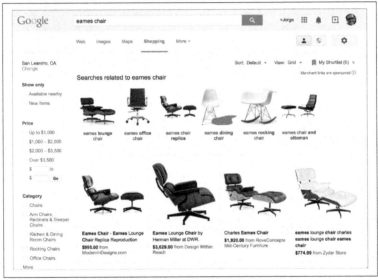

Figure 8-26. Google Shopping's visual search results

Social Navigation

With the rise of massive social networks like Facebook and Twitter, social navigation has become an important approach to structuring information so that people can discover new information particularly tailored to their interests. Social navigation is built on the premise that value for the individual user can be derived from observing the actions of other users—especially those that have some meaningful relation to that individual.

At its simplest level, social navigation can help users discover content based on the popularity of individual items, whether by sheer volume of traffic or by implementing a user-driven voting system. Reddit, a content aggregation and discovery service, employs such a voting system—in fact, it is its primary differentiator (Figure 8-27).

Figure 8-27. The sequence in which stories are presented on Reddit's home page is defined by the up- or down-votes of registered site users

Other systems depend on much richer and more complex social algorithms. For example, many of Facebook's navigation structures consist of dynamically generated lists of content items: from the sequence of posts that appear in the user's main timeline to lists of suggested pages and other Facebook users you may know (Figure 8-28). While the exact nature of these algorithms is not publicly known (it is part of Facebook's "secret sauce"), the content selection and the sequence it is presented in is clearly reliant on the user's "social graph" (the list of that individual's contacts on Facebook).

Figure 8-28. Facebook presents the user with a variety of algorithmically generated lists of navigation links that are influenced by the social graph; the ad selection is also algorithmically determined based on the user's profile (Facebook knows that Jorge is in the San Francisco Bay area, and that it is Valentine's Day)

We expect that as more people and devices become connected through these networks, dynamically generated social navigation systems will become increasingly complex, sophisticated, and useful. As a result, organizations will find new ways of tailoring the navigation structures of information environments to better serve the needs of individual users. However, we must be careful to not go overboard: systems that are *too* precisely tuned to the preferences of any one particular user's social groups can easily devolve into echo chambers that downplay alternative points of view. It's also important to keep in mind that global navigation structures play an important role in placemaking; people need to share some level of common, consistent structure when visiting the information environment over time. As with all information architecture, a balance is called for.

Recap

Let's recap what we learned in this chapter:

- We use navigation systems to chart our course, determine our position, and find our way back; they provide a sense of context and comfort as we explore new places.

- The surface layer of navigation—what people actually interact with—is changing very fast.

- There are various types of navigation systems; three common ones are global, local, and contextual systems.

- The tools we use to explore information environments—such as web browsers—provide their own navigation mechanisms.

- Building context—allowing users to locate their positions within the system—is a critical function of navigation systems.

- Global navigation systems are intended to be present on every page or screen in the information environment.

- Local navigation systems complement global ones, and allow users to explore the immediate area where they are.

- Contextual navigation systems occur in context of the content being presented in the environment, and support associative learning by allowing users to explore the relationships between items.

- There are also various supplemental navigation systems we can use, such as sitemaps, indexes, and guides.

And now we move on to search systems, which allow people to find what they are looking for in your information environment.

CHAPTER 9

Search Systems

> *The ultimate search engine would basically understand*
> *everything in the world, and it would always give you the*
> *right thing. And we're a long, long ways from that.*
> —*Larry Page*

In this chapter, we'll cover:

- Determining whether your product needs a search system
- The basic anatomy of a search system
- What to make searchable
- A basic understanding of retrieval algorithms
- How to present retrieval results
- Search interface design
- Where to learn more

Chapter 8 helped you understand how to create the best navigation system possible for your information environment. This chapter describes another form of finding information: searching. Searching (and more broadly, information retrieval) is an expansive, challenging, and well-established field, and we can only scratch the surface here. We'll limit our discussion to what makes up a search system, when to implement search systems, and some practical advice on how to design a search interface and display search results.

This chapter often uses examples of search systems that allow you to search various different types of information environments, ranging from the entire Web to mobile phone apps. Although these tools tend to index a very broad collection of content, it's nonetheless extremely useful to study them.

Does Your Product Need Search?

Before we delve into search systems, we need to make a point: think twice before you make your product searchable.

Your information environment should, of course, support the finding of its information. But as the preceding chapters demonstrate, there are other ways to support finding. And be careful not to assume, as many do, that a search engine alone will satisfy all users' information needs. While many users want to search, some are natural browsers, preferring to forgo filling in that little search box and hitting the "search" button. We suggest you consider the following issues before committing to a search system:

Amount of content in the information environment
How much content is enough to merit the use of a search engine? It's hard to say. It could be 5, 50, or 500 content items; no specific number serves as a standard threshold. What's more important is the type of information need that's typical of your product's users. For example, users of a technical support website often have a specific kind of information in mind, and are more likely to require search than users of an online banking app. If your product is more like a library than a software application, then search probably makes sense. If that's the case, then consider the volume of content, balancing the time required to set up and maintain a search system with the payoff it will bring to your product's users.

Focus on more useful navigation systems
Because many developers see search engines as the solution to the problems users have when trying to find information in their products, search engines become Band-Aids for poorly designed navigation systems and other architectural weaknesses. If you see yourself falling into this trap, you should probably suspend implementing your search system until you fix your navigation system's problems. You'll find that search systems often perform better if they can take advantage of aspects of strong navigation systems, such as the controlled vocabulary terms used to tag content. And users will often benefit even

more from using both types of finding if they work together well. Of course, your product's navigation might be a disaster for political reasons, such as an inability among your organization's decision makers to agree on a system-wide navigation system. In such cases, reality trumps what ought to be, and search might indeed be your best alternative.

Time and know-how to optimize the search system

Search engines are fairly easy to get up and running, but they are difficult to implement effectively. As a user of the Web, you've certainly seen incomprehensible search interfaces, and we're sure that your queries have retrieved some pretty inscrutable results. This is often due to a lack of planning by the site's developer, who probably installed the search engine with its default settings, pointed it at the site, and forgot about it. If you don't plan on putting some significant time into configuring your search engine properly, reconsider your decision to implement it.

Other alternatives

Search may be a good way to serve your product's users, but other ways may work better. For example, if you don't have the technical expertise or confidence to configure a search engine or the money to shell out for one, consider providing an index instead. Both indexes and search engines help users who know what they're looking for. While an index can be a heck of a lot of work, it is typically created and maintained manually, which makes it easier to implement. You could also provide access to a third-party search engine, such as Google's. (While this is a cost-effective alternative, it has downsides: for one, search becomes separate from other means of finding, leading to a disjointed experience. For another, delegated search can't generate the same data—and insights—from search analytics.)

Users' preferred ways of interacting

It may already be clear that your users would rather browse than search. For example, users of a handmade crafts site may prefer browsing thumbnails of cards instead of searching. Or perhaps users do want to search, but searching is a lower priority for them, and it should be for you as you consider how to spend your information architecture development budget.

Now that we've got our warnings and threats out of the way, let's discuss when you should implement search systems. Many information environments—websites, especially—aren't planned out in much detail before they're built. Instead, they grow organically. This may be all right for smaller systems that aren't likely to expand much, but for ones that become popular, more and more content and functional features get piled on haphazardly, leading to a navigation nightmare. The following issues will help you decide when your environment has reached the point of needing a search system:

Search helps when you have too much information to browse

There's a good analogy with physical architecture here. Powell's Books (*http://www.powells.com*), which claims to be the largest bookstore in the world, covers an entire city block (68,000 square feet) in Portland, Oregon. We guess that it started as a single small storefront on that block, but as the business grew, the owners knocked a doorway through the wall into the next storefront, and so on, until it occupied the whole block. The result is a hodgepodge of chambers, halls with odd turns, and unexpected stairways. This chaotic labyrinth is a charming place to wander and browse, but if you're searching for a particular title, good luck. It will be difficult to find what you're looking for, although if you're really lucky you might serendipitously stumble onto something better.

Yahoo! once was a web version of Powell's. At first, everything was there and fairly easy to find. Why? Because Yahoo!, like the Web, was relatively small. At its inception, Yahoo! pointed to a few hundred Internet resources, made accessible through an easily browsable subject hierarchy. No search option was available, something unimaginable to Yahoo! users today. But things soon changed. Yahoo! had an excellent technical architecture that allowed site owners to easily self-register their sites, but Yahoo!'s information architecture couldn't keep up with the increasing volume of resources that were added daily. Eventually, the subject hierarchy became too cumbersome to navigate, and Yahoo! installed a search system as an alternative way of finding information. In 2014, Yahoo! discontinued its browsable site directory altogether.

Your information environment probably isn't as large as Yahoo!, but it's probably experienced a similar evolution. Has your content outstripped your browsing systems? Do your site's users go insane trying to spot the right link on your hugely long category pages? Then perhaps the time has come for search.

Search helps fragmented sites

Powell's room after room after room of books is also a good analogy for the silos of content that make up so many intranets and large public websites. As is so often the case, each business unit has gone ahead and done its own thing, developing content haphazardly with few (if any) standards, and probably no metadata to support any sort of reasonable browsing.

If this describes your situation, you have a long road ahead of you, and search won't solve all of your problems—let alone your users' problems. But your priority should be to set up a search system to perform full-text indexing of as much system content as possible, even across such traditional silos as company departments. Even if it's only a stopgap, search will address your users' dire need for finding information regardless of which business unit actually owns it. Search will also help you to get a better handle on what content is actually out there.

Search is a learning tool

Through search-log analysis, which we touched on in Chapter 7, you can gather useful data on what users actually want from your information environment, and how they articulate their needs (in the form of search queries). Over time, you can analyze this valuable data to diagnose and tune your search system, other aspects of its information architecture, the performance of its content, and many other areas as well.

Search should be there because users expect it to be there

Your product probably doesn't contain as much content as Yahoo!, but if it's substantial, it probably merits a search engine. There are good reasons for this. Users won't always be willing to browse through its structures; their time is limited, and their cognitive-overload threshold is lower than you think. Interestingly, sometimes users won't browse for the wrong reasons— that is, they search when they don't necessarily know what to search for and would be better served by browsing. But perhaps most of all, users expect that little search box wherever they go. It's a default convention, and it's hard to stand against the wave of expectations.

Search can tame dynamism

You should also consider creating a search system for your product if it contains highly dynamic content. For example, an online newspaper might be adding dozens of story files daily via a commercial newsfeed or some other form of content syndication. For this reason, its team probably wouldn't have the time each day to manually catalog its content or maintain elaborate tables of contents and site indexes. A search engine could help by automatically indexing the contents of the site once or many times daily. Automating this process ensures that users have quality access to the newspaper's content, and the team can spend time doing things other than manually indexing and linking the story files as they come in.

Search System Anatomy

On its surface, search seems quite straightforward. Look for the box with the search button, enter and submit your query, and mutter a little prayer while the results load. If your prayers are answered, you'll find some useful results and can go on with your life.

Of course, there's a lot going on under the hood. A search engine application has indexed the content of the information environment. All of it? Some of it? As a user, you'll probably never know. And what parts of the content? Usually the search engine can find the full text of each document. But a search engine can also index information associated with each document—like titles, controlled vocabulary terms, etc.—depending on how it's been configured. And then there's the search interface, your window on the search engine's index. What you type there is looked up in the index; if things go well, results that match your query are returned.

A lot is going on here. There are the guts of the search engine itself; aside from tools for indexing and spidering, there are algorithms for processing your query into something the software can understand, and for ranking the results. There are interfaces, too: ones for entering queries (everything from simple search boxes to advanced natural-language, voice-driven interfaces like Siri) and others for displaying results (including decisions on what to show for each result, and how to display the entire set of results). Further complicating the picture, there may be variations in query languages (e.g., whether or not Boolean operators like AND, OR, and NOT can be used) and query builders (e.g., spell checkers) that can improve upon a query.

Obviously, there's a lot to search that doesn't meet the eye. Additionally, there's your query, which itself usually isn't very straightforward. Where does your query come from? Your mind senses a gap that needs to be filled with information, but isn't always sure how to express what it's looking for. Searching is often iterative—not just because we don't always like the results we retrieve, but often because it takes us a few tries to get the words right for our query. You then interact with a search interface, heading for the simple, Google-like box or, if you're "advanced," grappling with the advanced search interface. And finally, you interact with the results, hopefully quickly determining which results are worth clicking through, which to ignore, and whether or not you should go back and try modifying your search. Figure 9-1 shows some of these pathways.

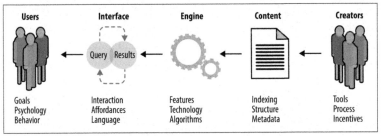

Figure 9-1. The basic anatomy of a search system (image adapted from Search Patterns: Design for Discovery, by Peter Morville and Jeffery Callender)

That's the 50,000-foot view of what's happening in a search system. Most of the technical details can be left to your IT staff; you are more concerned with factors that affect retrieval performance than with the technical guts of a search engine. That said, it's important that the team responsible for the environment's information architecture be part of the search system selection and implementation processes. The team must be prepared to argue strongly for owning at least an equal responsibility for selecting and implementing the search engine that will best serve users, rather than the one that runs on someone's favorite platform or is written in someone's favorite programming language.

Choosing What to Index

Let's assume that you've already chosen a search engine. What content should you index for searching? You can point your search engine at your content, tell it to index the full text of every document it finds, and let it do its thing. That's a large part of the value of search systems—they can be comprehensive and can cover a huge amount of content quickly.

But indexing everything doesn't always serve users well. In a large, complex environment chock-full of heterogeneous subsystems and databases, you may want to allow users to search the silo of technical reports or the staff directory without muddying their search results with the latest HR newsletter articles on the addition of fish sticks to the cafeteria menu. The creation of *search zones*—pockets of more homogeneous content—reduces the apples-and-oranges effect and allows users to focus their searches.

Choosing what to make searchable isn't limited to selecting the right search zones. Each document or record in a collection has some sort of structure, whether rendered in a markup language like HTML or database fields. In turn, that structure stores content components: pieces or "atoms" of content that are typically smaller than a document. Some of that structure—say, an author's name—may be leveraged by a search engine, while other parts—such as the legal disclaimer at the bottom of each page—might be left out.

Finally, if you've conducted an inventory and analysis of your content, you already have some sense of what content is "good." You might have identified your valuable content by manually tagging it or through some other mechanism. You might consider making this "good" stuff searchable on its own, in addition to being part of the global search. You might even program your search engine to search this "good" stuff first, and expand to search the rest of the content if that first pass doesn't retrieve useful results. For example, if most of an ecommerce site's users are looking for products, those could be searched by default, and the search could then be expanded to cover the whole site as part of a revised search option.

In this section, we'll discuss issues of selecting what should be searchable both at a coarse level of granularity (search zones) and at the more atomic level of searching within documents (content components).

Determining Search Zones

Search zones are subsets of an information environment that have been indexed separately from the rest of the content. When a user searches a search zone, he has, through interaction with the environment, already identified himself as interested in that particular information. Ideally, the search zones correspond to his specific needs, and the result is a better search experience. By eliminating content that is irrelevant to his need, the user should retrieve fewer, more relevant, results.

In Windows 8.1, shown in Figure 9-2, users can select search zones based on the type of content they are looking for (Settings, Files) and—somewhat awkwardly—by its location (Web images, Web videos), with "Web" implying that the "Settings" and "Files" options refer to settings and files on your computer. (Note that "Everywhere" is the default selection.) But what if the user wants to search for something other than videos or images on the Web? Or, inversely, wants to search for videos or images on her computer?

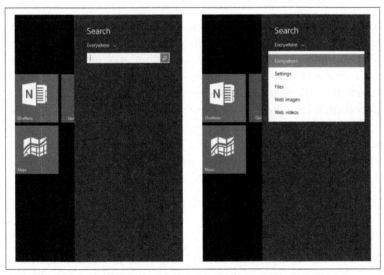

Figure 9-2. Search zones in Windows 8.1

Although both the search box and the search result screen in Windows 8.1 present a single and consistent user interface for all searches, behind the scenes the system is rendering results from two very different search zones: the user's computer system in the case of settings and files, and the entire Web (via Microsoft's Bing search engine) in the case of images and videos.

You can create search zones in as many ways as you can physically segregate documents or logically tag them. Your decisions in selecting your environment's organization schemes often help you determine search zones as well. So, our old friends from Chapter 6 can also be the basis of search zones:

- Content type
- Audience
- Role
- Subject/topic
- Geography
- Chronology
- Author
- Department/business unit

And so on. Like browsing systems, search zones allow a large body of content to be sliced and diced in useful new ways, providing users with multiple "views" of the environment and its content. But, naturally, search zones are a double-edged sword. Narrowing one's search through search zones can improve results, but interacting with them adds a layer of complexity. So be careful: many users will ignore search zones when they begin their searches, opting to enter a simple search against the global index. Users might not bother with your meticulously created search zones until they're taking their second pass at a search, via an advanced search interface.

Following are a few ways to slice and dice.

Navigation versus destination

Most content-heavy information environments contain, at minimum, two major types of pages or screens: *navigation pages* and *destination pages*. Destination pages contain the actual information you want: sports scores, book reviews, software documentation, and so on. Navigation pages may include main pages, search pages, and pages that help you browse the environment. The primary purpose of navigation pages is to get you to the destination pages.

When a user searches an information environment, it's fair to assume that he is looking for destination pages. If navigation pages are included in the retrieval process, they will just clutter up the retrieval results.

Let's take a simple example: your company sells electronics accessories via its website. The destination pages consist of descriptions, pricing, and ordering information, one page for each product. Also, a number of navigation pages help users find products, such as listings of products for different device types (e.g., tablets versus smartphones), listings of products for different types of accessories (e.g., screen protectors, cases), and listings of different device manufacturers (e.g., Apple, Samsung, LG). If the user is searching for Mophie iPhone cases, what's likely to happen? Instead of simply retrieving the Mophie's product page, she might have to wade through all of these pages:

- iPhone cases index page
- External batteries index page
- Apple devices products index page
- Mophie products index page
- Android products index page
- Mophie iPhone products index page

The user's search retrieves the right destination page (i.e., the Mophie iPhone product page), but also five more that are purely navigation pages. In other words, 83% of the retrieval obstructs the user's ability to find the most useful result.

Of course, indexing similar content isn't always easy, because "similar" is a highly relative term. It's not always clear where to draw the line between navigation and destination pages—in some cases, a page can be considered both. That's why it's important to test out navigation/destination distinctions before actually applying them. The weakness of the navigation/destination approach is that it is essentially an exact organization scheme (discussed in Chapter 6) that requires the pages to be either destination or navigation. In the following three approaches, the organization schemes are ambiguous, and therefore more forgiving of pages that fit into multiple categories.

Indexing for specific audiences

If you've already decided to create an architecture that uses an audience-oriented organization scheme, it may make sense to create search zones by audience breakdown as well. We found this a useful approach for the original Library of Michigan website.

The Library of Michigan has three primary audiences: members of the Michigan state legislature and their staffs, Michigan libraries and their librarians, and the citizens of Michigan. The information needed from this site is different for each of these audiences; for example, each has a very different circulation policy.

So we created four indexes: one for each of the three audiences, and one unified index of the entire site in case the audience-specific indexes didn't do the trick for a particular search. Table 9-1 shows the results from running a query on the word "circulation" against each of the four indexes.

Table 9-1. Query results

Index	Documents retrieved	Retrieval reduced by
Unified	40	—
Legislature area	18	55%
Libraries area	24	40%
Citizens area	9	78%

As with any search zone, less overlap between indexes improves performance. If the retrieval results were reduced by a very small figure—say, 10% or 20%—it might not be worth the overhead of creating separate audience-oriented indexes. But in this case, much of the site's content is specific to individual audiences.

Indexing by topic

The Mayo Clinic employs topical search zones on its website. For example, if you're looking for a doctor to help with your rehabilitation, you might select the "Doctors & Medical Staff" search zone, as shown in Figure 9-3.

The 88 results retrieved may sound like a lot, but if you'd searched the entire site, the total would have been 1,470 results, many dealing with topic areas that aren't germane to identifying a physician.

Figure 9-3. Executing a search against the "Doctors & Medical Staff" search zone

Indexing recent content

Chronologically organized content allows for perhaps the easiest implementation of search zones. (Not surprisingly, it's a common example of search zones.) Because dated materials aren't generally ambiguous and date information is typically easy to come by, creating search zones by date—even ad hoc zones—is straightforward.

The search interface of the *New York Times* provides a useful illustration of filtering by date range (Figure 9-4).

Regular users can return to the site and check up on the news using one of a number of chronological search zones (e.g., today's news, past week, past 30 days, past 90 days, past year, and since 1851). Additionally, users who are looking for news within a particular date range or on a specific date can essentially generate an ad hoc search zone.

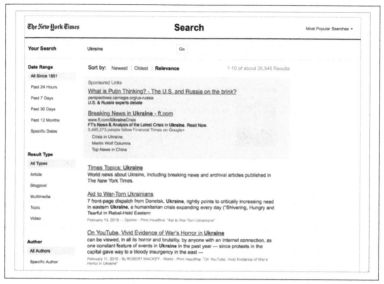

Figure 9-4. There are many ways to narrow your New York Times search by date

Selecting Content Components to Index

Just as it's often useful to provide access to subsets of your site's content, it's valuable to allow users to search specific components of your documents. By doing so, you'll enable users to retrieve more specific, precise results. And if your documents have administrative or other content components that aren't especially meaningful to users, these can be excluded from the search.

In the Yelp business listing shown in Figure 9-5, there are more content components than meet the eye. There is a business name, operating hours, images, a link to the business's website, and some attributes that are invisible to users. There are also content components that we don't want to search, such as the reviews and tips toward the bottom of the screen. These could confuse a user's search results; for example, if a review included the name of a competing restaurant. (A great by-product of the advent of content management systems and logical markup languages is that it's now much easier to leave out content that shouldn't be indexed, like navigation options, advertisements, disclaimers, and other stuff that might show up in document headers and footers.)

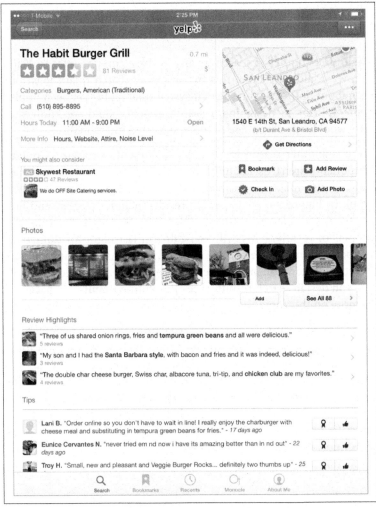

Figure 9-5. Yelp's business listings are jam-packed with various content components, some visible and some not

Yelp's search system allows users to take advantage of the information environment's structure, supporting searches by the following content components, among others:

- Business name
- Categories (e.g., Burgers, American)
- Ambiance and attire (e.g., casual, formal, etc.)

- Noise level

- Location

Would users bother to search by any of these components? In Yelp's case, we could determine this by reviewing search query logs. But what about in the case of a search system that hadn't yet been implemented? Prior to designing a search system, could we know that users would take advantage of this specialized functionality?

There is another reason to exploit a document's structure. Content components aren't useful only for enabling more precise searches; they can also make the format of search results much more meaningful. In Figure 9-6, Yelp's search results include category and listing titles ("Boulevard Burger," "Burgers, Breakfast & Brunch"), snippets of reviews ("My wife & I came in last night for dinner..."), number of reviews, average ratings, and locations. Indexing numerous content components for retrieval provides added flexibility in how you design search results. (See "Presenting Results" on page 233 for more on this topic.)

This leads to a difficult paradox: even if users would benefit from such souped-up search functionality, they likely won't ever ask for it during initial user research. Typically, users don't have much understanding of the intricacies and capabilities of search systems. Developing use cases and scenarios might unearth some reasons to support this level of detailed search functionality, but it might be better to instead examine other search interfaces that your site's users find valuable, and determine whether to provide a similar type of functionality.

Figure 9-6. Title, rating, and location are content components displayed for each result

Search Algorithms

Search engines find information in many ways. In fact, there are about 40 different retrieval algorithms alone, most of which have been around for decades. We're not going to cover them all here; if

you'd like to learn more, read any of the standard texts on information retrieval.[1]

We bring up the topic because it's important to realize that a
retrieval algorithm is essentially a tool, and just like other tools, specific algorithms help solve specific problems. And as retrieval algorithms are at the heart of search engines, it's important to note that
there is absolutely no single search engine that will meet all of your
users' information needs. Remember that fact the next time you
hear a search engine vendor claim that their product's brand-new
proprietary algorithm is the solution to all information problems.

Pattern-Matching Algorithms

Most retrieval algorithms employ pattern matching; that is, they
compare the user's query with an index of, typically, the full texts of
your system's documents, looking for the same string of text. When
a matching string is found, the source document is added to the
retrieval set. So, a user types the textual query "electric guitar," and
documents that include the text string "electric guitar" are retrieved.
It all sounds quite simple. But this matching process can work in
many different ways to produce different results.

Recall and precision

Some algorithms return numerous results of varying relevance,
while some return just a few high-quality results. The terms for
these opposite ends of the spectrum are *recall* and *precision*.
Figure 9-7 shows formulas for calculating them (note the difference
in the denominators).

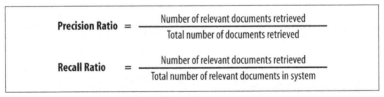

$$\text{Precision Ratio} = \frac{\text{Number of relevant documents retrieved}}{\text{Total number of documents retrieved}}$$

$$\text{Recall Ratio} = \frac{\text{Number of relevant documents retrieved}}{\text{Total number of relevant documents in system}}$$

Figure 9-7. Precision and recall ratios

---

[1] A good starting point is *Modern Information Retrieval* by Ricardo Baeza-Yates and
Berthier Ribeiro-Neto (Boston: Addison-Wesley, 2011).

Are your system's users doing legal research, learning about the current state of scientific research in a field, or performing due diligence about an acquisition? In these cases, they'll want high recall. Each of the hundreds or thousands (or more?) results retrieved will have some relevance to the user's search, although perhaps not very much. As an example, users who are "ego-surfing" will want to see every mention of their names—they're hoping for high recall. The problem, of course, is that along with good results come plenty of irrelevant ones.

On the other hand, a user who is looking for two or three really good articles on how to get stains out of a wool carpet will be hoping for high-precision results. It doesn't matter how many relevant articles there are if you get a good enough answer right away.

Wouldn't it be nice to have both recall and precision at the same time? Lots and lots of very high-quality results? Sadly, you can't have your cake and eat it, too: recall and precision are inversely related. You'll need to decide what balance of the two will be most beneficial to your users. You can then select a search engine with an algorithm biased toward either recall or precision, or perhaps configure an engine to accommodate one or the other.

For example, a search tool might provide automatic stemming, which expands a term to include other terms that share the same root (or stem). If the stemming mechanism is very strong, it might treat the search term "computer" as sharing the same root ("comput") as "computers," "computation," "computational," and "computing." Strong stemming in effect expands the user's query by searching for documents that include any of those terms. This enhanced query will retrieve more related documents, meaning higher recall.

Conversely, no stemming means the query "computer" retrieves only documents with the term "computer" and ignores other variants. Weak stemming might expand the query only to include plurals, retrieving documents that include "computer" or "computers." With weak stemming or no stemming, precision is higher and recall is lower. Which way should you go with your search system—high recall or high precision? The answer depends on what kinds of information needs your users have.

Another consideration is how structured the content is. Are there fields, rendered in HTML or XML or perhaps in a document record, that the search engine can "see" and therefore search? If so, searching for "William Faulkner" in the author field will result in higher precision, assuming we're looking for books authored by Faulkner. Otherwise, we're left with searching the full text of each document and finding results where "William Faulkner" may be mentioned, whether or not he was the author.

Other Approaches

When you already have a "good" document on hand, some algorithms will convert that document into the equivalent of a query (this approach is typically known as *document similarity*). "Stop words" (e.g., "the," "is," and "he") are stripped out of the good document, leaving a useful set of semantically rich terms that, ideally, represent the document well. These terms are then converted into a query that should retrieve similar results. An alternative approach is to present results that have been indexed with similar metadata. In Figure 9-8, hovering over individual search results in the Duck-DuckGo search engine offers more matches for the search terms in the same domain as that particular result.

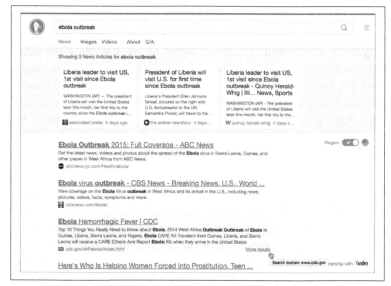

Figure 9-8. DuckDuckGo search results are accompanied by a link to "More results" within the same domain

Approaches such as collaborative filtering and citation searching go even further to help expand results from a single relevant document.

In the following example from CiteSeer (see Figure 9-9), we've identified an article that we like: "Application Fault Level Tolerance in Heterogeneous Networks of Workstations." CiteSeer automatically finds documents in a number of ways:

Cited by
> What other papers cite this one? The relationship between cited and citing papers implies some degree of mutual relevance. Perhaps the authors even know each other.

Active bibliography (related documents)
> Conversely, this paper cites others in its own bibliography, implying a similar type of shared relevance.

Related documents from co-citation
> Another twist on citation, co-citation assumes that if documents appear together in the bibliographies of other papers, they probably have something in common.

Figure 9-9. CiteSeer provides multiple ways to expand from a single search result

There are other retrieval algorithms, more than we can cover here. What's most important is to remember that the main purpose of these algorithms is to identify the best pool of documents to be presented as search results. But "best" is subjective, and you'll need to have a good grasp of what users hope to find when they're searching your site. Once you have a sense of what they wish to retrieve, begin your quest for a search tool with a retrieval algorithm that might address your users' information needs.

Query Builders

Besides search algorithms themselves, there are many other means of affecting the outcome of a search. *Query builders* are tools that can soup up a query's performance. They are often invisible to users, who may not understand their value or how to use them. Common examples include:

Spell checkers
> These allow users to misspell terms and still retrieve the right results by automatically correcting search terms. For example, "accomodation" would be treated as "accommodation," ensuring retrieval of results that contain the correct term.

Phonetic tools
> Phonetic tools (the best-known of which is "Soundex") are especially useful when searching for a name. They can expand a query on "Smith" to include results with the term "Smyth."

Stemming tools
> Stemming tools allow users to enter a term (e.g., "lodge") and retrieve documents that contain variant terms with the same stem (e.g., "lodging," "lodger").

Natural language processing tools
> These can examine the syntactic nature of a query—for example, is it a "how to" question or a "who is" question?—and use that knowledge to narrow retrieval. For example, Siri uses natural language processing to figure out if it should trigger a web search or a bad joke (Figure 9-10).

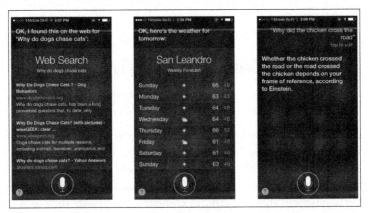

Figure 9-10. Siri uses natural language processing to determine whether the user wants to do a web search, look at the weather app, or hear a bad joke

Controlled vocabularies and thesauri
> Covered in detail in Chapter 10, these tools leverage the semantic nature of a query by automatically including synonyms within the query.

Spell checkers correct for an almost universal problem among searchers and are well worth considering for your search system. (Look over your search logs, and you'll be amazed by the preponderance of typos and misspellings in search queries.)

The other query builders have their pros and cons, addressing different information needs in different situations. Once again, a sense of your users' information needs will help you select which approaches make the most sense for you; additionally, keep in mind that your search engine may or may not support these query builders.

Presenting Results

What happens after your search engine has assembled the results to display? There are many ways to present results, so once again you'll need to make some choices. And as usual, the mysterious art of understanding your content and how users want to use it should drive your selection process.

When you are configuring the way your search engine displays results, there are two main issues to consider: which content components to display for each retrieved document, and how to list or group those results.

Which Content Components to Display

Display less information to users who know what they're looking for, and more information to users who aren't sure what they want.

A variant on that simple approach is to show users who are clear on what they're looking for only *representational* content components, such as a title or author, to help them quickly distinguish the result they're seeking. Users who aren't as certain of what they're looking for will benefit from *descriptive* content components such as a summary, part of an abstract, or keywords to get a sense of what their search results are about. You can also provide users some choice of what to display; again, consider your users' most common information needs before setting a default. For example, the Yelp iPad app allows the user to view search results as listings, a location map, or images (Figure 9-11).

Figure 9-11. The Yelp iPad app allows users to select three different ways of viewing search results: as listings, as locations on a map, or as images

When it's hard to distinguish retrieved documents because of a commonly displayed field (e.g., the title), show more information, such as a page number, to help the user differentiate between results.

Another take on the same concept is shown in Figure 9-12, which displays multiple versions of the same book. Some of the distinctions are meaningful: you'll want to know which items are available in the library. Some aren't so helpful; for example, you might not care as much about the cover.

Figure 9-12. Content components help distinguish multiple versions of the same book

How much information to display per result is also a function of how large a typical result set is. Perhaps you don't have that much content, or most users' queries are so specific that they retrieve only a small number of results. If you think that users would like more information in such cases, then it may be worth displaying more content components per result. But keep in mind that regardless of how many ways you indicate that there are more results than fit on one screen, many (if not most) users will never venture past that first screen. So don't go overboard with providing lots of content per result, as the first few results may obscure the rest of the retrieval.

Which content components you display for each result also depends on which components are available in each document (i.e., how your content is structured) and on how the content will be used. Users of phone directories, for example, want phone numbers first and foremost. So it makes sense to show them the information from the phone number field in the result itself, as opposed to forcing them to click through to another document to find this information (see Figure 9-13).

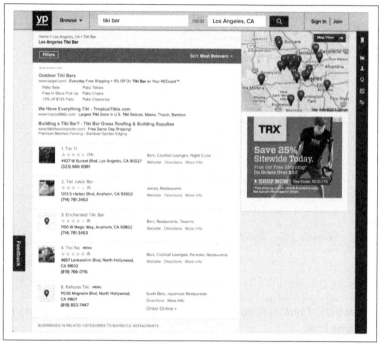

Figure 9-13. A Yellow Pages search doesn't force us to click through for a phone number

If you don't have much structure to draw from or if your engine is searching full text, showing the query terms within the "context" of the document's text is a useful variation on this theme (see Figure 9-14). In this example, The Verge highlights the query terms by using a bold font within the sentence they appear in—an excellent practice, as it helps the user quickly scan the results page for the relevant part of each result.

FEATURE

Up close with Glow's crazy laser light earbuds

By Sean O'Kane on February 19, 2015 11:27 am

Big **headphones** give companies plenty of space to create a distinct look for their brand, like Beats does with its iconic lowercase 'b' or Marshall does with its gui...

ARTICLE

MKBHD reviews Audio-Technica's high-end M70X **headphones**

By Ross Miller on February 17, 2015 04:30 pm

...addition to making him an accessory to drone murder, we're featuring more of our YouTube partner and his videos on The Verge. In the market for $400 **headphones**? MKBHD has published his take on Audio-Technica's ATH-M70X. It's a good overview of both the M70X and its little brother the M50X, which came out las...

ARTICLE

15 things we learned from The New Yorker's Jony Ive profile

By Jacob Kastrenakes on February 16, 2015 11:06 am

...ner." Tim Cook may not love Beats' hardware design Cook loves to talk about Beats Music and its playlists. We haven't heard him talk about Beats **headphones** very much. This might be the reason why: When I spoke to Cook, he lauded

Figure 9-14. The Verge bolds search query result instances in their surrounding sentences to show their context

How Many Documents to Display

How many documents are displayed depends mostly on two factors. If your engine is configured to display a lot of information for each retrieved document, you'll want to consider having a smaller retrieval set, and vice versa. Additionally, a user's screen resolution, connectivity speed, and browser settings will affect the number of results that can be displayed effectively. It may be safest to err on the side of simplicity—by showing a small number of results—while providing a variety of settings that users can select based on their own needs.

We suggest that you let users know the total number of retrieved documents so they have a sense of how many documents remain as they sift through search results. Also consider providing a results navigation system to help them move through the results. In Figure 9-15, Reuters provides such a navigation system, displaying the total number of results and enabling users to move through the result set 10 items at a time.

In many cases, the moment a user is confronted by a large result set is the moment he decides the number of results is too large. This is a golden opportunity to provide the user with the option of revising and narrowing his search. Reuters achieves this quite simply by repeating the query in the search box.

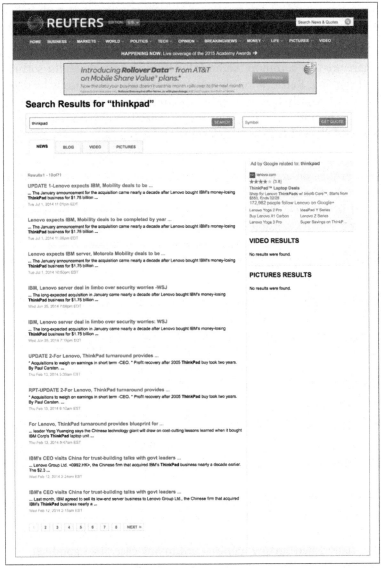

Figure 9-15. Reuters allows you to jump ahead through screens of 10 results at a time

Listing Results

Now that you have a group of search results and a sense of which content components you wish to display for each, in what order should these results be listed? Again, much of the answer depends upon what kind of information needs your users start with, what sort of results they are hoping to receive, and how they would like to use the results.

There are two common methods for listing retrieval results: sorting and ranking. Retrieval results can be sorted chronologically by date, or alphabetically by any number of content component types (e.g., by title, by author, or by department). They can also be ranked by a retrieval algorithm (e.g., by relevance or popularity).

Sorting is especially helpful to users who are looking to make a decision or take an action. For example, users who are comparing a list of products might want to sort by price or another feature to help them make their choice. Any content component can be used for sorting, but it's sensible to provide users with the option to sort on components that will actually help them accomplish tasks. Which ones are task oriented and which aren't, of course, depends upon each unique situation.

Ranking is more useful when there is a need to understand information or learn something. Ranking is typically used to describe retrieved documents' relevance, from most to least. Users look to learn from those documents that are most relevant. Of course, as we shall see, relevance is relative, and you should choose relevance ranking approaches carefully. Users will generally assume that the top few results are best.

The following sections provide examples of both sorting and ranking, as well as some ideas on what might make the most sense for your users.

Sorting by alphabet

Just about any content component can be sorted alphabetically (see Figure 9-16). This is a good general-purpose sorting approach—especially when sorting names—and in any case, it's a good bet that most users are familiar with the order of the alphabet! It works best to omit initial articles such as "a" and "the" from the sort order (certain search engines provide this option); users are likely to look for "The Naked Bungee Jumping Guide" under "N" rather than "T."

Figure 9-16. Baseball-Reference.com displays search results in alphabetical order

Sorting by chronology

If your content (or your user's query) is time sensitive, chronological sorts are a useful approach. And you can often draw on a filesystem's built-in dating if you have no other sources of date information.

If your site provides access to press releases or other news-oriented information, sorting by reverse chronological order makes good sense (see Figure 9-17 and Figure 9-18). Chronological order is less common and can be useful for presenting historical data.

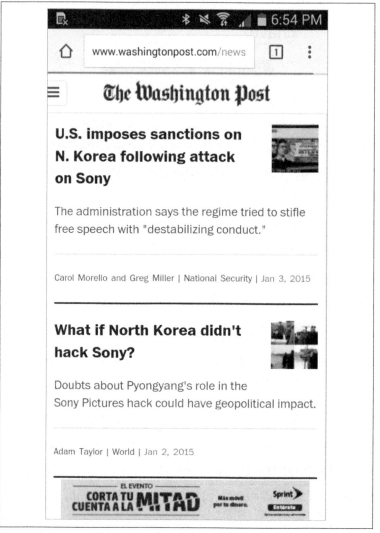

Figure 9-17. The Washington Post's default list ordering is by reverse chronological order...

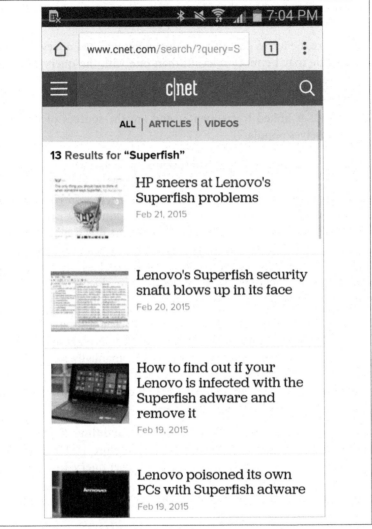

Figure 9-18. ...as is CNET's

Ranking by relevance

Relevance-ranking algorithms (there are many flavors) are typically based on one or more of the following:

- How many of the query's terms occur in the retrieved document
- How frequently those terms occur in that document

- How close together those terms occur (e.g., are they adjacent, in the same sentence, or in the same paragraph?)

- Where the terms occur (e.g., a document with the query term in its title may be more relevant than one with the query term in its body)

- The popularity of the document where the query terms appear (e.g., is it linked to frequently, and are the sources of its links themselves popular?)

Different relevance-ranking approaches make sense for different types of content, but with most search engines, the content you're searching is apples and oranges. So, for example, Document A might be ranked higher than Document B, but Document B is definitely more relevant. Why? Because while Document B is a bibliographic citation to a really relevant work, Document A is a long document that just happens to contain many instances of the terms in the search query. The more heterogeneous your documents are, the more careful you'll need to be with relevance ranking.

Indexing by humans is another means of establishing relevance. Keyword and descriptor fields can be searched, leveraging the value judgments of human indexers. For example, manually selected recommendations—popularly known as "best bets"—can be returned as relevant results. In Figure 9-19, the first set of results was associated with the query "Ukraine" in advance.

Requiring an investment of human expertise and time, the best bets approach isn't trivial to implement and therefore isn't necessarily suitable to be developed for each and every user query. Instead, recommendations are typically used for the most common queries (as determined by search log analysis) and combined with automatically generated search results.

Figure 9-19. A search of the BBC's site retrieves a set of manually tagged documents as well as automatic results; the recommendations are called "Editor's Choice" rather than "best bets"

Ranking by popularity

Popularity is the source of Google's popularity.

Put another way, Google is successful in large part because it ranks results by which ones are the most popular. It does so by factoring in how many links there are to a retrieved document. Google also distinguishes the quality of these links: a link from a site that itself receives many links is worth more than a link from a little-known site. This algorithm, which is part of Google's "secret sauce" for presenting search results, is known as PageRank.

There are other ways to determine popularity, but keep in mind that small sites or collections of separate, nonlinked sites (often referred to as "silos") don't necessarily take advantage of popularity as well as large, multisite environments with many users. The latter have a wide scope of usage and a richer set of links. A smaller system isn't likely to have enough variation in the popularity of different documents to merit this approach, while in a "silo" environment, little cross-pollination results in few links between sites. It's also worth noting that, to calculate relevance, Google uses many other criteria in addition to PageRank.

Ranking by users' or experts' ratings

In an increasing number of situations, users are willing to rate the value of information. User ratings can be used as the basis of retrieval result ordering. In the case of Yelp (see Figure 9-20), these ratings—based on users' reviews of businesses listed in the system— are integral to helping users judge the value of an item, and form the foundation of an entire information economy. Of course, Yelp has a lot of users who don't shrink from expressing their opinions, so there is a rich collection of judgments to draw on for ranking.

Most sites don't have a sufficient volume of motivated users to employ valuable user ratings. However, if you have the opportunity to use this data, it can be helpful to display user ratings with a document, if not as part of a presentation algorithm.

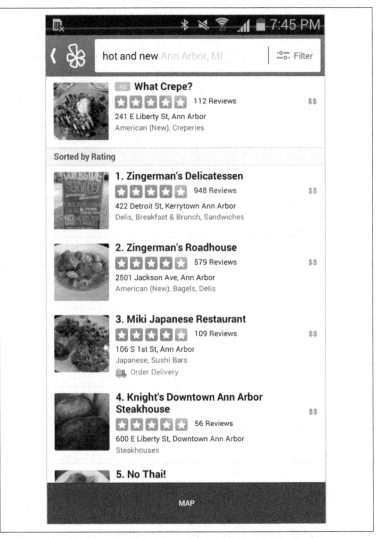

Figure 9-20. User ratings fuel the ranking of these Yelp results

Ranking by pay-for-placement

Advertising has become the predominant business model for publishing online, so it is no surprise that pay-for-placement (PFP) has become commonplace in many search systems. Although the previous Yelp example showed results sorted by user rankings, the first result on the list actually has a lower ranking than the others; it owes its position at the top of the list solely to the fact that it is a paid advertisement.

If your system aggregates content from a number of different vendors, you might consider implementing PFP to present search results. If users are shopping, they might also appreciate this approach—with the assumption being that the most stable, successful sites are the ones that can afford the highest placement. This is somewhat like selecting the plumber with the largest advertisement in the yellow pages to fix your toilet.

Grouping Results

Despite all the ways we can list results, no single approach is perfect. Hybrid approaches that combine different types of sorting—such as Google's—show a lot of promise, but you typically need to be in the business of creating search engines to have this level of involvement with a tool. In any case, our information environments are typically getting larger, not smaller. Search result sets will accordingly get larger as well, and so will the probability that those ideal results will be buried far beyond the point where users give up looking.

However, one alternative approach to sorting and ranking holds promise: clustering retrieved results by some common aspect. An excellent study by researchers at Microsoft and the University of California at Berkeley shows improved performance when results are clustered by category as well as by a ranked list.[2] How can we cluster results? The obvious ways are, unfortunately, the least useful: we can use existing metadata, like document type (e.g., *.doc*, *.pdf*) and file creation/modification date, to allow us to divide search results into clusters. Much more useful are clusters derived from

---

2 Susan T. Dumais, Edward Cutrell, and Hao Chen, "Optimizing search by showing results in context" (*Proceedings of CHI '01, Human Factors in Computing Systems*, 2001, 277–284)."

manually applied metadata, like topic, audience, language, and product family. Unfortunately, approaches based on manual effort can be prohibitively expensive.

In Figure 9-21, Forrester contextualizes the query "user experience" with roles such as "Marketing Leadership" and specific date ranges.

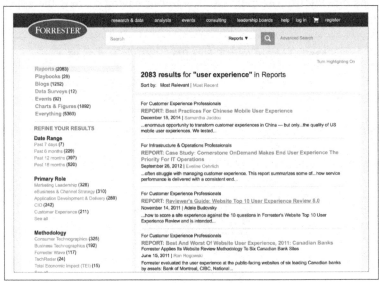

Figure 9-21. Forrester contextualizes search results for the query "user experience"

These clusters provide context for search results; selecting the category that seems to fit your interest best allows you to work with a significantly smaller retrieval set and (ideally) a set of documents that come from the same topical domain. This approach is much like generating search zones on the fly.

Acting on Results

You've provided the user with a set of search results. What happens next? Certainly, she could continue to search, revising her query and her idea of what she's looking for along the way. Or, heavens, she might have found what she was looking for and be ready to move on. Contextual inquiry and task-analysis techniques will help you understand what users might want to do with their results. The following sections discuss a few common options.

Call to action

Some search results can be acted on directly, without having to jump through intermediary steps. In these cases, it is often desirable to include a call-to-action button or link along with individual search results. For example, the iOS App Store allows the user to "GET" apps directly from search results, without having to view the apps' description screens and user reviews (Figure 9-22).

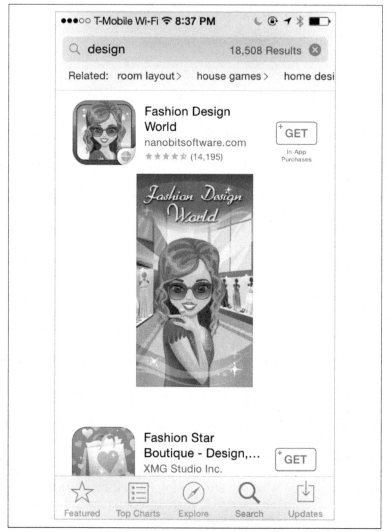

Figure 9-22. Search results in the iOS App Store include a "GET" button (which lists the app's price when it is not free)

Select a subset of results

Sometimes when you're searching you want to take more than one document along with you. You want to "shop" for documents just like you shop for books at Amazon. And if you're sorting through dozens or hundreds of results, you may need a way to mark the documents you like so you don't forget or lose track of them.

A shopping cart feature can be quite useful in search-intensive environments such as library catalogs. In Figure 9-23, users can "save" a subset of their retrieval and then manipulate those results in their "shelves" once they're done searching.

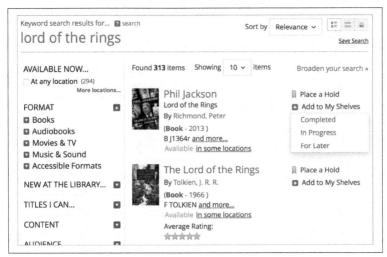

Figure 9-23. The San Francisco Public Library allows users to add search results to three "shelves": "Completed," "In Progress," and "For Later"

Save a search

In some cases, it's the search itself, not the results, that you're interested in "keeping." Saved searches are especially useful in dynamic domains that you'd like to track over time; you can manually re-execute a saved search on a regular basis, or schedule that query to automatically be rerun regularly. Note that the example in Figure 9-23 includes a "Save Search" link in the upper-right corner of the search results display; the user can name saved search sets for later retrieval.

Designing the Search Interface

All the factors we've discussed so far—what to search, what to retrieve, and how to present the results—come together in the search interface. And with so much variation among users and search technology functions, there can be no single ideal search interface. Although the literature of information retrieval includes many studies of search interface design, many variables preclude the emergence of a "right way" to design search interfaces. Here are a few of the variables on the table:

Level of searching expertise and motivation

Are users comfortable with specialized query languages (e.g., Boolean operators), or do they prefer natural language? Do they need a simple or a high-powered interface? Do they want to work hard to make their searches truly successful, or are they happy with "good enough" results? How many iterations are they willing to try?

Type of information need

Do users want just a taste, or are they doing comprehensive research? What content components can help them make good decisions about clicking through to a document? Should the results be brief, or should they provide extensive detail for each document? And how detailed a query are users willing to provide to express their needs?

Type of information being searched

Is the information made up of structured fields or full text? Is it navigation pages, destination pages, or both? Is it written in HTML or other formats, including nontextual? Is the content dynamic or more static? Does it come tagged with metadata, full of fields, or is it full text?

Amount of information being searched

Will users be overwhelmed by the number of documents retrieved? How many results is the "right number"? That's a lot to consider. Luckily, we can provide basic advice that you should consider when designing a search interface.

In the early days of the Web, many search engines emulated the functionality of the "traditional" search engines used for online library catalogs and databases, or were ported directly from those environments. These traditional systems were often designed for researchers, librarians, and others who had some knowledge of and incentive for expressing their information needs in complex query languages. Therefore, many search systems at the time allowed the user to use Boolean operators, search fields, and so forth; in fact, users were often required to know and use these complex syntaxes.

As the Web's user base exploded, overall searching experience and expertise bottomed out, and the new breed of user wasn't especially patient. Users more typically just entered a term or two without any operators, pressed the "search" button, and hoped for the best.

The reaction of search engine developers was to bury the old fancy tricks in advanced search interfaces, or to make them invisible to users by building advanced functionality directly into the search engines. For example, Google makes a set of assumptions about what kind of results users want (through a relevance algorithm) and how they'd like those results presented (using a popularity algorithm). Google makes some good assumptions for web-wide searching, and that's why it's successful. However, most search systems, web-wide or local, don't work as well.

For that reason, the pendulum may eventually swing back to supporting users who, out of frustration, have become more search literate and are willing to spend more time learning a complex search interface and constructing a query. But for now, it's fair to assume that, unless your site's users are librarians, researchers, or specialized professionals (e.g., an attorney performing a patent search), they won't invest much time or effort into crafting well-considered queries. That means the burden of searching falls chiefly on the search engine, its interfaces, and how content is tagged and indexed. Therefore, it's best to keep your search interface as simple as possible: present users with a simple search box and a "search" button.

The Box

Your system is likely to have the ubiquitous search box, as shown in Figure 9-24.

Figure 9-24. The ubiquitous search box (in this case, from Apple)

Simple and clear. Type in some keywords ("lost iPhone") or a natural language expression ("Where can I find my iPhone?"), hit the Return (or Enter) button on your keyboard, and the whole site will be searched and results displayed.

Users make assumptions about how search interfaces work, and you may want to test for those as you design your own search system. Some common user assumptions include:

- "I can just type terms that describe what I'm looking for and the search engine will do the rest."
- "I don't have to type in those funny AND, OR, or NOT thingies."
- "I don't have to worry about synonyms for my term; if I'm looking for dogs, I just type 'dogs,' not 'canine' or 'canines.'"
- "Fielded searching? I don't have time to learn which fields I can search."
- "My query will search the entire site."

If your users have those assumptions and are not especially motivated to learn more about how your system's search works differently, then go with the flow. Give them the box. You certainly could provide a "help" page that explains how to create more advanced, precise queries, but users may rarely visit this page.

Instead, look for opportunities to *educate users when they're ready to learn*. The best time to do this is after the initial searches have been executed, when the users have reached a point of indecision or frustration. The initial hope that the first try would retrieve exactly what they were looking for has now faded. And when users are ready to revise their searches, they'll want to know how they can make those revisions. For example, if you search the eBay app for "watches" (see Figure 9-25), you'll likely get a few more results than you'd like.

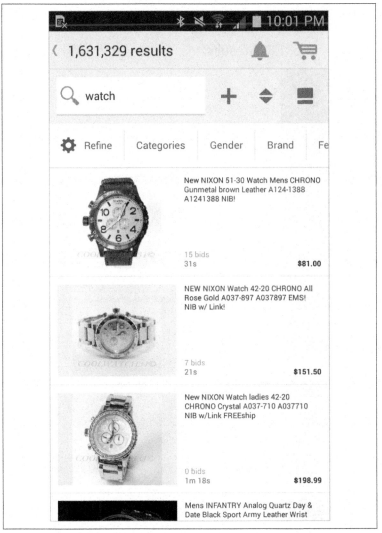

Figure 9-25. The eBay app's search results provide opportunities to revise your search...

At this point, eBay's search system goes beyond the box: it tells the user something to the effect of "Here are those 1,631,329 results that you asked for. Perhaps this is too many? If that's the case, consider revising your search using our souped-up 'Refine' interface, which allows you to narrow your search. Or, select from a list of categories to narrow your results further" (see Figure 9-26).

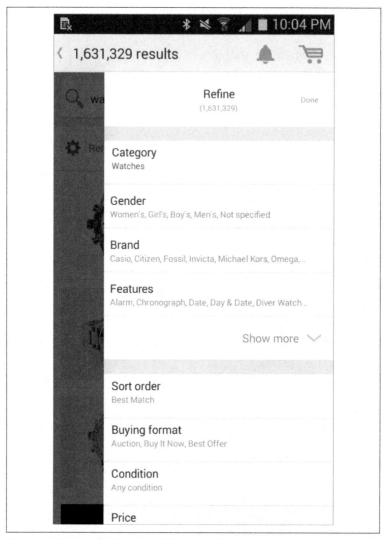

Figure 9-26. ...including the ability to refine your search by specifying various category-specific facets

In general, too many or too few (typically zero) search results are both good indicators for users to revise their searches; we'll cover more on this topic in the section "Supporting Revision" on page 260 later in this chapter.

Consider how your search box is presented. The box can cause confusion when it appears alongside other boxes. Unless your system's search functionality truly requires more than one field—as is the case with many travel-related services—it is best to keep search limited to a single box. (If more than one field is required, it's important that they be clearly labeled, as illustrated in Figure 9-27.)

Figure 9-27. Kayak's flight search form features clearly labeled fields

Consistent placement of the search box alongside other global navigation choices, along with the consistent use of a button labeled "search" that comes with that box, will go a long way toward ensuring that users at least know where to type their queries.

There are many assumptions behind that innocuous little search box, some made on the part of the user, and some by the designer who decides what functionality will be hidden behind that box. Determining what your users' assumptions are should drive the default settings that you set up when designing the simple search interface.

Autocomplete and Autosuggest

Autocomplete and autosuggest are widely used patterns for interacting with search systems. In both cases, a list of results is presented alongside the search box, preemptively prompting the user with possible matches based on the first few characters typed. These results are culled from search indexes, controlled vocabularies, manually configured match lists, or often all of the above. Displays range from very simple and straightforward text lists (in the case of autocomplete patterns) to popovers with highly customized layouts (Figure 9-28).

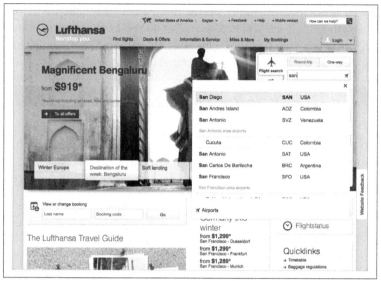

Figure 9-28. Like many airlines, Lufthansa presents a list of airports that match the first few characters the user types into the origin and destination search boxes

This technique is very useful, because it helps users identify potential matches based on partial or incomplete information. In some cases, it also gives them hints as to the way the system is structured, allowing them to make smarter searches by giving them the ability to explore the system right from the search box. Because of this, it has mostly supplanted the dedicated, advanced search mechanisms of yore.

Advanced Search

In the past, many websites provided advanced search interfaces as crutches for underfeatured or poorly configured search systems. In stark contrast to the search box, advanced search interfaces allow much more manipulation of the search system and are typically used by two types of users: advanced searchers (librarians, lawyers, doctoral students, medical researchers), and frustrated searchers who need to revise their initial searches (often users who've found that the search box didn't meet their needs). As search engines have improved, advanced search interfaces are increasingly focused on serving the former.

While they are less common today, advanced search interfaces provide flexibility and power to users who understand the structure of the information they are looking for. For example, the US Congress website allows knowledgeable users to configure extremely sophisticated searches using Boolean operators (Figure 9-29).

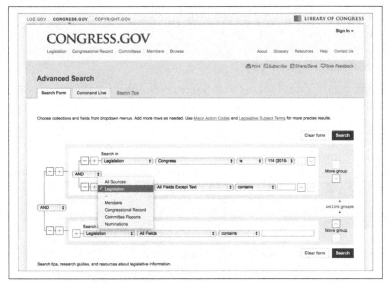

Figure 9-29. Congress.gov allows advanced users to build complex searches using Boolean operators

If your system could benefit from advanced search, a good rule of thumb is to expose your search engine's various heavy-duty search functions on the advanced page for those few users who want to have a go at them, but design your search system with the goal of making it unnecessary for the vast majority of searchers to ever need to go to the advanced search page.

Supporting Revision

We've touched on what can happen after the users find what they're looking for, when the search is done. But all too often that's not the case. Here are some guidelines to help your users hone their searches (and hopefully learn a little bit about your search system in the process).

Repeat search in results page

What was it I was looking for? Sometimes users are forgetful, especially after sifting through dozens of results. Displaying the initial search within the search box (as in Figure 9-30) can be quite useful: it restates the search that was just executed, and allows the user to modify it without reentering it.

Figure 9-30. In the Netflix Android app, the query is displayed on the results page and can be revised and reexecuted

Explain where results come from

It's useful to make clear what content was searched, especially if your search system supports multiple search zones (see Figure 9-31). This reminder can be handy if the user decides to broaden or narrow his search; more or fewer search zones can be used in a revised search.

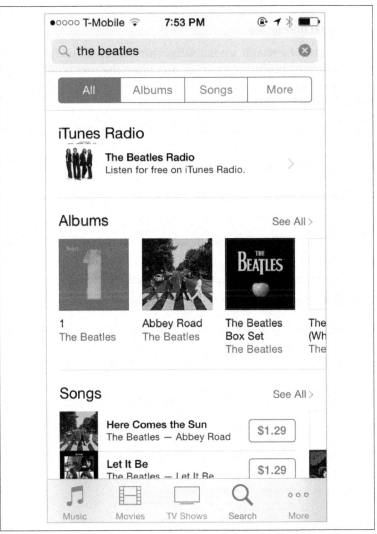

Figure 9-31. The iOS iTunes Store app search system shows you where you searched (i.e., "All"), and makes it easy to reach results from other search zones

Explain what the user did

If the results of a search are not satisfactory, it can be useful to state what happened behind the scenes, providing the user with a better understanding of the situation and a jumping-off point should she wish to revise her search.

Explaining "what happened" can include the two guidelines just mentioned, as well as:

- Restating the query
- Describing what content was searched
- Describing any filters that might be in place (e.g., date ranges)
- Showing implicit Boolean or other operators, such as a default AND
- Showing other current settings, such as the sort order
- Mentioning the number of results retrieved

In Figure 9-32, the *New York Times* site provides an excellent example of explaining to the user what just happened.

Figure 9-32. All aspects of the search are restated as part of these search results

Integrate searching with browsing

A key theme in this book is the need to integrate searching and browsing (think of them together as "finding"), but we won't belabor it here. Just remember to look for opportunities to connect your search and browse systems to allow users to easily jump back and forth.

As Figure 9-33 and Figure 9-34 illustrate, Barnes & Noble provides this functionality in both directions.

Figure 9-33. Searching leads to browsing: a search for "2001 a space odyssey" on the Barnes & Noble site retrieves categories as well as documents

Figure 9-34. And browsing leads to searching: navigate to the "Movies & TV" section, and you'll find the search box set to search that zone

When Users Get Stuck

You can strive to support iterative searching with fully integrated browsing and state-of-the-art retrieval and presentation algorithms, yet users still will fail time and time again. What should you do when presenting the user with zero results, or with way too many?

The latter case is a bit easier to address, because in most cases your search engine provides relevance-ranked results. In effect, winnowing oversized result sets is a form of search revision, and often the user will self-select when he is ready to stop reviewing results. But it is still useful to provide some instruction on how to narrow search results, as shown in Figure 9-35.

You can also help users narrow their results by allowing them to search within their current result sets. In Figure 9-36, the initial search for hotels in New York City retrieved over 600 results; we can "filter by hotel name" for particular brands to narrow our retrieval.

Figure 9-35. Congress.gov provides advice on how to narrow down searches

Figure 9-36. Priceline.com allows users to search within the result set

At the other end of the spectrum, zero hits is a bit more frustrating for users and challenging for information architects. We suggest you adopt a "no dead ends" policy to address this problem. "No dead ends" simply means that users always have another option, even if they've retrieved zero results. The options might include:

- A means of revising the search
- Search tips or other advice on how to improve the search
- A means of browsing (e.g., including the site's navigation system or sitemap)
- A human contact if searching and browsing won't work

It's worth noting that we've seen few (if any) search systems that meet all these criteria.

Where to Learn More

Although this is the longest chapter in this book, we've covered only the tip of the search system iceberg. If this piqued your interest, you may want to delve further into the field of information retrieval. Some of our favorite texts are:

- *Search Patterns: Design for Discovery* by Peter Morville and Jeffery Callender (Sebastopol, CA: O'Reilly, 2010)
- *Modern Information Retrieval* by Ricardo Baeza-Yates and Berthier Ribeiro-Neto (Boston: Addison-Wesley, 2011)
- *Concepts of Information Retrieval* by Miranda Lee Pao (Westport, CT: Libraries Unlimited, 1989); this title is out of print, but you may be able to find used copies on Amazon
- *On Search, the Series* (*http://bit.ly/on_search_the_series*) by Tim Bray, an excellent collection of essays on search written by the father of XML

If you're looking for more immediate and practical advice, the most useful site for learning about search tools is, naturally, Searchtools.com (*http://www.searchtools.com*), Avi Rappoport's compendium of installation and configuration advice, product listings, and industry news. Another excellent source is Danny Sullivan's Search Engine Watch (*http://www.searchenginewatch.com*), which focuses on web-wide searching but is quite relevant to site-wide searching nonetheless.

Recap

Let's recap what we learned in this chapter:

- Search is an important mechanism for finding information; however, it's not a given that your information environment requires a search system.

- Although search may appear simple—just type some words into the search box—there's a lot going on under the hood.

- Choosing what to index in your information environment is an important step when configuring your search system.

- There are many different types of search algorithms.

- There are also various different ways of presenting results back to the user.

- All of these factors—what to search, what to retrieve, and how to present the results—come together in the search interface.

Now we move on to discuss the final principle in our overview: thesauri, controlled vocabularies, and metadata.

CHAPTER 10

Thesauri, Controlled Vocabularies, and Metadata

The basic tool for the manipulation of reality is the manipulation of words.
—Philip K. Dick

In this chapter, we'll cover:

- Definitions of metadata and controlled vocabularies
- An overview of synonym rings, authority files, classification schemes, and thesauri
- Hierarchical, equivalence, and associative relationships
- Faceted classification and guided navigation

An interactive information environment—like a website—is a collection of interconnected systems with complex dependencies. A single link on a page can simultaneously be part of the site's structure, organization, labeling, navigation, and searching systems. It's useful to study these systems independently, but it's also crucial to consider how they interact. Reductionism will not tell us the whole truth.

Metadata and controlled vocabularies present a fascinating lens through which we can view the network of relationships between systems. In many large metadata-driven products, controlled vocabularies have become the glue that holds the systems together. A thesaurus on the backend can enable a more seamless and satisfying user experience on the frontend.

In addition, the practice of thesaurus design can help bridge the gap between past and present. The first thesauri were developed for libraries, museums, and government agencies long before the invention of the World Wide Web. We can draw upon these decades of experience, but we can't copy indiscriminately. The systems we design present new challenges and demand creative solutions.

But we're getting ahead of ourselves. Let's begin by defining some basic terms and concepts. Then we can work back toward the big picture.

Metadata

When it comes to definitions, metadata is a slippery fish. Describing it as "data about data" isn't very helpful. The following excerpt from Wikipedia (*https://en.wikipedia.org/wiki/Metadata*) takes us a little further:

> Metadata (metacontent) is defined as the data providing information about one or more aspects of the data, such as:
>
> - Means of creation of the data
> - Purpose of the data
> - Time and date of creation
> - Creator or author of the data
> - Location on a computer network where the data was created
> - Standards used
>
> For example, a digital image may include metadata that describe how large the picture is, the color depth, the image resolution, when the image was created, and other data. A text document's metadata may contain information about how long the document is, who the author is, when the document was written, and a short summary of the document.

Metadata tags are used to describe documents, pages, images, software, video and audio files, and other content objects for the purposes of improved navigation and retrieval. The keywords attribute of the HTML <meta> tag used by many websites provides a simple example. Authors can freely enter words and phrases that describe the content. These keywords are not displayed in the interface but are available for use by search engines:

```
<meta name="keywords" content="information architecture,
content management, knowledge management, user experience">
```

Many companies today are using metadata in more sophisticated ways. Leveraging content management software and controlled vocabularies, they create dynamic metadata-driven systems that support distributed authoring and powerful navigation. This metadata-driven model represents a profound change in how information environments are created and managed. Instead of asking, "Where do I place this document in the taxonomy?" we can now ask, "How do I describe this document?" The software and vocabulary systems take care of the rest.

Controlled Vocabularies

Vocabulary control comes in many shapes and sizes. At its most vague, it consists of any defined subset of natural language. At its simplest, a controlled vocabulary is a list of *equivalent terms* in the form of a synonym ring, or a *list of preferred terms* in the form of an authority file. Define relationships between terms (e.g., broader, narrower), and you've got a classification scheme. Model associative relationships between concepts (e.g., *See Also*, *See Related*), and you're working on a thesaurus. Figure 10-1 illustrates the relationships between different types of controlled vocabularies.

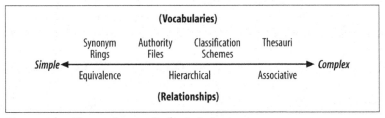

Figure 10-1. Types of controlled vocabularies

Because a full-blown thesaurus integrates all the relationships and capabilities of the simpler forms, let's explore each of these building blocks before taking a close look at the "Swiss Army knife" of controlled vocabularies.

Synonym Rings

A *synonym ring* (see Figure 10-2) connects a set of words that are defined as equivalent for the purposes of retrieval. In practice, these words are often not true synonyms. For example, imagine you're redesigning a consumer portal that provides ratings information about household products from several companies.

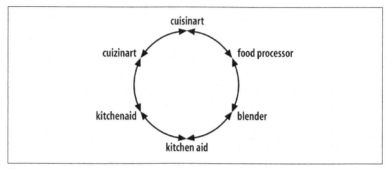

Figure 10-2. A synonym ring

When you examine the search logs and talk with users, you're likely to find that different people looking for the same thing are entering different terms. Someone who's buying a food processor may enter "blender" or one of several product names (or their common misspellings). Take a look at the content, and you're likely to find many of these same variations.

There may be no preferred terms, or at least no good reason to define them. Instead, you can use the out-of-the-box capabilities of a search engine to build synonym rings. This can be as simple as entering sets of equivalent words into a text file. When a user enters a word into the search engine, that word is checked against the text file. If the word is found, then the query is "exploded" to include all of the equivalent words. For example, in Boolean logic:

```
(kitchenaid) becomes (kitchenaid or "kitchen aid" or blender or
"food processor" or cuisinart or cuizinart)
```

What happens when you don't use synonym rings? Consider Figure 10-3, which shows the results of a search for "itouch" (a popular, yet unofficial, conflation of "iPod touch") on Frys.com. The search produces only two results, even though a search for "ipod touch" on the same site yields 648 results.

Figure 10-3. Results of searching Frys.com for "itouch" and "ipod touch," respectively

Other retailers provide synonyms for "itouch," leading to more useful results even though the user entered a "wrong" search term (Figure 10-4).

However, synonym rings can also introduce new problems. If the query term expansion operates behind the scenes, users can be confused by results that don't actually include their keywords. In addition, the use of synonym rings may result in less relevant results. This brings us back to the subject of precision and recall.

As you may remember from Chapter 9, *precision* refers to the relevance of documents within a given result set. To request high precision, you might say, "Show me only the most relevant documents." *Recall* refers to the proportion of relevant documents in the result set compared to all the relevant documents in the system. To request high recall, you might say, "Show me *all* the relevant documents." Let's revisit the precision and recall ratios we discussed in Chapter 9, which are presented again in Figure 10-5.

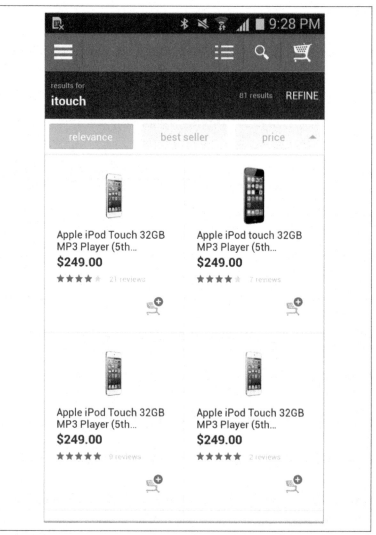

Figure 10-4. Searching for "itouch" in Target's Android app produces 81 results

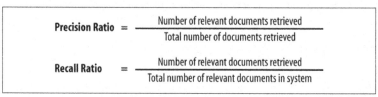

Precision Ratio = $\dfrac{\text{Number of relevant documents retrieved}}{\text{Total number of documents retrieved}}$

Recall Ratio = $\dfrac{\text{Number of relevant documents retrieved}}{\text{Total number of relevant documents in system}}$

Figure 10-5. Precision and recall ratios

While both high precision and high recall may be ideal, it's generally understood in the information retrieval field that you usually increase one at the expense of the other. This has important implications for the use of controlled vocabularies.

As you might guess, synonym rings can dramatically improve recall. In one study conducted at Bellcore in the 1980s, the use of synonym rings, or "unlimited aliasing," within a small test database increased recall from 20% to 80%.[1] However, synonym rings can also reduce precision. Good interface design and an understanding of user goals can help strike the right balance. For example, you might use synonym rings by default but order the exact keyword matches at the top of the search results list. Or, you might ignore synonym rings for initial searches but provide the option to "expand your search to include related terms" if there were few or no results.

In summary, synonym rings are a simple, useful form of vocabulary control. There is really no excuse for the conspicuous absence of this basic capability on many of today's largest information environments.

Authority Files

Strictly defined, an *authority file* is a list of preferred terms or acceptable values. It does not include variants or synonyms. Authority files have traditionally been used largely by libraries and government agencies to define the proper names for a set of entities within a limited domain.

In practice, authority files are commonly inclusive of both preferred and variant terms. In other words, authority files are synonym rings in which one term has been defined as the preferred term or acceptable value.

The two-letter codes that constitute the standard abbreviations for U.S. states as defined by the US Postal Service provide an instructive example. Using the purist definition, the authority file includes only the acceptable codes:

---

1 Thomas K. Landauer, *The Trouble with Computers: Usefulness, Usability, and Productivity* (Cambridge, MA: MIT Press, 1996).

```
AL, AK, AZ, AR, CA, CO, CT, DE, DC, FL, GA, HI, ID, IL, IN, IA,
KS, KY, LA, ME, MD, MA, MI, MN, MS, MO, MT, NE, NV, NH, NJ, NM,
NY, NC, ND, OH, OK, OR, PA, PR, RI, SC, SD, TN, TX, UT, VT, VA,
WA, WV, WI, WY
```

However, to make this list useful in most scenarios, it's necessary to include, at a minimum, a mapping to the names of states:

```
AL Alabama
AK Alaska
AZ Arizona
AR Arkansas
CA California
CO Colorado
CT Connecticut
  ...
```

To make this list even more useful in an information environment, it may be helpful to include common variants beyond the official state name:

```
CT Connecticut, Conn, Conneticut, Constitution State
```

At this point, we run into some important questions about the use and value of authority files in the environment. Because users can perform keyword searches that map many terms onto one concept, do we really need to define preferred terms, or can synonym rings handle things just fine by themselves? Why take that extra step to distinguish "CT" as the acceptable value?

First, there are a couple of backend reasons. An authority file can be a useful tool for content authors and indexers, enabling them to use the approved terms efficiently and consistently. Also, from a controlled vocabulary management perspective, the preferred term can serve as the unique identifier for each collection of equivalent terms, allowing for more efficient addition, deletion, and modification of variant terms.

There are also a number of ways that the selection of preferred terms can benefit the user. Consider Figure 10-6, where Drugstore.com is providing a mapping between the equivalent term "tilenol" and the authoritative brand name, "Tylenol." By showing users the preferred terms, you can educate them. In some cases, you'll be helping them to correct a misspelling. In others, you may be explaining industry terminology or building brand recognition.

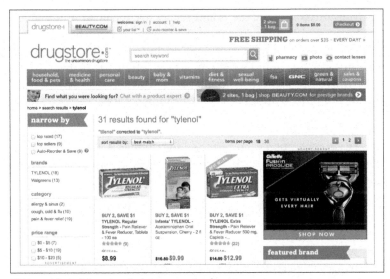

Figure 10-6. Mapping between equivalent terms

These "lessons" may be useful in very different contexts—perhaps during the next telephone conversation or in-store interaction a customer has with your organization. It's an opportunity to nudge everyone toward speaking the same language, without assuming or requiring such conformity within the search system. In effect, the search experience can be similar to an interaction with a sales professional, who understands the language of the customer and translates it back to the customer using the company or industry's preferred terminology.

Preferred terms are also important as the user switches from searching to browsing mode. When designing taxonomies, navigation bars, and indexes, it would be messy and overwhelming to present all of the synonyms, abbreviations, acronyms, and common misspellings for every term.

At Drugstore.com, only the brand names are included in the index (see Figure 10-7); equivalent terms like "tilenol" don't show up. This keeps the index relatively short and uncluttered and, in this example, reinforces the brand names. However, a trade-off is involved. In cases where the equivalent terms begin with different letters (e.g., aspirin and Bayer), there is value in creating pointers:

```
Aspirin see Bayer
```

Otherwise, when users look in the index under A for aspirin, they won't find Bayer. The use of pointers is called *term rotation*. Drugstore.com doesn't do it at all.

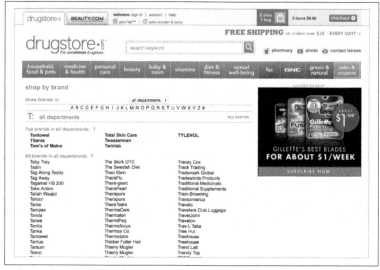

Figure 10-7. Brand index at Drugstore.com

In Figure 10-8, users looking for "Tylenol" on the US Federal Drug Administration website are guided to the generic term "acetaminophen." Such integration of the entry vocabulary can dramatically enhance the usefulness of the site index. However, it needs to be done selectively; otherwise, the index can become too long, harming overall usability. Once again, a careful balancing act is involved that requires research and good judgment.

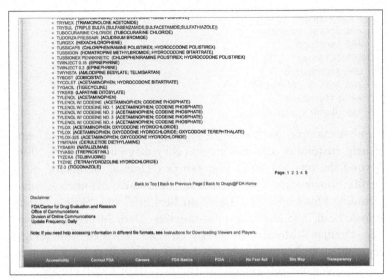

Figure 10-8. A site index with term rotation

Classification Schemes

We use *classification scheme* to mean an arrangement of preferred terms. These days, many people prefer to use *taxonomy* instead. Either way, it's important to recognize that these arrangements can take different shapes and serve multiple purposes, including:

- A frontend, browsable hierarchy that's a visible, integral part of the user interface
- A backend tool used by authors and indexers for organizing and tagging documents

Consider, for example, the Dewey Decimal Classification (DDC). First published in 1876, the DDC is now "the most widely used classification scheme in the world. Libraries in more than 135 countries use the DDC to organize and provide access to their collections."[2] In its purest form, the DDC is a hierarchical listing that begins with 10 top-level categories and drills down into great detail within each:

```
000 Computers, information, & general reference
100 Philosophy & psychology
```

2 From OCLC's "Introduction to the Dewey Decimal Classification" (*http://www.oclc.org/ dewey/about/about_the_ddc.htm*).

```
200 Religion
300 Social sciences
400 Language
500 Science
600 Technology
700 Arts & recreation
800 Literature
900 History & geography
```

Another example: Netflix uses a sophisticated classification scheme to help customers find new movies they may enjoy (Figure 10-9). Beyond the obvious, basic film genres ("Drama," "Comedy," etc.), Netflix movies are categorized in thousands of micro-genres, including broad ones like "Based on Real Life" and "With a Strong Female Lead," and highly specific ones like "Dark Suspenseful Gangster Dramas." Movies are analyzed and assigned "microtags" depending on features such as whether or not they have a happy ending. These microtags then inform the categorization process.[3]

Figure 10-9. Netflix categorizes movies using micro-genres, which allows the service to smartly suggest movies to customers

---

3 For an in-depth look at how Netflix's movie classification scheme works, see "How Netflix Reverse Engineered Hollywood" (*http://bit.ly/netflix_hollywood*) by Alexis C. Madrigal in *The Atlantic*.

Classification schemes can also be used in the context of searching. You can see in Figure 10-10 that Walmart's search results present "Departments" categories, which reinforces users' familiarity with Walmart's classification scheme.

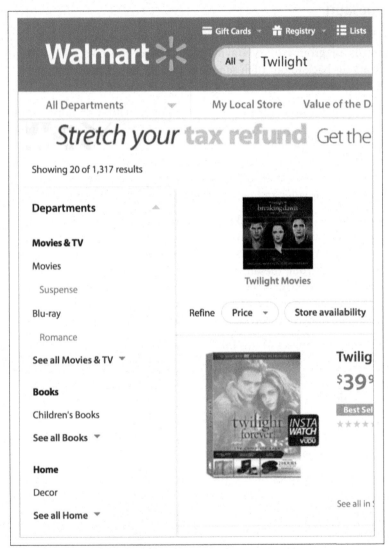

Figure 10-10. Category Matches at Walmart.com

The important point here is that classification schemes are not tied to a single view or instance. They can be used on both the backend and the frontend in all sorts of ways. We'll explore types of classification schemes in more detail later in this chapter, but first let's take a look at the "Swiss Army knife" of vocabulary control, the thesaurus.

Thesauri

The Oxford English Dictionary defines *thesaurus* as "a book that lists words in groups of synonyms and related concepts." This usage hearkens back to our high school English classes, when we chose big words from the thesaurus to impress our teachers.

Our species of thesaurus, the one integrated within an information environment to improve navigation and retrieval, shares a common heritage with the familiar reference text but has a different form and function. Like the reference book, our thesaurus is a semantic network of concepts, connecting words to their synonyms, homonyms, antonyms, broader and narrower terms, and related terms.

However, our thesaurus takes the form of an online database, tightly integrated with the user interface of a digital product or service. And though the traditional thesaurus helps people go from one word to many words, our thesaurus does the opposite. Its most important goal is synonym management—the mapping of many synonyms or word variants onto one preferred term or concept—so the ambiguities of language don't prevent people from finding what they need.

So, for the purposes of this book, a thesaurus is:

> A controlled vocabulary in which equivalence, hierarchical, and associative relationships are identified for purposes of improved retrieval.[4]

A thesaurus builds upon the constructs of the simpler controlled vocabularies, modeling these three fundamental types of semantic relationships.

As you can see from Figure 10-11, each preferred term becomes the center of its own semantic network. The *equivalence relationship* is focused on synonym management. The *hierarchical relationship* enables the classification of preferred terms into categories and subcategories. The associative relationship provides for meaningful

---

4 "Guidelines for the Construction, Format, and Management of Monolingual Thesauri," (*http://bit.ly/monolingual_thesauri*) ANSI/NISO Z39.19-1993 (R1998).

connections that aren't handled by the hierarchical or equivalence relationships. All three relationships can be useful in different ways for the purposes of information retrieval and navigation.

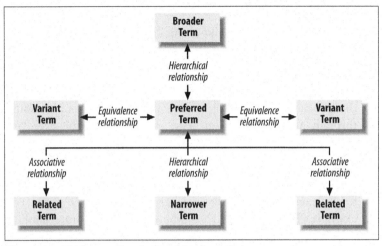

Figure 10-11. Semantic relationships in a thesaurus

Technical Lingo

If you're working with controlled vocabularies and thesauri, it's useful to know the core terminology used by experts in the field to communicate definitions and relationships. This specialized technical language can provide efficiency and specificity when communicating among experts. Just don't expect your users to recognize these terms. In the web environment, you can't require that users take a library science class before they use your information system. The core terminology includes the following:

Preferred Term (PT)
　Also known as the accepted term, acceptable value, subject heading, or descriptor. All relationships are defined with respect to the Preferred Term.

Variant Term (VT)
　Also known as entry terms or non-preferred terms, Variant Terms have been defined as equivalent to or loosely synonymous with the Preferred Term.

Broader Term (BT)

The Broader Term is the parent of the Preferred Term. It's one level higher in the hierarchy.

Narrower Term (NT)

A Narrower Term is a child of the Preferred Term. It's one level lower in the hierarchy.

Related Term (RT)

The Related Term is connected to the Preferred Term through the associative relationship. The relationship is often articulated through use of *See Also*. For example, Tylenol *See Also* Headache.

Use (U)

Traditional thesauri often employ the following syntax as a tool for indexers and users: Variant Term *Use* Preferred Term. For example, Tilenol *Use* Tylenol. Many people are more familiar with *See*, as in Tilenol *See* Tylenol.

Used For (UF)

This indicates the reciprocal relationship of Preferred Term *UF* Variant Term(s). It's used to show the full list of variants on the Preferred Term's record. For example, Tylenol *UF* Tilenol.

Scope Note (SN)

The Scope Note is essentially a specific type of definition of the Preferred Term, used to deliberately restrict the meaning of that term in order to rule out ambiguity as much as possible.

As we've seen, the preferred term is the center of its own semantic universe. Of course, a preferred term in one display is likely to be a broader, narrower, related, or even variant term in another display (see Figure 10-12).

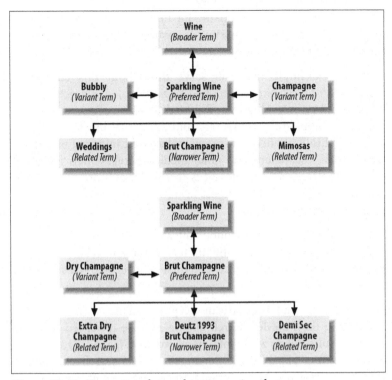

Figure 10-12. Semantic relationships in a wine thesaurus

Depending upon your experience with the classification of wines, you may already be questioning the selection of preferred terms and semantic relationships in this example. Should "sparkling wine" really be the preferred term? If so, why? Because it's a more popular term? Because it's the technically correct term? And aren't there better related terms than "weddings" and "mimosas"? Why were those chosen? The truth is that there aren't any "right" answers to these questions, and there's no "right" way to design a thesaurus. There will always be a strong element of professional judgment informed by research. We'll come back to these questions and provide some guidelines for constructing "good" answers, but first let's check out a real thesaurus on the Web.

A Thesaurus in Action

It's often not obvious when a site is using a thesaurus. When it's well integrated, a thesaurus can be invisible to the untrained eye. You have to know what you're looking for to notice one. Think back to the Tilenol/Tylenol example. How many users even realize when the site adjusts for their misspelling?

One good example that will serve throughout this chapter is PubMed (*http://www.ncbi.nlm.nih.gov/pubmed*), a service of the National Library of Medicine. PubMed provides access to over 16 million citations from MEDLINE and additional life science journals. MEDLINE has been the premier electronic information service for doctors, researchers, and other medical professionals for many years. It leverages a huge thesaurus that includes more than 19,000 preferred terms or "main subject headings" and provides powerful searching capabilities.

PubMed provides a simpler public interface with free access to citations, but without access to the full text of the journal articles. Let's first take a look at the interface, and then dive beneath the surface to see what's going on.

Let's say we're studying African sleeping sickness. We enter that phrase into the PubMed search engine and are rewarded with the first 20 results out of 5,758 total items found (Figure 10-13). So far, there's nothing apparently different about this search experience. For all we know, we might have just searched the full text of all 24 million journal articles. To understand what's going on, we need to look deeper.

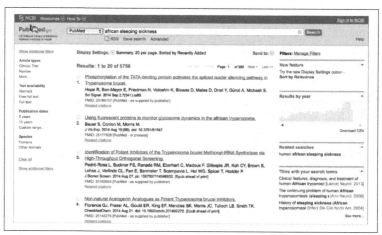

Figure 10-13. Search results on PubMed

In fact, we didn't search the full-text articles at all. Instead, we searched the metadata records for these articles, which include a combination of abstracts and subject headings (Figure 10-14).

Figure 10-14. Sample record with abstract in PubMed

When we select another item from our search results, we find a record with subject headings ("MeSH Terms") but no abstract (Figure 10-15).

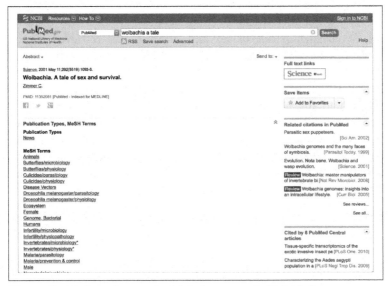

Figure 10-15. Sample record with index terms in PubMed

When we scroll down to look through the full list of terms, we see no entry for African sleeping sickness. What's going on? Why was this article retrieved? To answer that question, we need to switch gears and take a look at the MeSH Browser, an interface for navigating the structure and vocabulary of MeSH (Figure 10-16).

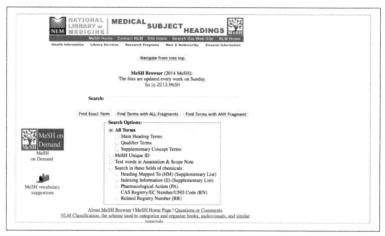

Figure 10-16. The MeSH Browser

The MeSH Browser enables us to navigate by browsing the hierarchical classification schemes within the thesaurus or by searching. If we try a search on "African sleeping sickness," we'll see why the article "Wolbachia. A tale of sex and survival" was retrieved in our search. "African sleeping sickness" is actually an entry term for the preferred term or MeSH heading, "Trypanosomiasis, African" (see Figure 10-17). When we searched PubMed, our variant term was mapped to the preferred term behind the scenes. Unfortunately, PubMed doesn't go further in leveraging the underlying MeSH thesaurus. It would be nice, for example, to turn all of those MeSH terms in our sample record into live links and provide enhanced searching and browsing capabilities, similar to those provided by Amazon, as shown in Figure 10-18.

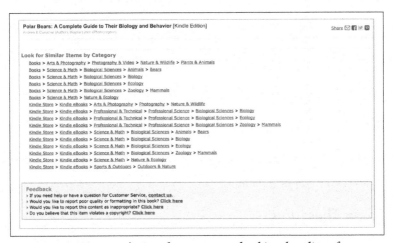

National Library of Medicine - Medical Subject Headings

2014 MeSH

MeSH Descriptor Data

Return to Entry Page

Standard View. Go to Concept View; Go to Expanded Concept View

MeSH Heading	Trypanosomiasis, African
Tree Number	C03.752.300.900.719
Annotation	for trypanosomiasis in tropical Africa caused by any species of Trypanosoma; coordinate with NEGLECTED DISEASES if pertinent; coordinate IM with TRYPANOSOMA BRUCEI GAMBIENSE (IM) for Gambian trypanosomiasis; entry term NAGANA; coordinate TRYPANOSOMIASIS, AFRICAN / vet (IM) with specific Trypanosoma species (IM) + animal disease term (IM) + specific animal (IM or NIM) + check tag ANIMALS; specify geographic term pertinent
Scope Note	A disease endemic among people and animals in Central Africa. It is caused by various species of trypanosomes, particularly T. gambiense and T. rhodesiense. Its second host is the TSETSE FLY. Involvement of the central nervous system produces "African sleeping sickness." Nagana is a rapidly fatal trypanosomiasis of horses and other animals.
Entry Term	African Sleeping Sickness
Entry Term	African Trypanosomiasis
Entry Term	Nagana
Allowable Qualifiers	BL CF CI CL CN CO DH DI DT EC EH EM EN EP ET GE HI IM ME MI MO NU PA PC PP PS PX RA RH RI RT SU TH TM UR US VE VI
Online Note	use TRYPANOSOMIASIS, AFRICAN to search NAGANA 1975-94; use TRYPANOSOMIASIS, AFRICAN/VE 1972-74; use TRYPANOSOMIASIS, BOVINE 1968-72
History Note	NAGANA was heading 1991-94; was see under TRYPANOSOMIASIS, AFRICAN 1973-90; was see under TRYPANOSOMIASIS, BOVINE 1968-mid 72
Date of Entry	19990101
Unique ID	D014353

MeSH Tree Structures

Parasitic Diseases [C03]
  Protozoan Infections [C03.752]
    Euglenozoa Infections [C03.752.300]
      Trypanosomiasis [C03.752.300.900]
        Chagas Disease [C03.752.300.900.200] +
        Dourine [C03.752.300.900.226]
      ▶ Trypanosomiasis, African [C03.752.300.900.719]
        Trypanosomiasis, Bovine [C03.752.300.900.802]

Return to Entry Page   Link to NLM Cataloging Classification

Figure 10-17. MeSH record for trypanosomiasis (top and bottom of page)

Polar Bears: A Complete Guide to Their Biology and Behavior [Kindle Edition]
Andrew E Derocher (Author), Wayne Lynch (Photographer)   Share ✉ 🔗 🐦

Look for Similar Items by Category
Books > Arts & Photography > Photography & Video > Nature & Wildlife > Plants & Animals
Books > Science & Math > Biological Sciences > Animals > Bears
Books > Science & Math > Biological Sciences > Biology
Books > Science & Math > Biological Sciences > Ecology
Books > Science & Math > Biological Sciences > Zoology > Mammals
Books > Science & Math > Nature & Ecology
Kindle Store > Kindle eBooks > Arts & Photography > Photography > Nature & Wildlife
Kindle Store > Kindle eBooks > Professional & Technical > Professional Science > Biological Sciences > Biology
Kindle Store > Kindle eBooks > Professional & Technical > Professional Science > Biological Sciences > Ecology
Kindle Store > Kindle eBooks > Professional & Technical > Professional Science > Biological Sciences > Zoology > Mammals
Kindle Store > Kindle eBooks > Science & Math > Biological Sciences > Animals > Bears
Kindle Store > Kindle eBooks > Science & Math > Biological Sciences > Biology
Kindle Store > Kindle eBooks > Science & Math > Biological Sciences > Ecology
Kindle Store > Kindle eBooks > Science & Math > Biological Sciences > Zoology > Mammals
Kindle Store > Kindle eBooks > Science & Math > Nature & Ecology
Kindle Store > Kindle eBooks > Sports & Outdoors > Outdoors & Nature

Feedback
▸ If you need help or have a question for Customer Service, contact us.
▸ Would you like to report poor quality or formatting in this book? Click here
▸ Would you like to report this content as inappropriate? Click here
▸ Do you believe that this item violates a copyright? Click here

Figure 10-18. Amazon's use of structure and subject headings for enhanced navigation

In this example, Amazon leverages the hierarchical classification scheme and subject headings to provide powerful options for browsing, allowing users to iteratively refine their queries. This surely could be a useful enhancement to PubMed.

One of the advantages to using a thesaurus is that you have tremendous power and flexibility to shape and refine the user interface over time. You can't take advantage of all the capabilities at once, but you can user-test different features, learning and adjusting as you go. PubMed may not have leveraged the full power of the MEDLINE thesaurus so far, but it's nice to have that rich network of semantic relationships to draw upon as design and development continues.

Types of Thesauri

Should you decide to build a thesaurus for your system, you'll need to choose from among three types: a classic thesaurus, an indexing thesaurus, and a searching thesaurus (Figure 10-19). This decision should be based on how you intend to use the thesaurus, and it will have major implications for design.

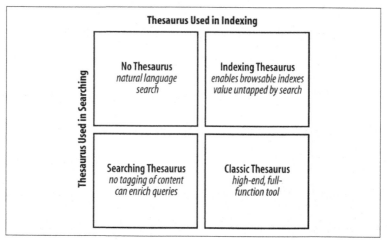

Figure 10-19. Types of thesauri

Classic Thesaurus

A classic thesaurus is used at the point of indexing and at the point of searching. Indexers use the thesaurus to map variant terms to preferred terms when performing document-level indexing. Searchers use the thesaurus for retrieval, whether or not they're aware of the role it plays in their search experience. Query terms are matched against the rich vocabulary of the thesaurus, enabling synonym management, hierarchical browsing, and associative linking. This is the full-bodied, fully integrated thesaurus we've referred to for much of this chapter.

Indexing Thesaurus

However, building a classic thesaurus is not always necessary or possible. Consider a scenario in which you have the ability to develop a controlled vocabulary and index documents, but you're not able to build the synonym-management capability into the search experience. Perhaps another department owns the search engine and won't work with you, or perhaps the engine won't support this functionality without major customization.

Whatever the case, you're able to perform controlled vocabulary indexing, but you're not able to leverage that work at the point of searching and map users' variant terms to preferred terms. This is a serious weakness, but there are a few reasons why an indexing thesaurus may be better than nothing:

- It structures the indexing process, promoting consistency and efficiency. The indexers can work as an integrated unit, given a shared understanding of preferred terms and indexing guidelines.
- It allows you to build browsable indexes of preferred terms, enabling users to find all documents about a particular subject or product through a single point of access.

Such consistency of indexing can provide real value for information systems with captive audiences. When dealing with an intranet application that's used by the same people on a regular basis, you can expect these users to learn the preferred terms over time. In such an environment, indexing consistency begins to rival indexing quality in value.

And finally, an indexing thesaurus positions you nicely to take the next step up to a classic thesaurus. With a vocabulary developed and applied to your collection of documents, you can focus your energies on integration at the user interface level. This may begin with the addition of an entry vocabulary to your browsable indexes and will hopefully bring searching into the fold, so the full value of the thesaurus is used to power the searching and browsing experience.

Searching Thesaurus

Sometimes a classic thesaurus isn't practical because of issues on the content side of the equation that prevent document-level indexing. Perhaps you're dealing with third-party content or dynamic news that's changing every day. Perhaps you're simply faced with so much content that manual indexing costs would be astronomical. (In this case, you may be able to go with a classic thesaurus approach that leverages automated categorization software.) Whatever the case, there are many web and intranet environments in which controlled vocabulary indexing of the full document collection just isn't going to happen. This doesn't mean that a thesaurus isn't still a viable option to improve the user experience.

A searching thesaurus leverages a controlled vocabulary at the point of searching but not at the point of indexing. For example, when a user enters a term into the search engine, a searching thesaurus can map that term onto the controlled vocabulary before executing the query against the full-text index. The thesaurus may simply perform equivalence term explosion, as we've seen in the case of synonym rings, or it may go beyond the equivalence relationship, exploding down the hierarchy to include all narrower terms (traditionally known as "posting down"). These methods will obviously enhance recall at the expense of precision.

You also have the option of giving more power and control to the users—asking them whether they'd like to use any combination of preferred, variant, broader, narrower, or associative terms in their queries. When integrated carefully into the search interface and search result screens, this can effectively arm users with the ability to narrow, broaden, and adjust their searches as needed.

A searching thesaurus can also provide greater browsing flexibility. You can allow your users to browse part or all of your thesaurus, navigating the equivalence, hierarchical, and associative relationships. Terms (or the combination of preferred and variant terms) can be used as predefined or "canned" queries to be run against the full-text index. In other words, your thesaurus can become a true portal, providing a new way to navigate and gain access to a potentially enormous volume of content. A major advantage of the searching thesaurus is that its development and maintenance costs are essentially independent of the volume of content. On the other hand, it does put much greater demands on the quality of equivalence and mapping.

If you'd like to learn more about searching thesauri, try these articles:

- James D. Anderson and Frederick A. Rowley, "Building End User Thesauri from Full Text," *Proc. 2nd ASIS SIG/CR Classification Research Workshop*, 1991, 1–10.
- Marcia J. Bates, "Design for a Subject Search Interface and Online Thesaurus for a Very Large Records Management Database," *Proc. 53rd ASIS Annual Meeting 27*, 1990, 20–28.

Thesaurus Standards

As we explained earlier, people have been developing thesauri for many years. In their 1993 article "The Evolution of Guidelines for Thesaurus Construction,"[5] David A. Krooks and F.W. Lancaster suggested that "the majority of basic problems of thesaurus construction had already been identified and solved by 1967."

This rich history lets us draw from a number of national and international standards, covering the construction of monolingual (single-language) thesauri. For example:

- ISO 2788 (1974, 1985, 1986, International)
- BS 5723 (1987, British)
- AFNOR NFZ 47–100 (1981, French)
- DIN 1463 (1987—1993, German)
- ANSI/NISO Z39.19 (1994, 1998, 2005, 2010, American)

In this book, we draw primarily from the original US standard, ANSI/NISO Z39.19-2005, which is very similar to the International standard, ISO 2788. The ANSI/NISO standard is entitled "Guidelines for the Construction, Format and Management of Monolingual Thesauri." The term "guidelines" in the title is very telling. Consider

---

5 *Libri* 43:4, 2009, 326–342

what software vendor Oracle (*http://bit.ly/intermedia_text*) has to say about its interpretation of this standard:

> The phrase...thesaurus standard is somewhat misleading. The computing industry considers a "standard" to be a specification of behavior or interface. These standards do not specify anything. If you are looking for a thesaurus function interface, or a standard thesaurus file format, you won't find it here. Instead, these are guidelines for thesaurus compilers—compiler being an actual human, not a program.
>
> What Oracle has done is taken the ideas in these guidelines and in ANSI Z39.19...and used them as the basis for a specification of our own creation...So, Oracle supports ISO-2788 relationships or ISO-2788 compliant thesauri.

As you'll see when we explore a few examples, the ANSI/NISO standard presents simple guidelines that are very difficult to apply. The standard provides a valuable conceptual framework and in some cases offers specific rules you can follow, but it absolutely does not remove the need for critical thinking, creativity, and risk taking in the process of thesaurus construction.

We strongly disagree with the suggestion by Krooks and Lancaster that the basic problems in this area have been solved, and we often disagree with guidelines in the ANSI/NISO standard. What's going on here? Are we just being difficult? No; what's really behind these tensions is the disruptive force of the Internet. We're in the midst of a transition from the thesaurus in its traditional form to a new paradigm embedded within networked information environments.

Traditional thesauri emerged within the academic and library communities. They were used in print form and were designed primarily for expert users. When we took library science courses back in the '80s and '90s, a major component of online information retrieval involved learning to navigate the immense volumes of printed thesauri in the library to identify subject descriptors for online searching of the Dialog information service. People had to be trained to use these tools, and the underlying assumption was that specialists would use them on a regular basis, becoming efficient and effective over time. The whole system was built around the relatively high cost of processor time and network bandwidth.

Then the world changed. We're now dealing with totally online systems. We can't ask our customers to run to the library before using our website. We're typically serving novice users with no formal training in online searching techniques. They're likely to be infrequent visitors, so they're not going to build up much familiarity with our site over time. And we're operating in the broader business environment, where the goals may be very different from those of academia and libraries.

Within this new paradigm, we're being challenged to figure out which of the old guidelines do and do not apply. It would be an awful waste to throw out valuable resources like the ANSI/NISO standard that are built upon decades of research and experience. There's a great deal there that's still relevant. However, it would also be a mistake to follow the guidelines blindly, akin to using a 1950s map to navigate today's highways.

Advantages to staying close to the standard include:

- There's good thinking and intelligence baked into these guidelines.
- Most thesaurus management software is designed to be compliant with ANSI/NISO, so sticking with the standard can be useful from a technology integration perspective.
- Compliance with the standard will provide a better chance of cross-database compatibility, so when your company merges with its competitor, you might have an easier time merging the two sets of vocabularies.

Our advice is to read the guidelines, follow them when they make sense, but be prepared to deviate from the standard when necessary. After all, it's these opportunities to break the rules that make our lives as information architects fun and exciting!

Semantic Relationships

What sets a thesaurus apart from the simpler controlled vocabularies is its rich array of semantic relationships. Let's explore each relationship more closely.

Equivalence

The equivalence relationship (Figure 10-20) is employed to connect preferred terms and their variants. While we may loosely refer to this as "synonym management," it's important to recognize that equivalence is a broader term than synonymy.

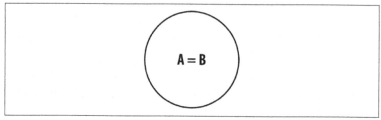

Figure 10-20. The equivalence relationship

Our goal is to group terms defined as "equivalent for the purposes of retrieval." This may include synonyms, near-synonyms, acronyms, abbreviations, lexical variants, and common misspellings. For example:

Preferred term
   Apple Watch Sport

Variant terms (equivalents)
   Apple Watch, iWatch, Smart watch, Smartwatch, Wearable computer, Galaxy Gear, Moto 360

In the case of a product database, it may also include the names of retired products and of competitors' products. Depending on the desired specificity of your controlled vocabulary, you may also fold more general and more specific terms into the equivalence relationship to avoid extra levels of hierarchy. The goal is to create a rich entry vocabulary that serves as a funnel, connecting users with the products, services, and content that they're looking for and that you want them to find.

Hierarchical

The hierarchical relationship (Figure 10-21) divides up the information space into categories and subcategories, relating broader and narrower concepts through the familiar parent–child relationship.

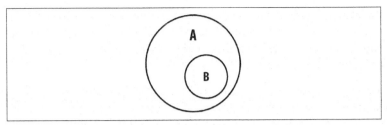

Figure 10-21. The hierarchical relationship

There are three subtypes of hierarchical relationship:

Generic
> This is the traditional class–species relationship we draw from biological taxonomies. Species B is a member of Class A and inherits the characteristics of its parent. For example, Bird *NT* Magpie.

Whole-part
> In this hierarchical relationship, B is a part of A. For example, Foot *NT* Big Toe.

Instance
> In this case, B is an instance or example of A. This relationship often includes proper names. For example, Seas *NT* Mediterranean Sea.

At first blush, the hierarchical relationship sounds pretty straightforward. However, anyone who's ever developed a hierarchy knows that it isn't as easy as it sounds. There are many different ways to hierarchically organize any given information space (e.g., by subject, by product category, or by geography). As we'll explain shortly, a *faceted* thesaurus supports the common need for multiple hierarchies. You also need to deal with the tricky issues of granularity, defining how many layers of hierarchy to develop.

Once again, we need to ground our work in the ultimate goal of enhancing the ability of our users to find what they need. The card-sorting methodologies (discussed in Chapter 11) can help you begin to shape your hierarchies based on user needs and behaviors.

Associative

The associative relationship (Figure 10-22) is often the trickiest, and by necessity is usually developed after you've made a good start on the other two relationship types. In thesaurus construction, associative relationships are often defined as strongly implied semantic connections that aren't captured within the equivalence or hierarchical relationships.

There is the notion that associative relationships should be "strongly implied." For example, Hammer *RT* Nail. In practice, however, defining these relationships is a highly subjective process.

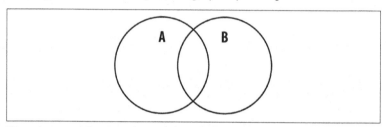

Figure 10-22. The associative relationship

The ANSI/NISO thesaurus discusses many associative relationship subtypes. Table 10-1 shows some examples.

Table 10-1. Examples of relationship subtypes

Relationship subtype	Example
Field of Study and Object of Study	Cardiology *RT* Heart
Process and its Agent	Termite Control *RT* Pesticides
Concepts and their Properties	Poisons *RT* Toxicity
Action and Product of Action	Eating *RT* Indigestion
Concepts Linked by Causal Dependence	Celebration *RT* New Year's Eve

In online commerce, the associative relationship provides an excellent vehicle for connecting customers to related products and services. Associative relationships allow what marketing folks call "cross-selling," allowing an ecommerce site, for example, to say "Hey, nice trousers! They'd go great with this shirt." When done well, these associative relationships can both enhance the user experience and further the goals of the business.

Preferred Terms

Terminology is critical. The following sections examine some aspects of terminology in detail.

Term Form

Defining the form of preferred terms is something that seems easy until you try it. All of a sudden, you find yourself plunged into heated arguments over grammatical minutiae. Should we use a noun or a verb? What's the "correct" spelling? Do we use the singular or plural form? Can an abbreviation be a preferred term? These debates can suck up large amounts of time and energy.

Fortunately, the ANSI/NISO thesaurus standard goes into great detail in this area. We recommend following these guidelines, while allowing for exceptions when there's a clear benefit. Some of the issues covered by the standard are shown in Table 10-2.

Table 10-2. Issues covered in the ANSI/NISO thesaurus standard

Topic	Our interpretation and advice
Grammatical form	The standard strongly encourages the use of nouns for preferred terms. This is a good default guideline, because users are better at understanding and remembering nouns than verbs or adjectives. However, in the real world, you'll encounter lots of good reasons to use verbs (i.e., task-oriented words) and adjectives (e.g., price, size, variety, color) in your controlled vocabularies.
Spelling	The standard notes that you can select a "defined authority," such as a specific dictionary or glossary, or you can choose to use your own "house style." You might also consider the most common spelling forms employed by your users. The most important thing here is that you make a decision and stick to it. Consistency will improve the lives of your indexers and users.
Singular and plural form	The standard recommends using the plural form of "count nouns" (e.g., cars, roads, maps). Conceptual nouns (e.g., math, biology) should remain in singular form. Search technology has rendered this less important than in the past. Once again, consistency is the goal in this case.
Abbreviations and acronyms	The guidelines suggest to default to popular use. For the most part, your preferred terms will be the full words. But in cases such as RADAR, IRS, 401K, MI, and TV, it may be better to use the acronym or abbreviation. You can always rely on your variant terms to guide users from one form to the other (e.g., Internal Revenue Service *See* IRS).

Term Selection

Of course, selection of a preferred term involves more than the form of the term; you've got to pick the right term in the first place. The ANSI/NISO standard won't help too much here. Consider the following excerpts:

- Section 3.0: "Literary warrant (occurrence of terms in documents) is the guiding principle for selection of the preferred (term)."
- Section 5.2.2: "Preferred terms should be selected to serve the needs of the majority of users."

This tension between literary warrant and user warrant can be resolved only by reviewing your goals and considering how the thesaurus will be integrated with the website. Do you want to use preferred terms to educate your users about the industry vocabulary? Will you be relying on preferred terms as your entry vocabulary (e.g., no variants in the index)? You'll need to answer these questions before deciding on the primary source of authority for term selection.

Term Definition

Within the thesaurus itself, we're striving for extreme specificity in our use of language. Remember, we're trying to control vocabulary. Beyond the selection of distinctive preferred terms, there are some tools for managing ambiguity.

Parenthetical term qualifiers provide a way to manage homographs. Depending on the context of your thesaurus, you may need to qualify the term "Cells" in some of the following ways:

- Cells (biology)
- Cells (electric)
- Cells (prison)

Scope notes provide another way to increase specificity. While they can sometimes look very much like definitions, scope notes are a different beast. They are intended to deliberately restrict meaning to one concept, whereas definitions often suggest multiple meanings. Scope notes are very useful in helping indexers to select the right preferred term. They can sometimes be leveraged in searching or results display to assist users as well.

Term Specificity

The specificity of terms is another difficult issue that all thesaurus designers must face. For example, should "knowledge management software" be represented as one term, two terms, or three terms? Here's what the standards have to say:

- ANSI/NISO Z39.19: "Each descriptor... should represent a single concept."
- ISO 2788: "It is a general rule that... compound terms should be factored (split) into simple elements."

Once again, the standards don't make your life easy. ANSI/NISO leaves you arguing over what constitutes a "single concept." ISO leads you toward uniterms (e.g., knowledge, management, software), which would probably be the wrong way to go in this example.

You need to strike a balance based on your context. Of particular importance is the size of the system. As the volume of content grows, it becomes increasingly necessary to use compound terms to increase precision. Otherwise, users get hundreds or thousands of hits for every search (and every preferred term).

The scope of content is also important. For example, if we're working on a website for *Knowledge Management* magazine, the single term "knowledge management software" or perhaps "software (knowledge management)" may be the way to go. However, if we're working on a broad IT site like CNET, it may be better to use "knowledge management" and "software" as independent preferred terms.

Polyhierarchy

In a strict hierarchy, each term appears in one and only one place. This was the original plan for the biological taxonomy. Each species was supposed to fit neatly into one branch of the tree of life:

```
kingdom:
        phylum:
                sub-phylum:
                        class:
                                order:
                                        family:
                                                species
```

However, things didn't go according to plan. In fact, biologists have been arguing for decades over the correct placement of various species. Some organisms have the audacity to exhibit characteristics of multiple categories.

If you're a purist, you can attempt to defend the ideal of strict hierarchy within your website. Or, if you're pragmatic, you can allow for some level of polyhierarchy, permitting some terms to be cross-listed in multiple categories. This is shown in Figure 10-23.

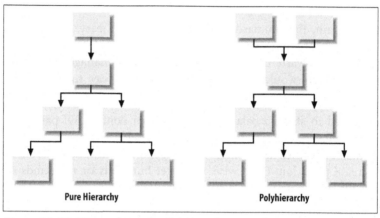

Figure 10-23. Hierarchy and polyhierarchy

When you're dealing with large information systems, polyhierarchy is unavoidable. As the number of documents grows, you need a greater level of precoordination (using compound terms) to increase precision, which forces polyhierarchy. For example, MEDLINE cross-lists viral pneumonia under both virus diseases and respiratory tract diseases (Figure 10-24).

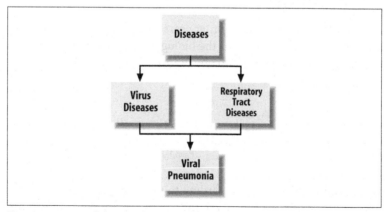

Figure 10-24. Polyhierarchy in MEDLINE

Wikipedia is another large information environment that makes extensive use of polyhierarchy. At the footer of most articles in the Wikipedia website is a box with links to the higher levels in the hierarchy that list that particular article (Figure 10-25).

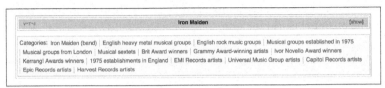

Figure 10-25. Polyhierarchy in Wikipedia

In the classification and placement of physical objects, polyhierarchy causes a problem. Physical objects can typically be in only one place at one time. The Library of Congress classification scheme was developed so that each book in a library could be placed (and found) in one and only one location on the shelves. In digital information systems, the only real challenge introduced by polyhierarchy is representing the navigational context. Most systems allow for the notion of primary and secondary locations within the hierarchy.

Faceted Classification

In the 1930s, an Indian librarian by the name of S.R. Ranganathan created a new type of classification system. Recognizing the problems and limitations of these top-down hierarchical solutions, Ranganathan built his system upon the notion that documents and objects have multiple dimensions, or *facets*.

The old model asks the question, "Where do I put this?" It's more closely tied to our experience in the physical world, with the idea of one place for each item. In contrast, the faceted approach asks the question, "How can I describe this?"

Like many librarians, Ranganathan was an idealist. He argued that you must build multiple "pure" taxonomies, using one principle of division at a time. He suggested five universal facets to be used for organizing everything:

- Personality
- Matter
- Energy

- Space
- Time

In our experience, the faceted approach has great value, but we don't tend to use Ranganathan's universal facets. Instead, common facets in the business world include:

- Topic
- Product
- Document type
- Audience
- Geography
- Price

Still confused about facets? See Figure 10-26. Here we're applying the structure of a fielded database to the more heterogeneous mix of documents and applications in a website. Rather than the one-taxonomy-fits-all approach, we're embracing the concept of multiple taxonomies that focus on different dimensions of the content.

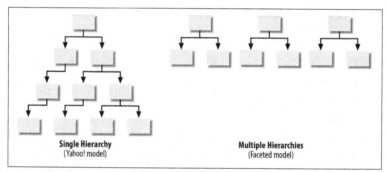

Figure 10-26. Single hierarchy versus multiple (faceted) hierarchies

Wine.com provides a simple example of faceted classification. Wine has several facets that we commonly mix and match in our selection process at restaurants and grocery stores, as shown in Table 10-3.

Table 10-3. Facets of wine

Facet	Sample controlled vocabulary values
Type	Red (Merlot, Pinot Noir), White (Chablis, Chardonnay), Sparkling, Pink, Dessert
Region (origin)	Australian, Californian, French, Italian
Winery (manufacturer)	Blackstone, Clos du Bois, Cakebread
Year	1969, 1990, 1999, 2000
Price	$3.99, $20.99, < $199, Cheap, Moderate, Expensive

Note that some facets are flat lists (e.g., price) whereas some must be represented hierarchically (e.g., type). When we look for a moderately priced Californian Merlot, we're unconsciously defining and combining facets. Wine.com leverages a faceted classification to enable this experience online. The mega-menu shown in Figure 10-27 presents various ways to browse, providing multiple paths to the same information.

Figure 10-27. Faceted classification at Wine.com

The Advanced Wine Search, shown in Figure 10-28, provides the ability to combine facets into the rich type of query we usually express in natural language.

Figure 10-28. Advanced Wine Search at Wine.com

The results page (Figure 10-29) has our list of moderately priced Californian Merlot wines. Note that not only are we able to leverage facets in the search, but we can also use the facets to sort results. Wine.com has added ratings from several magazines (RP = Robert Parker's *The Wine Advocate*, WS = *Wine Spectator*) as yet another facet.

Figure 10-29. Flexible search and results display

The designers of Wine.com have made decisions throughout the site about how and when to leverage facets within the interface. For example, you can't browse by ratings from individual magazines from the main page. Hopefully, these are informed decisions made by balancing an understanding of user needs (how people want to browse and search), business needs (how Wine.com can maximize sales of high-margin items), and the creation of meaningful contexts we described in Chapter 4.

The nice thing about a faceted classification approach is that it provides great power and flexibility. With the underlying descriptive metadata and structure in place, you can experiment with hundreds of ways to present navigation options. The interface can be tested and refined over time, while the faceted classification provides an enduring foundation.

Guided navigation was quickly embraced in the online retail arena, where there's a clear link between findability and profitability. In recent years, this hybrid search/browse model has been widely adopted across industry and in government, healthcare, publishing, and education. As Figure 10-30 shows, guided navigation is even being used to improve library catalogs. Ranganathan would be proud.

Figure 10-30. Guided navigation at the Ann Arbor Public Library website

In addition to the increasing mainstream implementation of controlled vocabularies, we're also enjoying a growing wealth of resources to support these efforts. Here are just a few:

- ANSI/NISO Z39.19-2005, "Guidelines for the Construction, Format, and Management of Monolingual Controlled Vocabularies" (*http://bit.ly/monolingual_thesauri*); completely rewritten (and renamed) in 2005
- "Controlled Vocabularies: A Glosso-Thesaurus" (*http://bit.ly/glosso-thesaurus*), by Fred Leise, Karl Fast, and Mike Steckel
- Dublin Core Metadata Initiative (*http://dublincore.org*)
- Flamenco Search Interface Project (*http://flamenco.berkeley.edu*)
- Glossary of terms relating to thesauri (*http://www.willpowerinfo.co.uk/glossary.htm*)
- Taxonomy Warehouse (*http://www.taxonomywarehouse.com/*)
- Online Thesauri and Authority Files (*http://bit.ly/online_thesauri*)

Metadata, controlled vocabularies, and thesauri are increasingly becoming the building blocks of most major websites and intranets. Single-taxonomy solutions are giving way to more flexible, faceted approaches. Put simply, if you're designing an information architecture, we see facets in your future![6]

Recap

Let's recap what we learned in this chapter:

- Thesauri, controlled vocabularies, and metadata operate on the backend of an information environment to enable a more seamless and satisfying experience on the frontend.
- Metadata tags are used to describe documents, pages, images, software, video and audio files, and other content objects for the purposes of improved navigation and retrieval.

---

6 For more about Wine.com, and faceted classification, see see Peter's 2001 article "The Speed of Information Architecture" (*http://bit.ly/speed_of_ia*).

- Controlled vocabularies are subsets of natural language; they include synonym rings, authority files, classification schemes, and thesauri.

- These systems allow you to structure and map language so that people can more easily find information.

- Faceted classification and polyhierarchy allow you to make information available in more than one way, allowing people to find their own routes to the stuff they're looking for.

With this look at thesauri, controlled vocabularies, and metadata, we conclude the "basic principles" part of the book. Now that you know the basic components that constitute an IA, we can see how these systems come together to produce effective and engaging information environments.

PART III

Getting Information Architecture Done

So far, we've focused on concepts and components. Now we're going to shift gears and explore the process and methods for creating information architectures.

If it were just a matter of whipping up a few standard sitemaps, our jobs would be easy. But as we've explained, information architecture doesn't happen in a vacuum. The design of complex information environments requires interdisciplinary teams that include interaction designers, software developers, content strategists, usability engineers, and other experts.

Effective collaboration requires agreement on a structured development process. Even for smaller projects, when teams are tiny and individuals fill multiple roles, tackling the right challenges at the right time is critical to success. The following chapters provide an overview of the process and the challenges you'll encounter along the way. Our focus on the early stages of research, strategy, and design, rather than the later stages of implementation and administration, belies our consulting background. While the vast majority of our experiences have involved strategy and design for fast-paced information architecture projects, we are true believers in the importance of nailing the details in implementation and building sustainable architectures. The dedicated in-house staff who protect and perfect information architectures over the long haul are the unsung heroes of the field.

CHAPTER 11

Research

Research is formalized curiosity. It is poking and prying with a purpose.
—Zora Neale Hurston

In this chapter, we'll cover:

- Integrating IA into the development process
- How and why to study people, context, and content
- Research methods including stakeholder interviews, heuristic evaluations, user testing, and card sorting

In the early days of website design, many companies employed a one-step process called "Code HTML." Everyone wanted to jump right in and build the site. People had no patience for research or strategy. We remember one eager client asking us in the middle of a planning session, "So when are we going to start the real work?" Fortunately, after several years of painful lessons, there's a growing realization that designing information environments is hard work and requires a phased approach, such as the one shown in Figure 11-1.

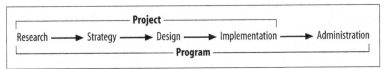

Figure 11-1. The process of information architecture development

Now, you may be thinking, "This looks an awful lot like a waterfall process—and we're agile!" In the case of information architecture, we believe this to be a false dilemma. Agile processes work best when the team knows the goal they're reaching for. ("Are we building a cathedral, or a garage?") Following the process outlined here helps the team understand the big picture that they are building toward. As with other aspects of the design, the information architecture needs to be refined and iterated on as the product gets built, and changes will inevitably happen as the product meets real-world conditions. (We are reminded of President Eisenhower's line: "In preparing for battle I have always found that plans are useless, but planning is indispensable.")

With that said, let's examine each phase of the process. The *research* phase begins with a review of existing background materials and meetings with the strategy team, aimed at gaining a high-level understanding of the goals and business context, the existing information architecture, the content, and the intended audiences. It then quickly moves into a series of studies, employing a variety of methods to explore the information ecology.

This research provides a contextual understanding that forms the foundation for development of an information architecture *strategy*. From a top-down perspective, this strategy defines the highest two or three levels of the information environment's organization and navigation structures. From a bottom-up perspective, it suggests candidate document types and a rough metadata schema. This strategy provides a high-level framework for the information architecture, establishing a direction and scope that will guide the project through implementation.

Design is where you shape a high-level strategy into an information architecture, creating detailed sitemaps, wireframes, and metadata schema that will be used by graphic designers, programmers, content authors, and the production team. The *design* phase is obviously where most of the work of information architecture is done. That said, quantity cannot drive out quality. Poor design execution can ruin the best strategy. For us, the meat is in the middle and the devil is in the details.

Implementation is where your designs are put to the test as the system is built, tested, and launched. This phase involves organizing and tagging documents, testing and troubleshooting, and developing documentation and training programs to ensure that the information architecture can be maintained effectively over time.

And last but not least is *administration*, the continuous evaluation and improvement of the system's information architecture. Administration includes the daily tasks of tagging new documents and weeding out old ones. It also requires monitoring usage and user feedback, identifying opportunities to improve through major or minor adjustments. Effective administration can make a good information environment great.

Admittedly, this is a simplified view of the process. Clear lines rarely exist between phases, and few projects begin with a clean slate. Budgets, schedules, and politics will inevitably force you off the path and into the woods. We don't aim to provide a paint-by-numbers design guide. The real world is far too messy. Instead, we present a framework and some tools and methods that may be useful when applied selectively within your environment.

Before we begin, we'll offer a word of encouragement. Much of this work looks tedious and boring when taken out of context. Not all of us can get jazzed up about poring over search logs and analyzing content. But when you do this work in the real world, it can be surprisingly engaging. And when that magic light bulb turns on, revealing a pattern that suggests a solution, you'll be glad you took the time to do it right.

A Research Framework

Good research means asking the right questions. And choosing the right questions requires a conceptual framework of the broader environment. Our faithful three-circle diagram (Figure 11-2), which we introduced in Chapter 2, has been invaluable in helping us shape a balanced approach to research. It helps us to decide where to shine the flashlight, and to understand what we see. Consequently, we have used this model to organize our exploration of the research process.

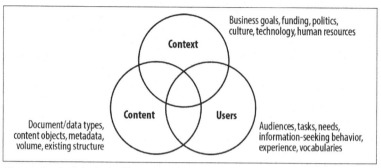

Figure 11-2. A balanced approach to research

We begin with an overview of tools and methods for research (see Figure 11-3). Obviously, it won't make sense or be possible to use every tool on every project. And, of course, you should absolutely seek out and try methods we haven't covered. Our goal is to provide you with a map and a compass. The journey is left to you.

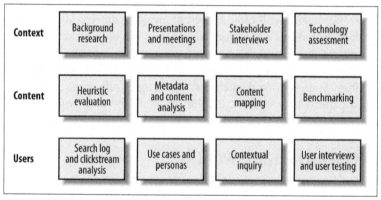

Figure 11-3. Tools and methods for research

Context

For practical purposes, an investigation of the business context can be a good place to start. It's critical to begin projects with a clear understanding of the goals and an appreciation of the political environment. Ignoring business realities is just as dangerous as ignoring users. A perfectly usable website or app that fails to support business goals won't last long. The term "user-centered design" is valuable insofar as it moves the pendulum away from executive-centered design, but don't let that pendulum swing too far.

Of course, context isn't just about politics. We also need to understand goals, budgets, schedules, technology infrastructure, human resources, and corporate culture. Legal issues can also be important, particularly in heavily regulated industries. All of these factors can and should influence the shape of the information architecture strategy.

Getting Buy-In

Research is not a one-way street. While conducting your investigation, it's important to recognize the value of building awareness and support for your project. After all, you're not a scientist studying rats. Your human subjects will have their own set of questions and concerns. For example:

- Who are you and why are you asking me these questions?
- What's information architecture and why should I care?
- What's your methodology and how does it relate to my work?

The way you answer these questions will influence the level of support you receive throughout the project. Because most large information environments depend upon interdepartmental collaboration and decentralized content ownership, it's impossible to succeed without broad buy-in. For this reason, you'll want to weave elements of presentation and persuasion throughout the research process.

Background Research

When a project begins, you should have all sorts of questions:

- What are the short- and long-term goals?
- What's the business plan? What are the politics?
- What's the schedule and budget?
- Who are the intended audiences?
- Why will people come? Why will they come back?
- What types of tasks should users be able to perform?
- How will content be created and managed, and by whom?
- What's the technical infrastructure?
- What worked in the past? What didn't?

But just asking the right questions is not enough. You need to ask them of the right people in the right way at the right time. You must be very focused in how you use people's time and realistic about who can answer which questions.

Consequently, it's good to begin with a review of background materials. Sometimes the best way to learn about the future is to dig into the past. Get your hands on any documents that relate to the site's mission, vision, goals, intended audiences, and content. Also, try to find documents that provide a broader picture of the management structure and culture. For example, organization charts are really valuable if you're an outside consultant, particularly when working on intranets; they capture an important component of the internal users' mental model of the organization and will help you determine potential stakeholders and user groups for interviews and testing.

 A revealing exercise is to compare the vision that preceded the current product with the actual product itself. In some cases, we've seen elaborate PowerPoint presentations, hundreds of pages long, that paint a tremendously ambitious picture of what the information environment should be. And then we've looked to the actual product and found a small, poorly designed website with limited functionality. This gap between vision and reality is a red flag, suggesting misunderstanding between the managers who produce the slides and the team who must build the product. Great visions are useless without the time, money, and expertise to implement them. In these cases, you'll need to rein in expectations quickly.

Introductory Presentations

When you're kicking off a project, it's worth taking time for an introductory presentation. It's good to get authors, software developers, interaction designers, visual designers, marketing folks, and managers all on the same page in understanding the following issues:

- What is information architecture and why is it important?
- How will the information architecture relate to the other components of the information environment and to the organization itself?
- What are the major milestones and deliverables?

These presentations and the discussions they provoke can identify potential land mines and foster productive relationships between teams. They are especially useful in building a common vocabulary that helps people communicate with one another more successfully.

Research Meetings

In the early 1990s, we held full-day marathon meetings with our clients' web teams to learn as much as possible about mission, vision, audience, content, and infrastructure, and to begin fleshing out a framework for the information architecture. In those days of small, centralized web design teams, one mammoth research meeting would often suffice. Today, the design and production of information-rich products and services is often more complicated, involving several teams drawn from different departments. This distributed reality may call for a series of targeted research meetings. Consider the following three meetings and their agendas.

Strategy team meeting

In many organizations today, there's a centralized strategy team or working group that's been tasked with management of digital products and channels. It's this strategy team that sets the high-level goals, defining the mission, vision, intended audience, content, and functionality. This is the group that deals with the big balancing act between centralization and autonomy.

Because of the need to establish trust and respect, face-to-face meetings with this team are essential. Only by having these meetings will you learn about the real goals of the project and the hidden land mines in your path. And only during face-to-face conversations will you reach a comfort level that allows both you and your colleagues to ask the difficult but necessary questions.

It's important to keep these meetings small and informal. Five to seven people is ideal. If the group gets too large, political correctness takes over and people won't talk. As far as the agenda goes, you'll want to hit on some of the following questions:

- What are the goals for this system?
- Who are the intended audiences?
- What is the planned content and functionality?
- What channel(s) will people use to access the system?
- Who will be involved in this effort?
- When do you need to show results?
- What obstacles do you anticipate?

However, the key in these meetings is to follow your nose. Be ready to dig deeper into the most interesting and important topics that come up. The worst thing you can do is rigidly stick to a formal agenda. Think of yourself as the facilitator, not the dictator. And don't be afraid to let the discussion wander a bit. You'll learn more, and everyone will have a more enjoyable meeting.

Content management meeting

The content owners and managers are the people you'll want to engage in detailed discussions about the nature of the content and the content management process. These people typically have lots of hands-on experience and a perspective more informed by bottom-up realities. If you can establish a rapport, you might learn a lot about the culture and politics of the organization as well. Questions for these folks include:

- What are the formal and informal policies regarding content inclusion?
- Is there a content management system (CMS) that handles authoring and publishing?
- Do those systems use controlled vocabularies and attributes to manage content?
- How is content entered into the system, and by whom?
- What technology is being used?
- What content does each owner handle?
- What is the purpose of the content? What are the goals and vision behind this content area?

- Who is the audience?
- How will the audience access the system?
- What is the format of the content? Is it dynamic or static?
- Who maintains the content?
- What future content or services are planned?
- Where does content originate? How is it weeded?
- What legal issues impact the content management process?

Information technology meeting

You should meet with the system administrators and software developers early on to learn about the existing and planned technical infrastructure that will support the product. This provides a good opportunity to discuss the relationships between information architecture and technical infrastructure, as well as to build trust and respect. Remember, you depend on these folks to forge the connection between ideas and implementation. Questions include:

- Will we be able to leverage content management software?
- How can we create the necessary infrastructure to support tagging?
- Does the CMS handle automated categorization of documents?
- What about automated index generation?
- What about personalization?
- How flexible is the search engine?
- Will the search engine support integration of a thesaurus?
- How do we get regular access to search logs and usage analytics?

Unfortunately, the IT groups in many organizations are swamped with work and don't have the time to support information architecture and usability efforts. It's important to identify this problem early and develop a practical, realistic solution. Otherwise, your whole effort can stall when implementation time arrives.

Stakeholder Interviews

Interviews with opinion leaders or stakeholders are often one of the most valuable components of the business context research. These interviews with senior executives and managers from a variety of departments and business units allow for broader participation in the process and bring new perspectives, ideas, and resources to the table.

During these interviews, the designer asks the opinion leaders open-ended questions about their assessment of the current information environment and their vision for the organization and its website or app. It's worth taking the time to explain your project to these folks—their political support may be more important in the long haul than the answers they give during the interview. Sample questions for an intranet project include:

- What is your role in the organization? What does your team do?
- In an optimal world, how would your company use the intranet to build competitive advantage?
- In your opinion, what are the key challenges your company intranet faces?
- What enterprise-wide initiatives are occurring that the intranet strategy team should know about?
- Do you use the existing intranet? If not, why not? If so, what parts of the intranet do you use? How often?
- How do you access the intranet?
- What incentives exist for departments and employees to share knowledge?
- What are the critical success factors for the intranet?
- How will these factors be measured? What's the ROI?
- What are the top three priorities for the intranet redesign?
- If you could tell the intranet strategy team one thing, what would it be?
- What question should we have asked that we didn't?

As with the strategy team meeting, these sessions should be informal discussions. Let the stakeholders tell you what's on their minds.

Beyond interviews, *contextual inquiries* are another useful ethnographic research method for understanding the business context. Instead of simply interviewing stakeholders or users, the researcher observes them going about their business in their workplace and asks them questions to keep the interaction focused on the topics that are within the design team's scope. We'll delve more deeply on contextual inquiry as a research method later in this chapter.

Technology Assessment

In our dream world, we would design our information architectures independent of technology, and then a team of system administrators and software developers would build the infrastructure and tools to support our vision.

In the real world, this doesn't happen very often. Usually, we must work with the tools and infrastructure already in place. This means that we need to assess the IT environment at the very beginning of a project so that our strategies and designs are grounded in reality.

This is why it's critical to talk with IT folks up front. You'll want to understand what's in place, what's in process, and who's available to help. Then you can perform a gap analysis, identifying the disconnects between business goals, user needs, and the practical limitations of the existing technology infrastructure.

You can then see if there are any commercially available tools that might help to close these gaps, and you can initiate a process to determine whether it's practical to integrate them within the context of the current project. Either way, it's much better to come to terms with these IT issues early on.

Content

We define content broadly as "the stuff in your information environment." This may include documents, data, applications, eservices, images, audio and video files, web pages, archived email messages, and more. And we include future stuff in this definition as well as present stuff.

Users need to be able to *find* content before they can use it—findability precedes usability. And if you want to create findable objects, you must spend some time studying those objects. You'll need to identify what distinguishes one object from another, and how document structure and metadata influence findability. You'll want to balance this bottom-up research with a top-down look at the existing information architecture.

If you are fortunate enough to be able to work alongside content strategists in your project, they are likely to bring up some of the following tools and techniques in the course of your research. If not, consider the following as a high-level introduction to some of the content-related issues you need to be aware of.

Heuristic Evaluation

Many projects involve redesigning existing information environments rather than creating new ones. In such cases, you're granted the opportunity to stand on the shoulders of those who came before you. Unfortunately, this opportunity is often missed because of people's propensity to focus on faults and their desire to start with a clean slate. We regularly hear our clients trashing their own websites, explaining that the current site is a disaster and we shouldn't waste our time looking at it. This is a classic case of throwing out the baby with the bathwater. Whenever possible, try to learn from the existing environment and identify what's worth keeping. One way to jump-start this process is to conduct a heuristic evaluation.

A *heuristic evaluation* is an expert critique that tests a product or service against a set of design guidelines. It's usually best to have someone outside the organization perform this critique, so this person is able to look with fresh eyes and be largely unburdened with political considerations. Ideally, the heuristic evaluation should occur before a review of background materials to avoid bias.

At its simplest, a heuristic evaluation of an information architecture involves one expert reviewing an information environment and identifying major problems and opportunities for improvement. This expert brings to the table an unwritten set of assumptions about what does and doesn't work, drawing upon experiences with many projects in many organizations.

This practice is similar to the physician's model of diagnosis and prescription. If your child has a sore throat, the doctor will rarely consult a reference book or perform extensive medical tests. Based on the patient's complaints, the visible symptoms, and her knowledge of common ailments, the doctor will make an educated guess as to the problem and its solution. These guesses are not always right, but this single-expert model of heuristic evaluation often provides a good balance between cost and quality.

At the more rigorous and expensive end of the spectrum, a heuristic evaluation can be a multi-expert review that tests a system against a written list of principles and guidelines.[1] This list may include such common-sense guidelines as:

- The environment should provide multiple ways to access the same information.
- Indexes and sitemaps should be employed to supplement the taxonomy.
- The navigation system should provide users with a sense of context.
- The environment should consistently use language appropriate for the audience.
- Searching and browsing should be integrated and reinforce each other.

Each expert reviews the environment independently and makes notes on how it fares with respect to each of these criteria. The experts then compare notes, discuss differences in their responses, and work toward a consensus. This reduces the likelihood that personal opinion will play too strong a role, and creates the opportunity to draw experts from different disciplines. Each will see very different problems and opportunities. This approach obviously costs more, so depending on the scope of your project, you'll need to strike a balance in terms of number of experts and the formality of the evaluation.

Content Analysis

Content analysis is a defining component of the bottom-up approach to information architecture, involving careful review of documents and objects (the "stuff" we mentioned earlier) that actually exist in your information environment. What you find in the analysis may not match the visions, quantity, or quality articulated by the strategy team and the opinion leaders in the organization. You'll need to identify and address these gaps between top-down vision and bottom-up reality as part of your review.

---

1 For a good example of such a list, see Jakob Nielsen's "Ten Usability Heuristics" (*http://bit.ly/usability_heuristics*).

Content analysis can take the shape of an informal survey or a detailed audit. Early in the research phase, a high-level content survey is a useful tool for learning about the scope and nature of content. Later in the process, a page-by-page content inventory and audit can produce a roadmap for migration to a content management system, or at least facilitate an organized approach to page-level authoring and design, with the end result being more valuable content and a better overall user experience.

Gathering content

To begin, you'll need to find, print, and analyze a representative sample of the system's content. We suggest avoiding an overly scientific approach to sample definition—there's no formula or software package that will guarantee success. Instead, you should use some intuition and judgment, balancing the size of your sample against the time constraints of the project.

We recommend the "Noah's Ark" approach: try to capture a couple of each type of animal. In an information environment, our animals are stuff like white papers, annual reports, and online reimbursement forms; the difficult part is determining what constitutes a unique species. The following dimensions should help distinguish one beast from another so that you can work toward a diverse and useful content sample:

Format
> Aim for a broad mix of formats, such as textual documents, software applications, video and audio files, archived email messages, and so on. Try to include offline resources such as books, people, facilities, and organizations that are represented by surrogate records within the environment.

Document type
> Capturing a diverse set of document types should be a top priority. Examples include product catalog records, marketing brochures, press releases, news articles, blog posts, annual reports, technical reports, white papers, forms, online calculators, presentations, spreadsheets, and more.

Source
> Your sample should reflect the diverse sources of content. In a corporate website or intranet, this will mirror the organization chart. You'll want to make sure you've got samples from engi-

neering, marketing, customer support, finance, human resources, sales, research, etc. This is not just useful—it's also politically astute. If your information environment includes third-party content such as externally hosted blogs, Facebook pages, Twitter feeds, Tumblr, Instagram, electronic journals, APIs, or ASP services, then review those, too.

Subject

This is a tricky one, because you may not have a topical taxonomy for your information environment. You might look for a publicly available classification scheme or thesaurus for your industry. It's a good exercise to represent a broad range of subjects or topics in your content sample, but don't force it.

Existing architecture

Used together with these other dimensions, the existing structure of the information environment can be a great guide to diverse content types. Simply by following each of the major category links on the main page or in the global navigation bar, you can often reach a wide sample of content. However, keep in mind that you don't want your analysis to be overly influenced by the old architecture.

Consider what other dimensions might be useful for building a representative content sample for your particular environment. Possibilities include intended audience, document length, dynamism, language, use of page templates, and so on.

As you're balancing sample size against time and budget, consider the relative number of members of each species. For example, if the environment contains hundreds of technical reports, you certainly want a couple of examples. But if you find a single white paper, it's probably not worth including in your sample. On the other hand, you do need to factor in the importance of certain content types. There may not be many annual reports on your website, but they can be content-rich, frequently downloaded, and very important to investors. As always, your judgment is required.

A final factor to consider is the law of diminishing returns. While you're conducting content analysis, you'll often reach a point where you feel you're just not learning anything new. This may be a good signal to go with the sample you've got, or at least take a break. Content analysis is only useful insofar as it teaches you about the stuff in the environment and provides insights about how to get users to that stuff. Don't just go through the motions—it's unproductive (and incredibly boring!).

Analyzing content

What are you looking for during content analysis? What can you hope to learn? One of the side benefits of content analysis is familiarity with the subject matter that's important to an organization and the people it serves. This is particularly important for consultants who need to quickly become fluent in the language of their client. But the central purpose of content analysis is to provide data that's critical to creating a good user experience. It helps you reveal patterns and relationships within content and metadata that can be used to better structure, organize, and provide access to that content. That said, content analysis doesn't need to be scientific. Our approach is to start with a short list of things to look for, and then allow the content to shape the process as you move forward.

For example, for each content object, you might begin by noting the following:

Structural metadata
> Describe the information hierarchy of this object. Is there a title? Are there discrete sections or chunks of content? Might users want to independently access these chunks?

Descriptive metadata
> Think of all the different ways you might describe this object. How about topic, audience, and format? There should be at least a dozen different ways to describe many of the objects you study. Now is the time to get them all on the table.

Administrative metadata
> Describe how this object relates to business context. Who created it? Who owns it? When was it created? When should it be removed?

This short list will get you started. In some cases, the object will already have metadata—grab that, too. However, it's important not to lock into a predefined set of metadata fields. You want to allow the content to speak to you, suggesting new fields you might not have considered. You'll find it helpful to keep asking yourself these questions:

- What is this object?
- How can I describe this object for people and for machines?
- What distinguishes this object from others?
- How can I make this object findable for people and for machines?

Moving beyond individual items, also look for patterns and relationships that emerge as you study many content objects. Are certain groupings of content becoming apparent? Are you seeing clear hierarchical relationships? Are you recognizing the potential for associative relationships, perhaps finding disparate items that are linked by a common business process?

Because of the need to recognize patterns within the context of the full sample, content analysis is by necessity an iterative process. It may be on the second or third pass over a particular document that the lightbulb blinks on and you discover a truly innovative and useful solution.

With the exception of true bottom-up geeks (and we use this term respectfully), many people don't find content analysis especially thrilling or addictive. However, experience has proven that this careful, painstaking work can suggest new insights and produce winning information architecture strategies. In particular, content analysis will help you in the design phase, when you begin fleshing out document types and metadata schemas. But it also provides valuable input into the broader design of organization, labeling, navigation, and searching systems.

Content Mapping

Heuristic evaluation provides a top-down understanding of an information environment's organization and navigation structures, while content analysis provides a bottom-up understanding of its content objects. Now it's time to bridge these two perspectives by developing one or more *content maps*.

A content map is a visual representation of the existing information environment (see Figure 11-4). Content maps are typically high level and conceptual in nature. They are a tool for understanding, rather than a concrete design deliverable.

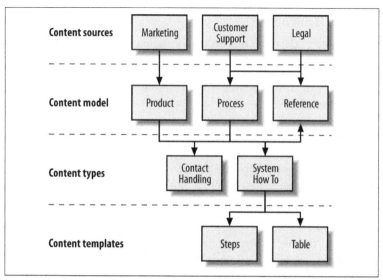

Figure 11-4. A small slice of a content map

Content maps vary widely. Some focus on content ownership and the publishing process. Some are used to visualize relationships between content categories. And others explore navigation pathways within content areas. The goal of creating a content map is to help you and your colleagues wrap your minds around the structure, organization, and location of existing content, and ultimately to spark ideas about how to provide improved access.

Benchmarking

We use the term *benchmark* informally to indicate a point of reference from which to make comparative measurements or judgments. In this context, benchmarking involves the systematic identification, evaluation, and comparison of information architecture features of the stuff in your information environment, such as websites, intranets, or apps.

These comparisons can be quantitative or qualitative. We might evaluate the number of seconds it takes a user to perform a task using competing websites, or take notes about the most interesting features of each site. Comparisons can be made between different websites (competitive benchmarking) or between different versions of the same website (before-and-after benchmarking). In both cases, we've found benchmarking to be a flexible and valuable tool.

Competitive benchmarking

Borrowing good ideas, whether they come from competitors, friends, enemies, or strangers, comes naturally to all of us. It's part of our competitive advantage as human beings. If we were all left to our own devices to invent the wheel, most of us would still be walking to work.

However, when we take these copycat shortcuts, we run the risk of borrowing bad ideas as well as good ones. This happens all the time in our field. Since the pioneering days of website design, people have repeatedly mistaken large financial outlays and strong marketing campaigns as signs of good information architecture. Careful benchmarking can catch this misdirected copycatting before it gets out of control.

For example, when we worked with a major financial services firm, we ran up against the notion that Fidelity Investments's longstanding position as a leader within the industry automatically conferred the gold standard upon its website. In several cases, we proposed significant improvements to our client's site but were blocked by the argument, "That's not how Fidelity does it."

To be sure, Fidelity is a major force in the financial services industry, with a broad array of services and world-class marketing. However, at the time, the information architecture of its site was a mess—it was not a model worth following. To our client's credit, they commissioned a formal benchmarking study, during which we evaluated and compared the features of several competing sites. During this study, Fidelity's failings became obvious, and we were able to move forward without that particular set of false assumptions.

The point here is that borrowing information architecture features from competitors can be valuable, but it must be done carefully, with consideration of context.

Before-and-after benchmarking

Benchmarking can also be applied to a single information environment over time to measure improvements. We can use it to answer such return-on-investment (ROI) questions as:

- How much did the intranet redesign reduce our employees' average time finding core documents?
- Has the website redesign improved our customers' ability to find the products they need?
- Which aspects of our redesign have had a negative impact on user efficiency or effectiveness?

Before-and-after benchmarking forces you to take the high-level goals expressed in your statement of mission and vision and tie them to specific, measurable criteria. This forced clarification and detail orientation will drive you toward a better information architecture design on the present project, in addition to providing a point of reference for evaluating success.

The advantages of before-and-after benchmarking include the following:

- Identifies and prioritizes information architecture features in the existing environment
- Encourages transition from broad generalizations (e.g., "Our site's navigation stinks") to specific, actionable definitions ("The label of this link should be updated because our testers didn't know what it meant")
- Creates a point of reference against which you can measure improvements

On the other hand, competitive benchmarking offers these benefits:

- Generates a laundry list of information architecture features, bringing lots of new ideas to table
- Encourages transition from broad generalizations (e.g., "Amazon is a good model") to specific, actionable definitions ("Amazon's personalization feature works well for frequent visitors")
- Challenges embedded assumptions (e.g., "We should be like Fidelity") and avoids copying the wrong features for the wrong reasons
- Establishes current position with respect to competitors and creates a point of reference against which to measure speed of improvement

Users

They're called users, respondents, visitors, actors, employees, customers, and more. They're counted as clicks, impressions, advertising revenues, and sales. Whatever you call them and however you count them, they are the ultimate judges of our information environments. Build a website that confuses customers, and they'll go elsewhere. Build an intranet that frustrates employees, and they won't use it.

This is the Internet's fast-forward brand of evolution. In the early years of the Web, Time Warner spent millions of dollars on a flashy, graphical extravaganza called Pathfinder. Users hated it, and a complete redesign followed months after the original launch. This was an expensive and embarrassingly public lesson in the importance of user-sensitive design.

So, we've established that people are powerful. They're also complex and unpredictable. You can't blindly apply lessons learned by Amazon to the information architecture design of Pfizer.com. You've got to consider the unique nature of the environment and of the people who will be using it.

There are many ways to study user populations.[2] Market research firms run focus groups to study branding preferences. Political pollsters use telephone surveys to gauge the public's feelings about candidates and issues. Usability firms conduct interviews to determine which icons and color schemes are most effective. Anthropologists observe people acting and interacting within their native environments to learn about their culture, behavior, and beliefs.

No single approach can stand alone as the one right way to learn about users and their needs, priorities, mental models, and information-seeking behavior. This is a multidimensional puzzle—you've got to look at it from many different perspectives to get a good sense of the whole. It's much better to conduct five interviews and five usability tests than to run one test ten times. Each approach is subject to the law of diminishing returns.

---

2 If you'd like to dig deeper, we recommend reading Joann Hackos and Janice Redish's *User and Task Analysis for Interface Design* (Hoboken, NJ: Wiley, 1998). And then, of course, there are all sorts of articles by usability guru Jakob Nielsen (*http://useit.com*).

As you consider integrating these user research methods into your design process, keep a couple of things in mind. First, observe the golden rule of discount usability engineering: any testing is better than no testing. Don't let budgets or schedules become an excuse. Second, remember that users can be your most powerful allies. It's easy for your colleagues and your boss to argue with you, but it's difficult for them to argue with their customers and with real user behavior. User research is an extremely effective political tool.

Usage Analysis

Most projects today involve redesigning an existing product. In these cases, it makes sense to begin by looking at data that shows how people have been using the system and where they've been running into problems.

Your content's usage data is a reasonable place to start. Most analytics software, such as Google Analytics, will provide the following reports:

Content performance
    The number of visits and interactions with content on the site over a given period. Examples include visits, pages viewed, navigation used, and more. This data shows what stuff is popular and helpful for users as well as what's not. By tracking this data over time, you can observe trends and tie content use to events such as advertising campaigns, the redesign of site navigation, and more.

Visitor information
    Analytics products claim they can tell you who is using your site. In reality, the information they provide is more general; it usually includes data points such as the referring sources of visitors (e.g., coming from a search engine, from another website, from social media, etc.), the countries their IP addresses are registered in, general capabilities of their web browsers, and so on.

Your analytics software may provide additional views into the usage data, indicating the times and dates when people are visiting, ratio of new users to previous visitors, and the types of browsers being used, as shown in Figure 11-5.

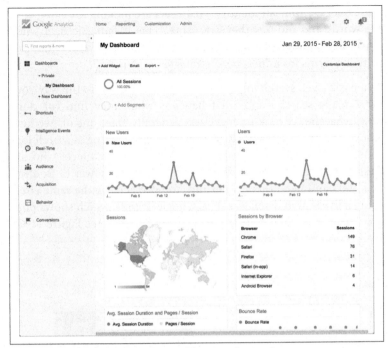

Figure 11-5. Usage data presented by Google Analytics

The path that users trace as they move through a website is known as the *clickstream*. You can trace where people come from (originating site), the path they take through your site, and where they go next (destination site). Along the way, you can learn how long they spend on each page of your site. This creates a tremendously rich datastream that can be fascinating to review, but is often difficult to act upon. What you really need to make clickstream data valuable is feedback from users explaining why they came to the site, what they found, and why they left. Some companies use pop-up surveys to capture this information as users are leaving the website.

Search Log Analysis

A simpler and extremely valuable approach involves the tracking and analysis of queries entered into the search engine.[3] By studying

---

3 For more in-depth information on search log analysis, we recommend Lou's book *Search Analytics for Your Site: Conversations with Your Customers* (Brooklyn, NY: Rosenfeld Media, 2011).

these queries, you can identify what users are looking for along with the words and phrases they are using. This is fantastic data when you're developing controlled vocabularies. It's also useful when prioritizing terms for a "best bets" strategy.

At a basic level, search log analysis will sensitize you to the way your users really search—and what happens when they find (or don't find) what they're looking for. Users generally enter one or two keywords, and sometimes don't spell them right. Looking at search logs provides a valuable education for information architects who are fresh out of school and all steamed up about the power of Boolean operators and parenthetical nesting. You can achieve the same effect using a live search display such as Google Trends, which shows popular terms that real people are using to search now (see Figure 11-6).

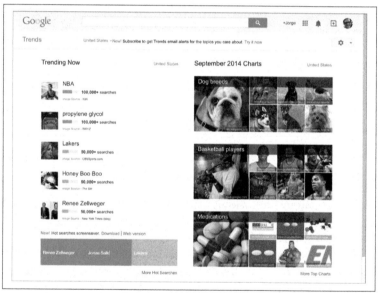

Figure 11-6. Google Trends

But with your own system's search logs, you can learn much more. At a bare minimum, you should be able to get a monthly report that shows how many times users searched on particular terms during that month, as shown here:

```
54 e-victor
53 keywords:"e-victor"
41 travel
41 keywords:"travel"
37 keywords:"jupiter"
```

```
37 jupiter31 esp
30 keywords:"esp"
28 keywords:"evictor"
28 evictor
28 keywords:"people finder"
28 people finder
27 fleet
27 keywords:"fleet"
27 payroll
26 eer
26 keywords:"eer"
26 keywords:"payroll"
26 digital badge
25 keywords:"digital badge"
```

But hopefully, you can work with your IT group to buy or build a more sophisticated query-analysis tool that allows you to filter by date, time, and IP address as well as discover what the searchers did after completing their searches. Figure 11-7 shows a good example of such a tool. This tool can help you answer the following questions:

- Which popular queries are retrieving zero results?
- Are these zero-hit users entering the wrong keywords, or are they looking for stuff that doesn't exist on your site?
- Which popular queries are retrieving hundreds of results?
- What are these hundred-hit users actually looking for?
- Which queries are becoming more popular? Less?

Based on the answers, you can take immediate and concrete steps to fix problems and improve information retrieval. You might add preferred and variant terms to your controlled vocabulary, change navigation labels on major pages, improve search tips, or edit content. Note that smart marketing groups are also getting interested in search logs as a valuable source of information about customer needs.

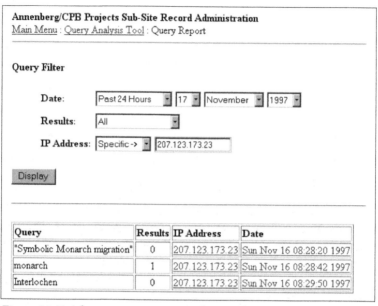

Figure 11-7. A homegrown query-analysis tool

Customer-Support Data

In addition to reviewing usage patterns, it's worth looking to the customer/technical support departments to see if they've been capturing and analyzing the problems, questions, and feedback from your product's customers. Help desk operators, call center representatives, librarians, and administrative assistants can also be rich sources of information; in many large corporations, these are the people to whom customers or employees turn for answers. That means they are the people who know the questions.

Participant Definition and Recruiting

All of the remaining user research methods, including surveys, focus groups, interviews, and ethnographic studies, require the selection of representative samples of users to participate in the research studies. With the possible exception of surveys, it's rarely possible to study every user of an information environment.

The definition and prioritization of intended and actual audiences for the environment is obviously a critical factor. As we discussed earlier, there are myriad ways of slicing and dicing these audiences.

Just as you define a primary hierarchy for your product, you also need to define a primary hierarchy for participant selection. This hierarchy should strike a balance between the traditional ways that an organization views its customers (e.g., home users, business users, value-added resellers) and the distinctions you are interested in (e.g., people familiar with the old site, people unfamiliar with the old site).

For large projects, you should consider working with a traditional market research firm that has experience defining audience categories, developing profiles of participants within those categories, recruiting participants, and handling logistics like facilities, incentives, and note taking.

Surveys

Surveys are a broad-and-shallow research tool that provide an opportunity to gather input from a large number of people relatively quickly and inexpensively. Surveys can be conducted via email, websites, telephone, mail, or in person, and can be used to gather qualitative or quantitative data.

When designing a survey, you'll need to limit the number of questions if you want a reasonable response rate. You may also need to guarantee anonymity and offer an incentive. Because there's little opportunity for follow-up questions or dialogue, surveys don't allow you to gather rich data about users' information-seeking behaviors. Instead, they are best used for identifying:

- Which content and tasks users find most valuable
- What frustrates users most about the current product
- What ideas users have for improvement
- The current level of user satisfaction

In addition to the inherent value of real users' opinions, the survey results will provide you with a powerful political tool. If 90% of users say that the employee directory is the most important and most frustrating intranet resource, that's a compelling argument for improving it.

Contextual Inquiry

Field study is an important component of research programs in a variety of disciplines, from animal behavior to anthropology. Environmental context is tightly interwoven with behavior—you can only learn so much about the bald eagle or the bottle-nosed dolphin by studying them in a lab. The same applies to people and their use of information technology. In fact, a growing number of anthropologists are being tapped by the business world to apply their ethnographic research methods to product design.

These methods of contextual inquiry can be useful to the creation of an information architecture.[4] For example, simply seeing the work spaces of users can be valuable in showing the spectrum of information resources they use on a daily basis (e.g., computer, phone, bulletin board, Post-it notes).

If possible, it's also valuable to watch people interact with a product during the normal course of business. If you're redesigning a mission-critical call center application that people interact with all day long, spend a few hours watching them. On the other hand, if you're redesigning a typical business website, this observational approach won't be practical given the sporadic nature of site use. Most people will visit only once every several weeks or months. In these cases, you'll need to rely on user testing, though you still may be able to run the tests in the user's natural habitat.

In some cases, it can be valuable to simply watch people work. Observing users performing normal daily tasks—going to meetings, taking phone calls, and so on—can provide insight into how the intranet or website might (or might not) help people be more productive. The difficult issue here (and, to some degree, with all the observation approaches) is that information architecture begins to bleed into knowledge management and business-process re-engineering. In an ideal world, the roles and responsibilities of departments, teams, and individuals would all be designed in an integrated fashion. In the real world (and particularly in large organizations), most projects are limited by the scope, schedule, and budget of these different departments. The folks responsible for

---

4 To learn more about contextual inquiry, we recommend reading Hugh Beyer and Karen Holtzblatt's *Contextual Design* (Burlington, MA: Morgan Kaufmann, 1997).

designing the information architecture rarely influence the way other departments do their work. For this reason, keep asking yourself throughout the research process whether you'll actually be able to act on the data. If you're going to get the job done, the answer better be yes.

Focus Groups

Focus groups are one of the most common and most abused tools for learning from users. When conducting focus groups, you gather groups of people who are actual or potential users of your product. In a typical focus-group session, you might ask a series of scripted questions about what users would like to see in the product, demonstrate a prototype or show the product itself, and then ask questions about the users' perception of the product and their recommendations for improvement.

Focus groups are great for generating ideas about possible content and function. By getting several people from your target audiences together and facilitating a brainstorming session, you can quickly find yourself with a laundry list of suggestions. However, focus groups don't work as well for information architecture as they do for, say, consumer product design or marketing. For example, people can tell you what they like, don't like, and wish for regarding their refrigerators, but most people don't have the understanding or language necessary to be articulate about information architectures.

Focus groups are also very poor vehicles for testing usability. A public demonstration does not come close to replicating the actual environment of a user who is interacting with a website or app. Understanding—and the contextual experience of "being there" described in Chapter 4—happens individually. Consequently, the suggestions of people in focus groups often do not carry much weight. Sadly, focus groups are often used only to prove that a particular approach does or doesn't work, and they can easily be influenced in one direction or another through the skillful selection and phrasing of questions.

User Research Sessions

Face-to-face sessions involving one user at a time are a central part of the user research process. However, these sessions can also be expensive and time-consuming. We've learned that you tend to get the most value out of these sessions by integrating two or more research methods. We typically combine an interview with either card sorting or user testing. This multi-method approach makes the most of our limited time with real people.

Interviews

We often begin and end user research sessions with a series of questions. Starting with a brief Q&A can put the participants at ease. This is a good time to ask about their overall priorities and needs with respect to the product. Questions at the end of the session can be used to follow up on issues that came up during the user testing. This is a good time to ask what frustrates the users about the current product and what suggestions they have for improvement. This final Q&A brings closure to the session. Here are some questions we've used for intranet projects in the past:

Background
- What do you do in your current role?
- What is your background?
- How long have you been with the company?

Information use
- What information do you need to do your job?
- What information is hardest to find?
- What do you do when you can't find something?

Intranet use
- Do you use the intranet?
- What is your impression of the intranet? Is it easy or hard to use?
- How do you find information on the intranet?
- Do you use customization or personalization features?

Document publishing
- Do you create documents that are used by other people or departments?
- Tell us what you know about the life cycle of your documents. What happens after you create them?

- Do you use content management tools to publish documents to the intranet?

Suggestions
- If you could change three things about the intranet, what would they be?
- If you could add three features to the website, what would they be?
- If you could tell the web strategy team three things, what would they be?

In determining what questions to ask, it's important to recognize that most people do not understand information architecture. They don't have the understanding or vocabulary to engage in a technical dialogue about existing or potential architectures. If you ask them if they like the current organization scheme or whether they think a thesaurus would improve the site's usability, you'll get blank stares or made-up answers. That's why we turn to another research method to yield the answers to these questions.

Card Sorting

Want to get your hands on some of the most powerful information architecture research tools in the world? Grab a stack of index cards, some Post-it notes, and a pen. Card sorting may be low-tech, but it's great for understanding your users.

What's involved? Not a whole lot, as you can see in Figure 11-8. Label a bunch of index cards with headings from categories, subcategories, and content within your website. About 20 to 25 cards is usually sufficient. Number the cards so that you can more easily analyze the data later. Ask users to sort this stack of cards into piles that make sense, and to label those piles using the Post-it notes. Ask them to think out loud while they work. Take good notes, and record the labels and contents of their piles. That's it!

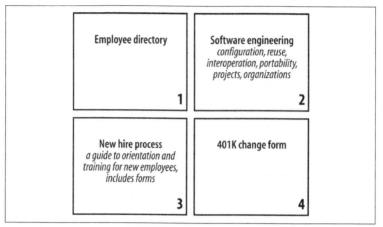

Figure 11-8. Sample index cards

Card-sorting studies can provide insight into people's mental models, illuminating the ways they often tacitly group, sort, and label tasks and content in their own heads. The simplicity of this method confers tremendous flexibility. In the earliest phases of research, you can employ exploratory, open-ended card-sorting methods like the one we just described. Later on, you can use closed card sorts in which users rely on your predefined labels to question or validate a prototype information architecture. You can also instruct people to sort the cards according to what's most important to them; they can even have a pile for "things I don't care about." The permutations are infinite. Consider the following dimensions of card sorting:

Open/closed
> In totally open card sorts, users write their own card and category labels. Totally closed sorts allow only prelabeled cards and categories. Open sorts are used for discovery. Closed sorts are used for validation. There's a lot of room in the middle. You'll need to set the balance according to your goals.

Phrasing
> The labels on your cards might be words, phrases, sentences, or categories with sample subcategories. You can even affix a picture. You might phrase the card labels as questions or answers, or use topic- or task-oriented words.

Granularity

Cards can be high level or detailed. Your labels might be main page categories or the names of subsites, or you may focus on specific documents or even content elements within documents.

Heterogeneity

Early on, you may want to cover a lot of ground by mixing apples and oranges (e.g., name of subsite, document title, subject heading) to elicit rich qualitative data. This will really get users talking as they puzzle over the heterogeneous mix of cards. Later, you may want high consistency (e.g., subject headings only) to produce quantitative data (e.g., 80% of users grouped these three items together).

Cross-listing

Are you fleshing out the primary hierarchy of the product or exploring alternate navigation paths? If it's the latter, you might allow your users to make copies of cards, cross-listing them in multiple categories. You might also ask them to write descriptive terms (i.e., metadata) on the cards or category labels.

Randomness

You can strategically select card labels to prove a hypothesis, or you can randomly select labels from a pool of possible labels. As always, your power to influence outcomes can be used for good or evil.

Quantitative/qualitative

Card sorting can be used as an interview instrument or as a data collection tool. We've found it most useful for gathering qualitative data. If you go the quantitative route, be careful to observe basic principles of the scientific method and avoid prejudicing the outcome.

Just as there are many ways to do card sorting, there are many ways to analyze the results. From a qualitative perspective, you should be learning and forming ideas during the tests, as users talk out loud about their reasoning, their questions, and their frustrations. By asking follow-up questions, you can dig into some specifics and gain a better understanding of opportunities for organizing and labeling content.

On the quantitative side, there are some obvious metrics to capture:

- The percentage of time that users place two cards together. A high level of association between items suggests a close affinity in users' mental models.

- The percentage of time a specific card is placed in the same category. This works well in closed sorts. For open sorts, you may need to normalize the category labels (e.g., Human Resources equals HR equals Admin/HR) to make this work.

These metrics can be represented visually in an *affinity modeling diagram* (see Figure 11-9) to show the clusters and the relationships between clusters. You may want to plug your data into analytics software and have it generate the visuals automatically. However, these automatically generated visualizations are often fairly complex and hard to understand. They tend to be better for identifying patterns than for communicating results.

When you're ready to present research results to your clients, you may want to create a simpler affinity model by hand. These manually generated diagrams provide an opportunity to focus on a few highlights of the card-sorting results.

In Figure 11-10, 80% of users grouped the "How to set DHTML event properties" card in the same pile as "Enterprise edition: Deployment," suggesting they should be closely linked on the site. Note that "Load balancing web servers" is a boundary spanner and should probably be referenced in both categories on the site.

When used wisely, affinity models can inform the brainstorming process and are useful for presenting research results and defending strategic decisions. However, it's important to avoid masking qualitative research with quantitative analysis. If you conducted only five user tests, the numbers may not be statistically meaningful. So although card sorts produce very seductive data sets, we've found them most useful for the qualitatively derived insights they provide.

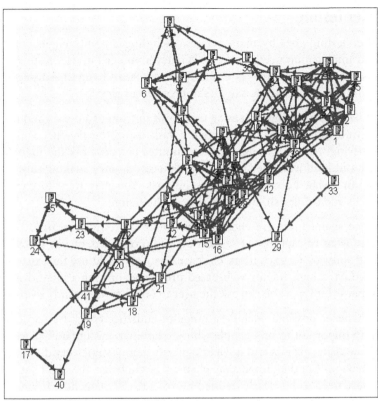

Figure 11-9. An automatically generated affinity model (prepared for Louis Rosenfeld and Michele de la Iglesia by Edward Vielmetti using InFlow 3.0 network analysis software from Valdis Krebs)

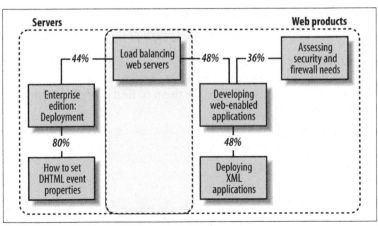

Figure 11-10. A handcrafted affinity model

User Testing

User testing goes by many names, including usability engineering and information needs analysis. Whatever you call it, user testing is fairly straightforward. As usability expert Steve Krug of Advanced Common Sense likes to say, "It's not rocket surgery."[5]

In basic user testing, you ask a user to sit in front of a device and try to find information or complete a task using the product you're studying. Allowing roughly three minutes per task, ask the user to talk out loud while he's navigating. Take good notes, making sure to capture what he says and where he goes. You may want to count clicks and bring a stopwatch to time each session.

Once again, there are endless ways to structure this research. You may want to capture the session on audio or video, or use specialized software to track users' clickstreams. You might use the existing product, a high-fidelity web-based prototype, or even a low-fidelity paper prototype. You can ask the user to only browse or only search.

Whenever possible, include a range of audience types. It's particularly important to mix people who are familiar and unfamiliar with the website; experts and novices typically demonstrate very different behavior. Another important element is choosing the right tasks. These need to be clearly defined by your research agenda. If you're in an exploratory phase, consider distributing your tasks along the following lines:

Easy to impossible
> It's often good to begin with an easy task to make the user feel confident and comfortable. Later, include some difficult or impossible tasks to see how the system performs under duress.

Known-item to exhaustive
> Ask users to find a specific answer or item (e.g., a customer support phone number). Also, ask them to find everything they can on a particular topic.

---

5 For pointers on how to perform rocket surgery, we refer you to Steve's book *Rocket Surgery Made Easy: The Do-It-Yourself Guide to Finding and Fixing Usability Problems* (San Francisco: New Riders, 2009).

Topic to task
> Ask some topical or subject-oriented questions (e.g., find something on microelectronics). Also, give them some tasks to complete (e.g., purchase a phone).

Artificial to real
> Although most of your tasks will be artificial, try to build in some realistic scenarios. Rather than saying "find printer X," provide a problem statement. For example, "You're starting a home business and have decided to purchase a printer." Encourage the user to role-play. Perhaps she will visit other websites, searching for third-party reviews of this printer.

As with content analysis, you'll also want to spread these tasks across multiple areas and levels of the product.

User testing typically provides a rich data set for analysis. You'll learn a great deal just by watching and listening. Obvious metrics include "number of clicks" and "time to find." These can be useful in before-and-after comparisons, hopefully to show how much you improved the site in your latest redesign. You'll also want to track common mistakes that lead users down the wrong paths.

If you're like us, you'll find these user tests highly energizing. There are few things more motivating to a user-sensitive professional than watching real people struggle and suffer with an existing product. You see the pain, you see what doesn't work, and you inevitably start creating all sorts of better solutions in your head. Don't ignore these great ideas. Don't convince yourself that creativity belongs only in the strategy phase. Strike while the iron's hot. Jot down ideas during the research sessions, talk with your colleagues and clients between sessions, and expand on the ideas as soon as you get a spare minute. You'll find these notes and discussions hugely valuable as you move into the strategy phase.

In Defense of Research

The design or redesign of any complex information environment should begin with research leading to the formation of an information architecture strategy. Through research, we aim to learn enough about the business goals, the users, and the information ecology to develop a solid strategy. By creating, presenting, and refining this strategy, we can work toward consensus on the direction and scope of the product's structure and organization.

This strategy will then serve as the roadmap for all subsequent design and implementation work. It will not only drive the information architecture process, but also guide the work of graphic designers, content authors, and software developers. While each of these teams will take different paths, the information architecture strategy ensures that everyone is headed toward a common destination.

Sometimes these are separate phases. Sometimes they are combined into a joint research and strategy phase. Either way, it's important to have the same team of people involved in performing the research and developing the strategy. In cases where these are done separately, the research team tends to lack direction and focus, seeking answers that are interesting but not necessarily actionable, while the strategy team lacks the richness of direct interaction with users, opinion leaders, and content. Only a small percentage of the hands-on learning can be conveyed through formal presentations and reports.

What happens if you don't make the time for research? There's no need to hazard a guess—we've seen firsthand the very messy results of uncoordinated web development projects. On one occasion, we were brought into a large-scale ecommerce project in midstream. The client had chosen to skip the research and strategy phases because they wanted to "move fast." Graphic designers had created beautiful page templates; content authors had restructured and indexed large numbers of articles; the technical team had selected and purchased a content management system. None of these components worked together. There was no shared vision for how to connect users and content. In fact, nobody could even agree on the primary goals of the website. The project entered what one participant eloquently called a "death spiral," as each team tried to convince the others that its vision was the right one. The client eventually pulled the plug, deciding it would be more efficient to start over rather than try to salvage the incompatible and fairly misguided efforts of each team.

Unfortunately, this scenario is not uncommon. In today's fast-paced world, everyone's looking for a shortcut. It can be very difficult to convince people, particularly senior managers with little hands-on web experience, of the importance of taking the time to do research and develop a solid strategy. If you're struggling with this problem, the next section might help.

Overcoming Research Resistance

In many corporate settings, mentioning the word research gets immediate resistance. Three common arguments include:

- We don't have the time or money.
- We already know what we want.
- We've already done research.

There are good reasons behind these arguments. Everyone operates under time and budget constraints. Everyone has opinions (sometimes good ones) about what's working and how to fix what's not. And for all but the newest projects, some level of prior research that applies to the current situation will already have been done. Fearing the perils of analysis paralysis, business managers tend to be very action oriented. "Let's skip the research and get started with the real work" is a familiar sentiment.

However, for any major design or redesign project, you must find a way to communicate the importance of conducting information architecture research. Without this careful investigation and experimentation aimed at the discovery of facts, you'll find yourself basing your strategy on the unstable foundation of biased opinion and faulty assumption. Let's review the common arguments for conducting information architecture research.

You're likely to save time and money by doing research

The propensity to skip research and dive into design is often the project manager's version of the paradox of the active user.[6] The immediate perception of progress feels good but often comes at the expense of overall efficiency and effectiveness. Because the information architecture forms the foundation of the entire information environment, mistakes made here will have a tremendous ripple effect.

---

6 Users choose the illusion of speed over real efficiency. This explains why people repeatedly enter keywords into search engines despite bad results. Browsing feels slower.

Our experience (summarized in Figure 11-11) constantly reinforces the idea that by spending the necessary time on research, you'll often shorten the design and implementation phases so much (by avoiding lots of arguments and redesigns along the way) that you actually shorten the completion time for the overall project.

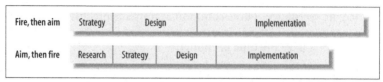

Figure 11-11. The paradox of the active manager

However, the biggest savings will come from the fact that your information environment will actually work, and you won't have to completely redesign it six months later.

Managers don't know what your users want

Most digital designers have "gotten the religion" when it comes to recognizing the importance of user-centered design. Many business managers have not. They confuse what they want, what their bosses want, and what they think users want with *what users actually want*. The best way to convert these nonbelievers is to involve them in some user testing. There's no substitute for the humbling experience of watching regular people try to use your product or service.

We need to do information architecture research

You need to ask unique questions in unique ways. Market research studies and general-purpose usability tests may provide useful data, but they're not enough. Also, you want the same people involved in both testing and design. Throwing old research reports over the wall has limited value.

Recap

Let's recap what we've learned in this chapter:

- Good research means asking the right questions, and choosing the right questions requires a conceptual framework of the broader environment.
- We use our Content/Context/Users conceptual framework as the basis of our research.
- When researching context, we're looking to understand goals, budgets, schedules, technology infrastructure, human resources, corporate culture, and politics.
- When researching content, we're looking to understand "the stuff in the information environment."
- When researching users, we're looking to understand the people—real, living human beings—who will be using the information environment.
- It can sometimes be difficult to convince stakeholders to include time for research in the project, but it's important that they do so.

Now let's examine the next step of the process: strategy.

CHAPTER 12
Strategy

Strategy 101 is about choices: You can't be all things to all people.
—Michael Porter

In this chapter, we'll cover:

- The elements of an information architecture strategy
- Guidelines for moving from research to strategy
- Using metaphors, scenarios, and conceptual diagrams to bring your strategy to life
- Project plans, presentations, and the strategy report (including a detailed example from Weather.com)

Research can be addictive: the more you learn, the more questions you have. This is why doctoral students sometimes take more than a decade to complete their dissertations. We rarely have that luxury: typically, we need to move from research to design according to schedules measured in weeks or months rather than years.

The bridge between research and design is an information architecture strategy. It's critical that you start thinking about how you're going to build that bridge before research begins, and keep thinking about it throughout the research process. Similarly, as you're building the bridge you need to continue your research efforts, continually testing and refining your assumptions.

In short, the line between research and strategy is blurred. It's not as simple as turning the page from Chapter 11 to Chapter 13. Though the process of moving from research to administration is linear at a high level, as shown in Figure 12-1 (also featured in Chapter 11), when you get down into the details this is a highly iterative, interactive process.

Figure 12-1. The process of information architecture development

You must repeatedly switch back and forth between roles, wearing both the researcher's hat and the strategist's hat against the backdrop of a budget and schedule. Oh, did we mention there's some stress involved? There's no question that this is hard work, but it can be fun and rewarding, too.

What Is an Information Architecture Strategy?

An information architecture strategy is a high-level conceptual framework for structuring and organizing an information environment. It provides the firm sense of direction and scope necessary to proceed with confidence into the design and implementation phases. It also facilitates discussion and helps get people on the same page before moving into the more expensive design phase. Just as the operating plans of each department should be driven by a unifying business strategy, your information architecture should be driven by a holistic IA strategy.

To succeed, you need a strategy that will work within the unique information ecology at hand. Based upon the results of your research into context, people, and content, you're striving to design a strategy that balances the needs and realities of each.

The information architecture strategy provides high-level recommendations regarding:

Information architecture administration
It's critical to look ahead to the end game and create a realistic strategy for developing and maintaining the information architecture. This covers the inevitable centralization versus decentralization questions that are closely tied to politics, the departmental structure, and content ownership. Are you look-

ing at a command-and-control model or a federated approach? Will your architecture deliver users to subsites or all the way through to content and applications? Can you trust content authors to apply metadata? Who will manage the controlled vocabularies?

Technology integration
The strategy must address opportunities to leverage existing tools and identify needs for additional technologies to develop or manage the information architecture. Key technology categories include search engines, content management, auto-classification, collaborative filtering, and personalization.

Top-down or bottom-up emphasis
Many factors influence where to focus your energies, including the current status of the product, the political environment, and the IA management model. For example, if there's already a solid top-down information architecture or a strong design team that "owns" the primary hierarchy, bottom up is probably the way to go.

Organization and labeling systems (top down)
This involves defining the major organization schemes for the environment (e.g., users must be able to navigate by product, by task, and by customer category) and then identifying the dominant organization scheme to serve as the primary hierarchy.

Document type identification (bottom up)
This involves identifying a suite of document and object types (e.g., article, report, white paper, financial calculator, online course module) and requires close collaboration with the content authoring and management teams.

Metadata field definition
This entails the definition of administrative, structural, and descriptive metadata fields. Some fields may be global (i.e., applied to every document), others may be local (i.e., applied only to documents within a particular subsite), and others may be associated only with a particular document type (e.g., for every news article, we need to identify the headline).

Navigation system design
The strategy must explain how the integrated and supplemental navigation systems will leverage the top-down and bottom-up

strategies. For example, search zones may allow users to leverage the top-down product hierarchy, while fielded searching may allow users to search for a particular white paper. This may also cover implications for customization and personalization capabilities.

While this may seem like a lot to cover, it's certainly not an exhaustive list. Each information ecology will place unique demands on you regarding what to include in the strategy and where to place emphasis. As always, you'll have to be creative and use good judgment.

The strategy is typically detailed in an information architecture strategy report, communicated in a high-level strategy presentation, and made actionable through a project plan for information architecture design. However, it's important to avoid placing too much focus on creating the perfect deliverables. Ultimately, an information architecture strategy must find understanding and acceptance within the minds of the designers, developers, authors, stakeholders, and anyone else involved in designing, building, and maintaining the product. Getting people to buy into your vision is critical to success.

Strategies Under Attack

While we're on the topic of buy-in, it's worth discussing some critical issues that crop up again and again when developing information architecture strategies. It's not unusual for a hostile stakeholder within a client's organization to ask the following questions during an interview:

- How can you develop an information architecture when we don't have a business strategy?

- How can you develop an information architecture before we have the content in place?

These questions can stop you in your tracks, especially when they're asked by a chief information officer or a vice president for business strategy within a Fortune 500 corporation. It's at times like that when you wish you'd read one of those books on how to deal with difficult people or how to disappear into thin air.

Fortunately, the lack of a written business plan or a complete content repository does not mean you need to fold up your sitemaps and go home. In all our years of consulting for Fortune 500 clients, we've never seen a business plan that was complete or up to date, and we've never seen a content collection that wouldn't undergo significant change within a 12-month period.

The reality is that you're dealing with a classic chicken-and-egg problem. There are no clean answers to the questions:

- What comes first, the business strategy or the information architecture?
- What comes first, the content or the information architecture?

Business strategies, content collections, and information architectures don't exist in a vacuum, and they don't hatch from the egg fully formed. They co-evolve in a highly interactive manner.

Developing an information architecture strategy is a wonderful way to expose gaps in business strategies and content collections. The process forces people to make difficult choices that they've thus far managed to avoid. Seemingly simple questions about organization and labeling issues can often set off a ripple effect that impacts business strategy or content policy. For example:

Innocent question posed by the designer:
   "In trying to design the hierarchy for this Consumers Energy website, I'm having a really hard time creating a structure that accommodates the content of Consumers Energy and its parent company, CMS Energy. Are you sure we shouldn't provide two different hierarchies and separate the content?"

Long-term implication of asking this question:
   This simple question started a discussion that led to a business decision to build two separate websites, providing a unique online identity and unique content collections for the two organizations:

   - *http://www.consumersenergy.com/*
   - *http://www.cmsenergy.com/*

This decision has held up over time. Go ahead and check the URLs.

There's a similar bidirectional relationship between business strategy and content policy. For example, a colleague of ours was involved in the information architecture design of the Australian Yellow Pages. The business strategy was focused on increasing revenues by introducing banner advertising. It soon became obvious that the content policy was a key factor in executing this strategy, and the strategy ultimately led to real success.

Ideally, you should work directly with the business strategy and content policy teams, exploring and defining the relationships between these three critical areas. Just as the business strategists and content managers should be open to the possibility that the development of an information architecture strategy may expose gaps or introduce new opportunities in their areas, you need to remember (and remind others) that the information architecture strategy is not set in stone either. As interaction designers and programmers become involved in later phases of the project, their work may expose gaps and introduce opportunities for improving the information architecture as well.

From Research to Strategy

You should start considering possible strategies for structuring and organizing the information environment before the research even begins. During the research phase, throughout the user interviews, content analysis, and benchmarking studies, you should be constantly testing and refining the hypotheses already in your head against the steady stream of data you're compiling. If you're really committed (or ready to be committed, depending on how you look at it), you'll be wrestling with organization structures and labeling schemes in the shower. By the way, that's a great place for a whiteboard!

In any case, you should never wait until the strategy phase to start thinking and talking within your team about strategy—that's a given. The more difficult timing issue involves deciding when to begin articulating, communicating, and testing your ideas about possible strategies. When do you create your first conceptual sitemaps and wireframes? When do you share them with clients? When do you test your assumptions in user interviews?

As usual, there's no easy answer. The research phase exists to challenge your (and everyone else's) preconceived notions regarding content, context, and users. You need a structured methodology in place to create the necessary space for learning. However, you'll reach a point in the research process when you begin to experience the law of diminishing returns. You're no longer learning anything new by asking the same questions in open-ended user interviews, and you're anxious to flesh out one or two hierarchies and start introducing your structures and labels to users, clients, and colleagues.

Whether or not the timing corresponds with the formal project plan, this is the point when you move from research to strategy. The emphasis shifts from open-ended learning to designing and testing. While you can continue to use research methodologies as you move through this phase, your focus should shift to articulating your ideas through visuals (conceptual sitemaps and wireframes), sharing those visuals with clients and colleagues in strategy meetings, and testing your organization structures and labeling schemes with users.

Developing the Strategy

The transition from research to strategy involves a shift from a primary focus on process to a balance between process and product. Methodology is still important, but the work products and deliverables you create by applying that methodology move toward the center of attention.

Moving from a mode of absorption to one of creation is often a difficult transition. No matter how much qualitative or quantitative research you've done, the development of an information architecture strategy is inherently a creative process, with all the associated messiness, frustration, pain, and fun.

Figure 12-2 presents an outline of the strategy development process and the resulting deliverables. Note the preponderance of arrows—this is a highly iterative and interactive process. Let's take a look at the four steps along the path: think, articulate, communicate, and test (TACT).

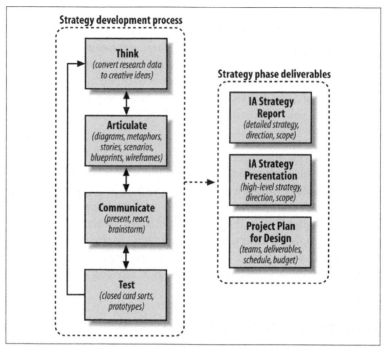

Figure 12-2. Developing the information architecture strategy with TACT

Think

The human mind is the ultimate black box. Nobody really understands the process by which input (e.g., research data) is converted into output (e.g., creative ideas). Our advice is to use whatever works best for you. Some people think best by themselves, while taking a long walk or doodling on a pad of paper. Others think best in a group setting. The key is to recognize that you need to create some time and space to digest all that you've learned during research and become ready to be productive.

Articulate

As your ideas begin to form, it's important to begin articulating them. It's best to start informally, scribbling diagrams and notes on paper or a whiteboard. Stay away from visual design software at this point; otherwise, you'll waste energy on layout and formatting when you should be focused on developing your ideas.

Once again, some people work best alone whereas others need a sounding board. We've seen teams of two or three designers work well together to flesh out ideas, collaborating around design of high-level visuals on a whiteboard. We've also seen environments where teams of eight or more people from a variety of backgrounds lock themselves in a room for day-long "collaborative design workshops." In our experience, these have been highly inefficient, unproductive exercises that lead to groupthink and exhaustion. Large group meetings may be good for brainstorming and sharing reactions, but not for designing complex systems.

Communicate

Eventually, you'll make the shift from creating ideas to communicating them. You'll need to identify the most effective ways to communicate these particular ideas to your target audience. Your toolbox may include metaphors, stories, use case scenarios, conceptual diagrams, sitemaps, wireframes, reports, and presentations. Let form follow function, selecting the right communication tools for your purpose.

It's often best to begin with informal communications with "safe" colleagues who will help you refine your ideas and build your confidence. You can then share your draft work products with "unsafe" colleagues, those people you can count on to ask hard questions and poke holes. This process should help you to develop your ideas (and confidence) so you're ready to present them to a broader group of clients or colleagues.

We've learned through much experience that it's good to communicate your ideas early and often. Many of us have a natural aversion to sharing partially formed ideas—our egos don't like the risk. One way to reduce your own sense of exposure is to suggest that this is a "strawman" work product, intended to provoke reactions and jump-start discussion. This explicit disclaimer will help everyone feel comfortable presenting and discussing alternate viewpoints and hopefully moving toward consensus. By proactively taking this collaborative approach, you'll end up with a better information architecture strategy and more agreement from your clients and colleagues.

Test

Whether you're operating on a shoestring budget or have a multimillion-dollar project, there's no excuse for not testing your ideas before you lock into an information architecture strategy. Even running an informal usability test on a friend is better than nothing.

Many of the methodologies covered during the research phase can be applied with minor modification to the testing of possible strategies. For example, you might present your draft work products to a few opinion leaders and stakeholders to make sure you're on the right track in terms of business context. Similarly, you might test your model against documents and applications not included in the content analysis sample to make sure your strategy will accommodate the full breadth and depth of content. However, we've found the most valuable methods for testing at this stage of the game to be variations of card sorting and task performance analysis.

Closed card sorting provides a great way to observe user reactions to your high-level organization and labeling schemes. Create "category cards" for each of your high-level categories, using your recommended category labels. Then select a few items that belong in each of those categories. You may want to run this exercise a few times with items at differing levels of granularity (e.g., second-level category labels, destination documents and applications). Jumble up the cards and ask users to sort them into the appropriate categories. As users perform this exercise and think out loud, you'll get a sense of whether your categories and labels are working for them.

Task performance analysis is also a useful approach. Rather than testing users' abilities to navigate the existing website as you did during research, you can now create paper or interactive prototypes for users to navigate. Designing these prototype tests can be tricky; you need to think carefully about what you want to test and how you can construct the test to yield trustworthy results.

At one end of the spectrum, you may want to isolate the high-level information architecture (e.g., categories, labels) from the interface components (e.g., graphic design, layout). You can get close to this ideal of testing the pure information architecture by presenting users with hierarchical menus and asking them to find some content or perform a task. For example, you could ask the user to find the current stock price of Cisco by navigating the following series of hierarchies:

- Arts & Humanities
- Business & Economy
- Computers & Internet

Of course, it's impossible to completely escape interface design implications. Simply deciding how to order these categories (e.g., alphabetically, by importance, or by popularity) will impact the results. More significantly, when presenting hierarchies, you need to make an interface decision regarding the presentation of sample second-level categories. Research shows that the presentation of second-level categories can substantially increase users' abilities to understand the contents of a major category. By adding second-level categories, you can increase the "scent" of information:[1]

- Arts & Humanities
- Literature, Photography, etc.
- Business & Economy
- B2B, Finance, Shopping, Jobs, etc.
- Computers & Internet
- Internet, WWW, Software, Games, etc.

Advantages of these stripped-down information architecture prototype tests include:

- Very little work is necessary to build the prototypes.
- The tests ensure that users focus primarily on information architecture and navigation rather than interface.

Disadvantages include:

- You risk thinking you've isolated information architecture from interface when you really haven't.
- You miss the opportunity to see how the interface might alter the users' experience of the information architecture.

---

1 The notion of *information scent* comes from an information-foraging theory developed at Xerox PARC.

At the other end of the spectrum is the fully designed interactive prototype. In most situations, this testing occurs later in the process. Developing these prototypes requires a great deal of work, some of it involving interface designers and software developers. Additionally, the tests themselves introduce so many variables that you often lose the ability to learn about user reactions to the information architecture.

We often run a combination of tests, some aimed at isolating pure hierarchy and some that use simple wireframes. Wireframes are not fully designed prototypes, but they do allow us to see how users interact with the information architecture when it's embedded within the broader context of a web page, as illustrated in Figure 12-3.

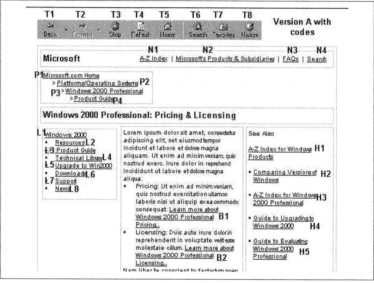

Figure 12-3. Sample wireframe with codes for tracking user choices during paper prototype testing

Ideally, these tests will validate the information architecture strategy that you've developed. Realistically, they will help you to identity problems with your strategy and provide some insight into refining that strategy.

Remember that strategy development should be an iterative process. Within the parameters of budget and schedule, the more you can move from "think" to "articulate" to "communicate" to "test" and back again, the more confident you'll be that your information architecture strategy is on the right track. You should also be prepared to encounter pushback from clients or colleagues who may balk at iterating on strategic direction. This is to be expected, yet risky, because it could lead to "safe" strategies that are either too high level or too vague to be of much use.

Work Products and Deliverables

Throughout this chapter, we've referred to a variety of work products and deliverables (e.g., sample architectures, organizational schemes, and labeling systems) that may prove useful in communicating an information architecture strategy. Let's explore the advantages, disadvantages, and proper uses of a few.

Metaphor Exploration

Metaphor is a powerful tool for communicating complex ideas and generating enthusiasm. By suggesting creative relationships or mapping the familiar onto the new, metaphors can be used to explain, excite, and persuade.[2] In 1992, vice-presidential candidate Al Gore popularized the term "information superhighway."[3] This term mapped the familiar metaphor of the physical highway infrastructure of the United States onto the new and unfamiliar concept of a national information infrastructure. Gore used this metaphor to excite the voters about his vision for the future. Although the term is oversimplified and went on to be horribly overused, it did inspire people to learn about and discuss the importance and direction of the global Internet.

Many types of metaphors can be applied in the design of information environments. Let's look at three of the most important ones:

---

2 For more about the use of metaphor, read George Lakoff and Mark Johnson's *Metaphors We Live By* (Chicago: University of Chicago Press, 2003).

3 According to Mark Stefik's *Internet Dreams: Archetypes, Myths, and Metaphors* (Cambridge, MA: MIT Press, 1997), "The information superhighway metaphor goes back to at least 1988, when Robert Kahn proposed building a high-speed national computer network he often likened to the interstate highway system."

Organizational metaphors

These leverage familiarity with one system's organization to convey quick understanding of a new system's organization. For example, when you visit an automobile dealership, you must choose to enter new car sales, used car sales, repairs and services, or parts and supplies. People have a mental model of how dealerships are organized. If you're creating a website for an automobile dealership, it may make sense to employ an organizational metaphor that draws from this model.

Functional metaphors

These make a connection between the tasks you can perform in a traditional environment and those you can perform in the new environment. For example, when you enter a traditional library, you can browse the shelves, search the catalog, or ask a librarian for help. Many library websites present these tasks as options for users, thereby employing a functional metaphor.

Visual metaphors

These leverage familiar graphic elements such as images, icons, and colors to create a connection to the new elements. For example, an online directory of business addresses and phone numbers might use a yellow background and telephone icons to invoke a connection with the familiar print-based yellow pages.

The process of metaphor exploration can really get the creative juices flowing. Working with your clients or colleagues, begin to brainstorm ideas for metaphors that might apply to your project. Think about how those metaphors might apply in organizational, functional, and visual ways. How would you organize a virtual bookstore, library, or museum? Is your environment similar to any of these? What are the differences? What tasks should users be able to perform? What should the site look like? You and your colleagues should really cut loose and have fun with this exercise. You'll be surprised by the brilliant ideas you come up with.

After this brainstorming session, you'll want to subject everyone's ideas to a more critical review. Start populating the rough metaphor-based architecture with random items from the expected content to see if they fit. Try one or two user scenarios to see if the metaphor holds up. While metaphor exploration is a useful process, you should not feel obligated to carry all or any of the ideas forward into the information architecture. The reality is that metaphors are great for getting ideas flowing during the conceptual design process, but can be problematic when carried forward to the product itself.

For example, the metaphor of a virtual community is one that has been taken too far in many cases. Some of these online communities have post offices, town halls, shopping centers, libraries, schools, and police stations. It becomes a real challenge for the user to figure out what types of activities take place in which "buildings." In such cases, the metaphor gets in the way of usability. You should try to ensure that any use of metaphor is empowering, not limiting.

In the early days of the Web, many sites experimented with organization schemes based on real-world metaphors. For example, when the Internet Public Library first launched (Figure 12-4), it used visual and organizational metaphors to provide access to the reference area. Users could browse the shelves or ask a question. However, the traditional library metaphor did not support integration of such things as a multiuser object-oriented environment ("MOO"), and eventually the entire site was redesigned. Applied in such a strong way, metaphors can quickly become limiting factors in architecture and design.

Figure 12-4. Metaphor use in the main page of the Internet Public Library (mid-1990s)

Also realize that people tend to fall in love with their own metaphors. Make sure everyone knows that this is just an exercise, and that it will rarely make sense to carry the metaphors into the information architecture design. For a lively discussion of the dangers of metaphor, see the chapter entitled "Metaphors, Idioms, and Affordances" in Alan Cooper et al.'s book *About Face: The Essentials of User Interface Design, Fourth Edition* (Hoboken, NJ: Wiley, 2014).

Scenarios

While architecture sitemaps are excellent tools for capturing an approach to information organization in a detailed and structured way, they do not tend to excite people. Because you want to convince your colleagues of the wisdom of your approach, you need to help them "envision" the environment as you see it in your mind's eye. Scenarios are great tools for helping people to understand how the user will navigate and experience your product, and may also help you generate new ideas for the architecture and navigation system.

To provide a multidimensional experience that shows the true potential for the environment, it is best to write a few scenarios that show how people with different needs and behaviors might navigate your product. Your user research is obviously an invaluable source of input for this process. Make sure you really take the time to wallow in the data before beginning to ask and answer these questions.

Who are the people using your product? Why and how will they want to use it? Will they be in a rush or will they want to explore? Try to select three or four major user "types," who will use the product in very different ways.[4] Based on your research, you can create a character who represents each type, giving each one a name, a profession, and a reason for using your product. Then begin to flesh out sample sessions in which those people use the product, highlighting the best features through your scenarios. If you've designed for a new customization feature, show how someone would use it.

This is a great opportunity to be creative. You'll probably find these scenarios to be easy and fun to write. And hopefully, they'll help convince your colleagues to invest in your ideas.

---

4 One popular way of doing this is through the use of *personas*, fictional people who represent typical users of the product. For more on personas, see Alan Cooper's book *The Inmates Are Running the Asylum* (Carmel, IN: Sams Publishing, 2004).

Sample scenario

Let's look at a brief sample scenario. Rosalind, a 10th grader in San Francisco, regularly visits the LiveFun website because she enjoys the interactive learning experience. She uses the site in both "investigative mode" and "serendipity mode."

For example, when her anatomy class was studying skeletal structure, she used the investigative mode to search for resources about the skeleton. She found the "interactive human skeleton" that let her test her knowledge of the correct names and functions of each bone. She bookmarked this page so she could return for a refresher the night before final exams.

When she's done with homework, Rosalind sometimes "surfs" through the site in serendipity mode. Her interest in poisonous snakes leads her to articles about how certain types of venom affect the human nervous system. One of these articles leads her into an interactive game that teaches her about other chemicals (such as alcohol) that are able to cross the blood-brain barrier. This game piques her interest in chemistry, and she switches into investigative mode to learn more.

This simple scenario shows why and how users may employ both searching and browsing within the website. More complex scenarios can be used to flesh out the possible needs of users from multiple audiences.

Case Studies and Stories

It's not easy to take a complex, abstract subject like information architecture and make it accessible to a diverse audience. When you're communicating with other designers, you can cut right to the chase, using a technical vocabulary that assumes familiarity and understanding. But when you're talking with a broader audience of clients and colleagues, you may need to be more creative in your communication approach in order to engage their interest and facilitate their understanding.

Case studies and stories can be a wonderful way to bring the concepts of information architecture to life. When trying to explain a recommended information architecture strategy, we find it very helpful to compare and contrast this case with past experiences, discussing what did and didn't work on past projects.

Conceptual Diagrams

Pictures are another way to bring abstract concepts to life. As an information architect, you often have to explain high-level concepts and systems that go beyond organization and labeling schemes.

For example, we often find ourselves needing to paint a picture of the broader information ecology within a business. When we work with an intranet team, it's not uncommon to find that they've succumbed over time to tunnel vision, seeing the intranet as the sole source of information for employees. You can tell them that this isn't true, but this really is a case where a picture is worth a thousand words.

The conceptual diagram in Figure 12-5 places the employee, rather than the intranet, at the center of the universe. The sizes of the "information clouds" roughly correspond to the importance of each resource as explained by employees during a series of user interviews. This diagram shows that people view personal networks and colleagues as the most important information resources, and see the current intranet as having relatively little value in their work lives. The diagram also presents a fragmented information environment, in which artificial boundaries of technology (media and format) or geography exist between pools of information. While it's possible to explain all of this verbally, we've found this type of visual to have a significant and lasting impact. It really gets the point across.[5]

---

5 For a more in-depth treatment of conceptual diagrams, see "How to Make a Concept Model" (*http://bit.ly/concept_model*) by Christina Wodtke.

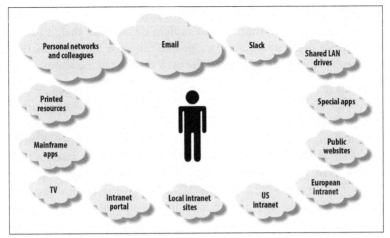

Figure 12-5. A conceptual diagram of how employees view the company's information ecology

Sitemaps and Wireframes

The collaborative brainstorming process is exciting, chaotic, and fun. However, sooner or later, you must hole up away from the crowd and begin to transform this chaos into order. Sitemaps (which show the relationships between pages and other content components) and wireframes (quick-and-dirty visuals that show the content and links of major pages on the website) are the architect's tools of choice for performing this transformation. We discuss sitemaps and wireframes in much greater detail in Chapter 13.

The Strategy Report

In our experience, this deliverable serves as the catalyst for the most detailed, comprehensive articulation of the information architecture strategy. The process of integrating the previous results, analysis, and ideas into a single written document forces tough decisions, intellectual honesty, and clear communication. Great ideas that don't fit within the broader framework must be discarded in the name of consistency and cohesiveness. Big, vague ideas must be broken down into components and explained so that all involved can understand their intention and implications.

For the design team, the strategy report is often the largest, hardest, and most important deliverable. It forces the team members to come together around a unified vision for the information architecture, and requires them to find ways to explain or illustrate that vision so that clients and colleagues (i.e., people who are not information architects) will understand what the heck they're talking about.

One of the hardest things about writing the report is organizing it. Here you face yet another chicken-and-egg problem. An information architecture strategy is not linear, but a report forces a linear presentation. "How will they understand this section if they haven't read that later section?" is a common question. There's rarely a perfect solution, but the problem can be dealt with in a couple of ways. First of all, by including high-level visuals in the report, you can paint a nonlinear big picture and follow up with linear textual explanations. Second, remember that a strategy report cannot and should not stand completely alone. You should always have an opportunity to verbally explain your ideas and answer questions. Ideally, you'll have a face-to-face information architecture strategy presentation; at a minimum, you should have a conference call to discuss reactions and answer questions.

The only thing harder and more abstract than writing an information architecture strategy report is trying to write about how to write one. To bring this subject to life, let's examine a real strategy report that Argus created for The Weather Channel (*http://www.weather.com/*) in 1999.

A Sample Strategy Report

The Weather.com website is a component of the broader Weather Channel family of services (including cable television, data and phone, radio and newspaper, and the Internet) that has provided timely weather information to the world since 1982. The Weather Channel's website is one of the most popular sites in the world, and features current conditions and forecasts for over 1,700 cities worldwide along with local and regional radars.

In 1999, The Weather Channel contracted Argus Associates to conduct research and recommend a strategy for improving the information architecture of Weather.com. Let's take a look at the table of contents of the final strategy report for this engagement (Figure 12-6).

Table of Contents

Executive Summary	1
Audiences & Mission/Vision for the Site	2
Lessons Learned from Benchmarking, User Interviews and Content Analysis	3
Local Weather Organization and Content	3
General Organization and Content	4
Navigation	5
Labeling	5
Features	6
Architectural Strategies & Approaches	7
Local Hub Architectural Strategy	8
Geographic Hub Architectural Strategy	10
Mockups of Content Areas	12
Customization & Personalization Strategy	21
Navigation Elements	25
Distributed Content Architectural Strategy	26
Content Management	31

Figure 12-6. Table of contents for the Weather.com strategy report

This table of contents should provide a rough sense of the size and scope of the strategy report. While some of our reports (including sitemaps and wireframes) have been more than 100 pages long, we encourage our teams to strive for fewer than 50. If it gets much longer than that, you run the risk that nobody will have the time or inclination to read it. The major sections of this report are fairly typical. Let's take a look at each one in turn.

Executive summary

The executive summary should provide a high-level outline of the goals and methodology, and present a 50,000-foot view of the major problems and major recommendations. The executive summary sets a tone for the entire document and should be written very carefully. It's helpful to think of this as the one page of the whole report that will be read by the big boss. You need to consider the political message you're sending, and generate enough interest to get people to continue reading.

The executive summary in Figure 12-7 does a nice job of accomplishing its objectives within one page. We were able to take such an upbeat tone because the Weather.com team was already well organized and had a fairly solid information architecture in place. This executive summary places an emphasis on recommendations for improving the information architecture to achieve greater competitive advantage.

Executive Summary

Weather.com contracted with Argus Associates, Inc. ("Argus") to develop recommendations for two top-level site architectural strategies, based on research on their audiences, competitors, content and an understanding of the company's strategic focus. Argus conducted user interviews, and performed benchmarking and content analysis to develop strategic recommendations for the site architecture.

The current Weather.com site garners huge numbers of hits and is the most recognized weather Web site on the Internet. The existing content on the site is attempting to please all audiences – those who want local weather, those who want to understand the weather, and those who only want weather information when it is convenient to get it. Although there is a great deal of valuable proprietary content, in addition to detailed weather data, it is essentially impossible to organize all of it in one site to fulfill the needs of all the audiences.

Consequently, our strategic recommendations are bi-fold:

- Develop a solid architecture that attracts and keeps users interested in accessing local weather and weather-related information, as well as providing a niche for users who want to understand more about the weather.

- Develop and promote Weather.com content for distribution to a wide variety of external sources including portals, software and hardware applications and specialized audiences. This will attract users who don't want to do much work to access the weather – convenience users – as well as users who are only interested in specific weather-related topics, e.g., gardening or stargazing.

The recommendations in this report address all 5 of the key focal areas noted as important for development of the Weather.com site:

- Making content more relevant to users – building a local hub architecture that allows users to access their local weather and related weather content from the same place.

- Improving personalization features – providing customization and personalization options that best suit weather users.

- Enhancing localization of the weather data – creating a local hub area that offers the most effective weather data, in an attracting layout.

- Developing customer loyalty – offering opportunities for users to customize weather data and content to suit their needs, distributing content to a wide variety of places outside the site and providing places for users interested in weather to talk to one another.

- Building and enhancing distribution opportunities – growing the user base by distributing Weather.com content via the Internet to a range of external sources.

By using the recommendations in this report to develop viable strategic solutions, Weather.com will be able to help all users find what they need more easily, attract a growing population of users and have these users return to the site. Weather.com is already in the lead of weather Web site development due to its branding and content – now it needs to use these recommendations to increase the narrowing gap between its site and competitor weather sites.

Figure 12-7. Executive summary for Weather.com

Audiences, mission, and vision for the site

It's important to define the audiences and goals of the site to make sure that the report (and the reader) is grounded by the broader context. This is a good place to restate the mission statement for the website.

The following is the mission statement from the Weather.com strategy report:

Weather.com will be the best weather web site on the Internet. As the dominant brand leader of weather information on the Internet, Weather.com will provide relevant, up-to-the-minute information about the weather to any user. The primary focus of the site is to provide localized weather data and value-added proprietary and exclusive weather and weather-related content, supported by significantly related non-proprietary content. Weather.com will employ technology that effectively leverages personalization and customization of content, and that allows us to meet user demands during extraordinary weather conditions.[6]

This is also a good place to define a vocabulary for discussing the roles of users and the audience segments. Figure 12-8 shows how this was accomplished for the Weather.com report.

Role	Abbreviation	Weather.com Audiences*
Care about weather only when it's convenient	Convenience	Commodity
Care about their city's forecast	My City	Planner: Scheduling, Activities
Care about other cities' forecast	Other Cities	Engaged: Caring, Tracking Planner: Scheduling, Activities
Care about weather anywhere and how it works	Understanding	Engaged: Understanding

* Taken from the Segmentation Study performed by Envision, 1996.

Figure 12-8. Audiences and roles for Weather.com

Lessons learned

This section forms the bridge between your research and analysis and your recommendations. By showing that your recommendations are grounded in the results of competitive research (benchmarking), user interviews, and content analysis, you will build confidence and credibility.

In the Weather.com report, we organized this section into five subcategories. Table 12-1 shows a sample observation from each.

---

6 Using business jargon such as "dominant brand leader" and "value-add proprietary... content" is sometimes unavoidable, but can cause confusion. As always, try to speak and write in ways that communicate clearly to your audience.

Table 12-1. Observations from the Weather.com report

Observation	Conclusion	Implications for site architecture
Local Organization and Content		
Users said they wanted to see their city's weather first. (User Interviews)	Local, local, local.	Access to local weather should be through a prominent search box and browsing via a map or links.
General Organization and Content		
On weather sites, seasonal content is often scattered among several content areas. (Benchmarking)	Ephemeral content does not live in distinct areas that have a place within the site architecture.	Topically related content should live in a discrete, devoted area, even if it is seasonal. This will assist in providing effective content management of all content areas.
Navigation		
Users couldn't decipher where local and global navigation took them within portal sites that contained weather as well as other content. (User Interviews & Benchmarking)	Weather is only a portion of the content, and consequently what would be global navigation on a devoted weather site becomes local, which confuses users.	Weather- and non-weather-related content navigation shouldn't be colocated within the navigation frame.
Observation Labeling		
Many labels didn't accurately describe the content area underneath. (Benchmarking)	Labels need to describe exactly what is under them.	Use description or scope notes to help clarify a label. Avoid colloquialism and jargon.
Features		
No weather sites are providing effective personalization; in fact, some are doing a very poor job at it. (Benchmarking)	Personalizing using anonymous tracking and content affinity is most effective.	Use Amazon as a benchmark for this. Provide options such as "the top 10 weather stories" or "the top 5 purchases made by users from Michigan." Link these from the local weather pages.

Architectural strategies and approaches

Now we get to the meat of the report—the explanation of the recommended architectural strategies and approaches. This is a fairly extensive section, so we can't include it in its entirety, but we'll present and briefly explain a few of the visuals used to illustrate the recommendations.

This report presents two strategies, *local hub* and *distributed content*, which are intended to be used in tandem. The local hub strategy centers on the fact that users are mainly focused on learning about their local weather. The conceptual blueprint in Figure 12-9 presents an information architecture built around this local hub strategy.

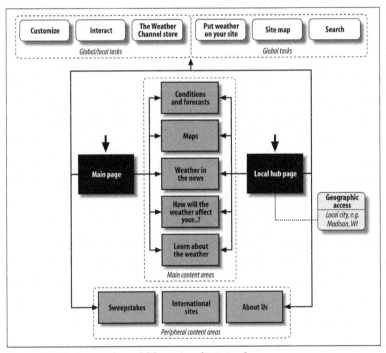

Figure 12-9. A conceptual blueprint for Weather.com

This blueprint is fairly difficult to understand without the accompanying text and context, some of which is shown in Figure 12-10. At a high level, it provides for geography-specific access (the local hub) and specifies major content areas and tasks that will ultimately be translated into navigation options on the local hub web page. These conceptual sitemaps are followed by a series of wireframes that further illustrate the key points.

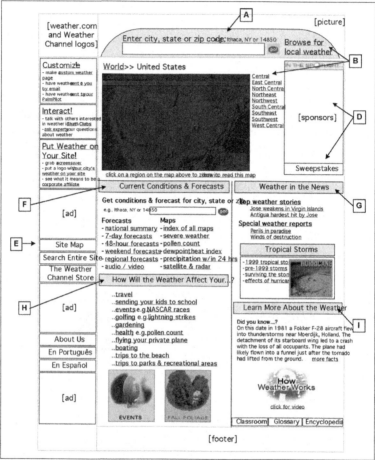

Figure 12-10. The accompanying wireframe for Weather.com

For each of the lettered callouts in the wireframe, we included a textual explanation. Table 12-2 shows two examples.

Table 12-2. Example descriptions for callouts in Weather.com wireframe

Code	Elements	Description	Implications (from lessons learned)
A	City, state, or zip code search box	Searching for local weather needs to be at the very top of the page. It should be prominent and obvious, or users will ignore it.	Access to local weather should be through a prominent search box and browsing via a map or links.
B	Find local weather (search, map, "breadcrumbs")	Users can click on the "Browse for local weather" link next to the search box, click on the map or the links to the right to access a region, or click on "World" to go up a geographic level. This allows users to navigate to weather at all levels. The map, if provided, cannot detract attention from the search box, which is the main method of access.	[Ditto]

On the other hand, the distributed content architectural strategy is centered on the fact that there are a wide variety of portals other than Weather.com through which users access weather information. For example, Yahoo! serves as a general portal for many users. Weather information is one component of a wide range of information needs for Yahoo! users.

The Weather Channel has partnerships with some of these portals, providing customized access to Weather.com content. The distributed content architectural strategy shown in Figure 12-11 presents a model for how to structure the information architecture for these partnerships.

One of the major goals of this architectural strategy is to get users to return to the place that contains all the content: the Weather.com website. When distributing content, it's not possible to offer users everything they need, so it's important to provide "teasers" to attract users to the site.

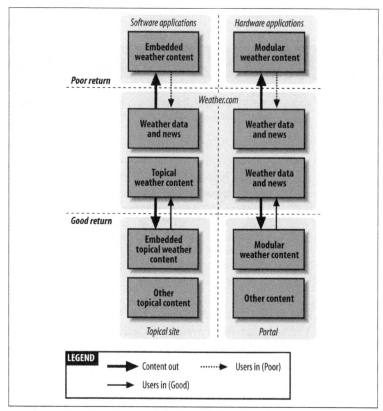

Figure 12-11. A distributed content architecture for Weather.com

This architectural diagram places emphasis on the rate of return to the Weather.com site. It makes the point that it's more likely that users will come to Weather.com from topical websites and general portals than from embedded software applications (e.g., a Java-based Miami heat index) or wireless hardware platforms (e.g., a desktop or phone).

Content management

The final section of this report provides a reality check by discussing how these information architecture recommendations will impact the content management infrastructure. Any discussion of content management is very context-sensitive, depending upon the people, technology, and content in question. If your organization has a dedicated content strategy team, you should work with them early in the process to ensure that the system's information architecture and content goals are closely aligned and support each other.[7]

In this particular report, we took a high-level pass at explaining the relationship between information architecture and content management. It begins with a brief description of the three components of effective content management, as follows:

Rules

These are the standardized, repeatable processes that help an organization manage and govern its content. Usually these are codified as workflows followed by staff to create, publish, and maintain content on the site. A workflow can be a part of, or external to, any content management software or other system that is purchased or developed. Additional process documents can include style guidelines and content standards, which are intended to help govern the creation and management of content over time.

Roles

These are the types of staff or other personnel that manage content. These people follow the processes, standards, and guidelines, as well as helping create, evangelize, and maintain them. There may be highly specified roles for people who create metadata, review or edit content, write content, act as a liaison with external content providers, or fix software when it breaks. There may be several people who have the same role (e.g., indexers, editors, or marketers).

Resources

These include the content itself in its various forms of creation, modification, or deletion, as well as the repository for holding static content and sources of dynamic data. They also include the content management software that helps facilitate the rules and roles.

We then go on to provide specific recommendations to Weather.com that might lead to more efficient content management. Here are just a few of the recommendations:

---

7 For a more in-depth treatment of content strategy, see Kristina Halvorson and Melissa Rach's *Content Strategy for the Web, Second Edition* (San Francisco: New Riders, 2012).

Templates

Much of the content that already exists on the site is dynamic data pulled from external sources (e.g., dew point, pollen count, and flight arrival times, which are all provided by external partners). Data is very well suited for templates—it's simple to build common structured pages that are used over and over for the same type of data. Paragraphs and sentences aren't as easily placed in templates because they are more variable by nature, although some document types can account for this (e.g., a news story template). Both static and dynamic content need structured navigation templates, which are a consistent frame where users can easily see the types of navigation: global, local, and contextual.

Metadata

Descriptive metadata needs to be created to more easily populate the site architecture with relevant content. For instance, each news story blurb on the "Weather in the News" main page should make use of the descriptive data shown in Table 12-3.

Table 12-3. Descriptive data for news story blurbs

Metadata element	Example
author	Terrell Johnson
publisher	Jody Fennell
title	Antigua hardest hit by Jose
date	Thu Oct 21 1999
expiration date	1031999 12:01:23
links	/news/102199/storyhtm
document type	news story, glossary term
subject area	tropical storm
keywords	Jose, Antigua, damage, intensity
related to	breaking weather, news stories, severe weather maps
geographic access levels	local city, local regional, national
geographic areas	Antigua, North Carolina, South Carolina

Thesaurus

Building a thesaurus for your metadata helps users find information more easily. For instance, if a user is unsure whether to use the term "tropical storm" or "hurricane," accessing a thesaurus can identify the preferred term. It will be useful to create thesauri for weather terms and geographic areas, as well as one that allows for normalization of the "keyword" metadata field for indexing purposes. Generally, thesauri are built for behind-the-scenes use by staff who are creating the metadata for content chunks (e.g., looking up which term to assign to a chunk), but they are also useful for helping people search and browse the site.

While this strategy report is obviously an older example, we think it illustrates well the points we've been making in this chapter. Because it is based on the Content/Context/Users framework, we can easily see how such a project could be approached differently today. Since we produced this report, the biggest change has happened to the context in which Weather.com operates. For example, mobile devices are much more popular and powerful today than they were in 1999, and as a result it can be assumed that a large percentage of users will be accessing the site using devices with much smaller screens and the ability to access the user's geographical location. The pervasiveness of social networks such as Facebook is also a contextual issue that would influence a strategy report such as this one if it were produced today. In short, the framework has stood the test of time: it's the conditions within the three categories of the framework that vary.

The Project Plan

We often find it useful to go beyond the content management discussion and actually create a project plan for information architecture design as part of the strategy phase deliverables.

This project plan can accomplish two major objectives. First, when developed in parallel with the strategy report, it forces the team to constantly ask questions such as:

- How will we accomplish that?
- How long will it take?
- Who will do it?
- What kinds of deliverables will be required?
- What are the dependencies?

This ensures that information architecture strategy is grounded in reality. The second objective of the project plan is to form the bridge between strategy and design. It can be integrated with plans from other teams (e.g., interaction design, content authoring, or application development) toward the development of a structured schedule for overall site design.

Given the common need to show some immediate progress, we usually provide short-term and long-term plans. In the short-term plan, we focus on low-hanging fruit, defining a process for design changes that can and should be made immediately to improve the information architecture. In the long-term plan, we present a methodology for fleshing out the information architecture, noting interdependencies with other teams where appropriate.

Presentations

You've done rigorous research and brilliant brainstorming. You've created a detailed, high-quality strategy report and a solid project plan. You've worked hard. You've successfully completed the strategy phase, right? Wrong!

We've learned through painful experience that information architecture deliverables can die a quiet death if they're left to fend for themselves. People are busy, have short attention spans, and generally don't enjoy reading 50-page information architecture strategy reports. Without some form of presentation and discussion, many of your best recommendations may never see the light of day.

It's often a good idea to make one or more presentations to the people who need to understand your recommendations. In some situations, this might take the form of a single presentation to the website or intranet strategy team. In other situations, you make dozens of presentations to various departments to achieve organization-wide understanding and buy-in. You need to think about these presentations from a sales perspective. Success is defined by the extent to which you can communicate and sell your ideas in a clear and compelling manner.

First, make sure you've got the basics down. Select some highlights of your recommendations that will really get the attention of the particular group you're talking to. Then, organize your thoughts into a logical order to create a smooth presentation.

After you've figured all that out, you can consider ways to bring the presentation to life. Visuals such as charts, graphs, and conceptual diagrams can make a big difference, as can the use of metaphor. Remember, you're selling ideas. Metaphor can be a powerful tool for transforming garden-variety ideas into contagious, self-replicating memes.

Consider this example. We were designing an information architecture strategy for the primary website of a Global 100 corporation. We had developed three possible strategies with the following working titles:

Umbrella Shell for Separate Hubs
Develop a broad but shallow umbrella website that directs users to independently maintained subsites or "hubs." Distributed control. Low cost, low usability.

Integrated Content Repository
Create a unified, structured database for all content, providing powerful, flexible, consistent searching and browsing. Centralized control. High cost, high usability.

Active Inter-Hub Management
Create standards for global metadata attributes, but allow for local subsite ("hub") attributes as well. Knit together with inter- and intra-hub guides. Federated model. Medium cost, medium usability.

The titles were very descriptive, but they didn't exactly roll off the tongue or stimulate interest. For our presentation, we came up with a musical metaphor that made this complex topic more fun and engaging (Table 12-4).

Table 12-4. Musical model for presenting strategy options

Model	Working title	Description	Comments
Competing boom boxes	Umbrella Shell for Separate Hubs	Whoever has the loudest music wins	The "Status Quo." Works for neither company nor customers.
Symphony	Integrated Content Repository	Many instruments acting as one; a big investment	A "Bet the Farm" approach that carries many risks.
Jazz band	Active Inter-Hub Management	A common key and beat; good teamwork; combination of tight rhythms and improvisation	Our favorite option. It provides rich functionality with less risk than the Symphony approach.

Not only can this use of metaphor make for a better immediate discussion, but people are more likely to talk about the ideas with colleagues after the presentation itself, spreading the concepts like a virus. For example, throughout this chapter we have been referring to strategy as a "bridge"—this is obviously a metaphor, meant to make abstract concepts more concrete and memorable. You, too, can use metaphors to make your strategy easier to discuss.

Now, finally, you can congratulate the visionary within you, take a brief rest, and prepare for the detail orientation of the design and documentation phase.

Recap

Let's recap what we've learned in this chapter:

- An information architecture strategy serves as a bridge between research and design.
- The IA strategy provides a high-level conceptual framework for structuring and organizing an information environment.
- You should start considering possible strategies for structuring and organizing the product before research begins.
- The main deliverable of the strategy phase is the strategy report.
- We find it useful to create a project plan for the design of the information architecture as part of the strategy phase.
- You're not done when you've created the report—you also need to present and discuss it with stakeholders.

CHAPTER 13

Design and Documentation

You can use an eraser on the drafting table
or a sledge hammer on the construction site.
—Frank Lloyd Wright

In this chapter, we'll cover:

- The role of diagrams in the design phase
- Why, when, and how to develop sitemaps and wireframes, the two most common types of IA diagrams
- How to map and inventory your content
- Content models and controlled vocabularies for connecting and managing granular content
- Ways to enhance your collaboration with other members of the design team
- Style guides for capturing your past decisions and guiding your future ones

When you cross the bridge from research and strategy into design, the landscape shifts dramatically. The emphasis moves from process to deliverables as your clients and colleagues expect you to move from thinking and talking to actually producing a clear, well-defined information architecture.

This can be an uneasy transition. You must relinquish the white lab coat of the researcher, leave behind the ivory tower of the strategist, and delve into the exposed territory of creativity and design. As you commit your ideas to paper, it can be scary to realize there's no going back. You are now actively shaping what will become the user experience. Your fears and discomforts will be diminished if you've had the time and resources to do the research and develop a strategy; if you're pushed straight into design (as is too often the case), you'll be entering the uncertain realm of intuition and gut instinct.

It's difficult to write about design because the work in this phase is so strongly defined by context and influenced by tacit knowledge. You may be working closely with a graphic designer to create a small website or app from the ground up. Or you may be building a controlled vocabulary and index as part of an enterprise-level redesign of a broad information environment that involves more than a hundred people. The design decisions you make and the deliverables you produce will be informed by the total sum of your experience.

In short, we're talking about the creative process. Ours is a vast, complex, and ever-changing canvas. Often, the best way to teach art is through the time-tested practice of show-and-tell. So, in this chapter, we'll use work products and deliverables to tell the story about what we do during the design phase.

Before we dive in, here's a caveat: although this chapter focuses on deliverables, process is as important during design as it is during research and strategy. This means that the techniques covered previously should be applied to these later phases, albeit with more concrete and detailed artifacts—ranging from vocabularies to wireframes to working prototypes—being tested.

And another caveat: for reasons beyond your control, you'll occasionally—even frequently—find yourself in the uncomfortable situation of bypassing research and strategy altogether, skipping headlong into the abyss of design. Deliverables are especially critical in this context; they're anchors that, by forcing the team to pause, capture, and review its work, regulate and moderate an out-of-control project. You can also use deliverables to unmask design problems and force the project to backtrack to research and design tasks that should have been handled much earlier.

Guidelines for Diagramming an Information Architecture

We are under extreme pressure to clearly represent the product of our work. Whether it's to help sell the value of information architecture to a potential client or to explain a design to a colleague, we rely upon visual representations to communicate what it is we actually do.

And yet information architectures—as we've mentioned many times—are abstract, conceptual things. Websites, in particular, are not finite; often you can't tell where one ends and the other begins. Subsites and the "invisible web" of databases further muddy the picture of what should and shouldn't be included in a specific architecture. Digital information itself can be organized and repurposed in an almost infinite number of ways, meaning that an architecture is typically multidimensional—and therefore exceedingly difficult to represent in a two-dimensional space such as a whiteboard or a sheet of paper.

So we're left with a nasty paradox: we're forced to demonstrate the value and essence of our work in a visual medium, though our work itself isn't especially visual.

There really is no ideal solution. The field of information architecture is too young and dynamic for its practitioners to have figured out how best to visually represent information architectures, much less agree upon a standard set of diagrams that work for all audiences in all situations.[1] And it's unlikely that the messages we wish to communicate will ever lend themselves easily to 8.5″ × 11″ sheets of paper.

Still, there are a couple of good guidelines to follow as you document your architecture:

---

[1] For an in-depth look at deliverables, we recommend Dan Brown's *Communicating Design: Developing Web Site Documentation for Design and Planning, Second Edition* (San Francisco: New Riders, 2010). Dan is an information architect whose work is highly respected by many practitioners.

Provide multiple "views" of an information architecture

Information environments are too complex to show all at once; a diagram that tries to be all things to all people is destined to fail. Instead, consider using a variety of techniques to display different aspects of the architecture. No single view takes in the whole picture, but the combination of multiple diagrams might come close.

Develop those views for specific audiences and needs

You might find that a visually stunning diagram is compelling to client prospects, therefore justifying its expense. However, it probably requires too many resources to use in a production environment, where diagrams may change multiple times per day. Whenever possible, determine what others need from your diagrams before creating them. For example, Keith Instone, an information architect formerly at IBM, created very different diagrams for communicating "upstream" with stakeholders and executives than for communicating "downstream" with designers and developers.

Whenever possible, present information architecture diagrams in person, especially when the audience is unfamiliar with them. If you can't be there in person, at least be there via videoconference or telephone. Again and again, we've witnessed (and suffered from) huge disconnects between what the diagram was intended to communicate and what it was actually understood to mean. This shouldn't be surprising, because, as we mentioned, there is no standard visual language to describe information architectures yet. So, be present to translate, explain, and (if necessary) defend your work.

Better yet, work in advance with whomever you're presenting your diagrams to—clients, managers, designers, programmers—so they can understand what they will need from them. You may find that your assumptions of how they would use your diagrams were quite wrong. We've seen a large, respected firm fired from a huge project because it took too many weeks to produce bound, color-printed, sexy diagrams. The client preferred (and requested) simple, even hand-drawn, sketches because it needed them as soon as possible.

As we've seen in previous chapters, the most frequently used diagrams are sitemaps and wireframes, which focus more on the structure of content than its semantic value. Because of this, sitemaps and wireframes are not as effective at conveying the semantic nature of content or labels. We'll discuss both types of diagrams in detail in the following sections, but first it's helpful to understand the visual language that these diagrams use.

Communicating Visually

Diagrams are useful for communicating the two basic aspects of an information system's structural elements.[2] Diagrams define:

Content components
> What constitutes a unit of content, and how those components should be grouped and sequenced

Connections between content components
> How content components are linked to enable actions such as navigating between them

No matter how complex your diagrams may ultimately become, their main goal will always be to communicate what your information environment's content components are and how they're connected.

A variety of visual vocabularies have emerged to help convey the complexity of information architecture in visual diagrams, each providing a clear set of terms and syntax to visually communicate components and their links. The best known and most influential visual vocabulary is Jesse James Garrett's (*http://www.jjg.net/ia/visvocab*), which has been translated into eight languages. Jesse's vocabulary anticipates and accommodates many uses, but perhaps the greatest reason for its success is its simplicity; just about anyone can use it to create diagrams, even by hand.

Visual vocabularies are at the heart of the many templates used to develop sitemaps and wireframes. Thanks to their developers' generosity, there are many free templates you can use to create your own deliverables; Table 13-1 provides useful examples. Each requires one of the common charting programs, like Microsoft's Visio (for Windows PCs) or Omni Group's OmniGraffle (for Macs).

---

2 Semantic aspects, like controlled vocabularies, don't lend themselves as easily to visual representation.

Table 13-1. Templates for common diagramming tools

Name	Creator	Application	URL
OmniGraffle Wireframe Stencils	Michael Angeles	OmniGraffle	*http://bit.ly/omnigraffle_wireframe*
Sitemap Stencil	Nick Finck	Visio	*http://www.nickfinck.com/stencils.html*
Wireframe Stencil	Nick Finck	Visio	*http://www.nickfinck.com/stencils.html*
Block Diagram Shapes Stencil	Matt Leacock, Bryce Glass, and Rich Fulcher	OmniGraffle	*http://www.paperplane.net/omnigraffle/*
Flow Map Shapes Stencil	Matt Leacock, Bryce Glass, and Rich Fulcher	OmniGraffle	*http://www.paperplane.net/omnigraffle/*

What if you're a nonvisual person who cringes at the idea of learning OmniGraffle? Or the people you're communicating your ideas to aren't visually oriented? Does your work *have* to be visual?

Absolutely not. As ugly as the results may be, you can render your sitemaps as outlines in a word processor or use a spreadsheet's cells in a similar fashion. You can write page descriptions that cover the same bases as your wireframes—just about anything can be rendered in text. Ultimately, these deliverables are first and foremost communication tools. You need to play to your own communication strengths and, more importantly, take advantage of whatever style works best for your audience.

But remember, there's a reason they say "a picture is worth a thousand words." The lines between information architecture and the more visual aspects of design are blurry, and at some point, you'll have to connect your IA concepts, however textual, to the work that is the responsibility of graphic designers and interaction designers. Hence, we spend most of our time in this chapter on visual means for communicating information architectures.

Sitemaps

Sitemaps show the relationships between information elements such as pages and other content components, and can be used to portray organization, navigation, and labeling systems. Both the diagram and the navigation system display the "shape" of the information space in overview, functioning as a condensed map for site developers and users, respectively.

High-Level Architecture Sitemaps

High-level sitemaps are often created as part of a top-down information architecture process (and they may also be produced during a project's strategy phase.) Starting with the main page, you might use the process of developing a sitemap to iteratively flesh out more and more of the architecture, adding subsidiary sections, increasing levels of detail, and working out the navigation from the top down. Sitemaps can also support bottom-up design, such as displaying a content model's content chunks and relationships; we discuss these uses later in the chapter.

The very act of shaping ideas into the more formal structure of a sitemap forces you to be realistic and practical. If brainstorming takes you to the top of the mountain, creating the sitemap can bring you back down to the valley of reality. Ideas that seemed brilliant on the whiteboard may not pan out when you attempt to organize them in a practical manner. It's easy to throw around concepts such as "personalization" and "adaptive information architectures." It's not so easy to define on paper exactly how these concepts will be applied to a specific product.

During the design phase, high-level sitemaps are most useful for exploring primary organization schemes and approaches. High-level sitemaps map out the organization and labeling of major areas, usually beginning with a bird's-eye view from the main page of the website. This exploration may involve several iterations as you further define the information architecture.

High-level sitemaps (like the one in Figure 13-1) are great for stimulating discussions focused on the organization and management of content as well as on the desired access pathways for users. These sitemaps can be drawn by hand, but we prefer to use diagramming software such as Visio or OmniGraffle. These tools not only help you to quickly lay out your architecture sitemaps, but can also help with site implementation and administration. They also lend your work a more professional look, which, sadly, can sometimes be more important than the quality of your actual design.

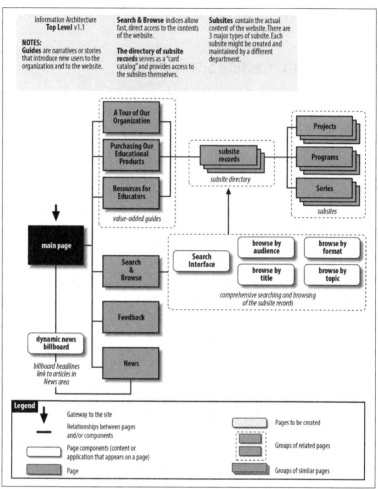

Figure 13-1. A high-level sitemap

Let's walk through the sitemap in Figure 13-1 as if we were presenting it to clients or colleagues. The building block of this architecture is the subsite. Within this company, the ownership and management of content is distributed among many individuals in different departments. There are already dozens of small and large websites, each with its own graphic identity and information architecture. Rather than trying to enforce one standard across this collection of sites, this sitemap suggests an "umbrella architecture" approach that allows for the existence of lots of heterogeneous subsites.

Moving up from the subsites, we see a directory of subsite records. This directory serves as a "card catalog" that provides easy access to the subsites. There is a record for each subsite; each record consists of fields such as *title*, *description*, *keywords*, *audience*, *format*, and *topic*, which describe the contents of that subsite.

By creating a standardized record for each subsite, we are actually creating a database of subsite records. This database approach enables both powerful known-item searching and exploratory browsing. As you can see from the Search & Browse page, users can search and browse by title, audience, format, and topic.

The sitemap also shows three guides. These guides take the form of simple narratives or "stories" that introduce new users to the site's sponsor and selected areas within the website.

Finally, we see a dynamic news billboard that rotates the display of featured news headlines and announcements. In addition to bringing some action to the main page, this billboard provides yet another way to access important content that might otherwise be buried within a subsite.

At this point in the discussion of the high-level sitemap, you are sure to face some questions. As you can see, sitemaps don't completely speak for themselves, and that's exactly what you want. High-level sitemaps are an excellent tool for explaining your architectural approaches and making sure that they're challenged by your client or manager. Questions such as "Do those guides really make sense, considering the company's new plans to target customers by region?" give you an excellent opportunity to gain buy-in from the client and to fireproof your design from similar questions that might arise much later in the process, when it'll be more expensive to make changes.

Presenting sitemaps in person allows you to immediately answer questions and address concerns, as well as to explore new ideas while they're still fresh. You might also consider augmenting your sitemaps with a brief text document to explain your thinking and answer the most likely questions right on the spot. At the very least, consider providing a "Notes" area (as we do in this example) to briefly explain basic concepts.

Digging Deeper into Sitemaps

As you create sitemaps, it's important to avoid getting locked into a particular type of layout. Instead, let form follow function. Notice the difference between Figures 13-2 and 13-3.

Figure 13-2 provides a holistic view of the information architecture for a global consulting firm. It's part of an initiative to build support for the overall vision of unified access to member firms' content and services. In contrast, Figure 13-3 focuses on a single aspect of navigation for The Weather Channel's website, aiming to show how users will be able to move between local and national weather reports and news. Both sitemaps are high level and conceptual in nature, yet each takes on a unique form to suit its purpose.

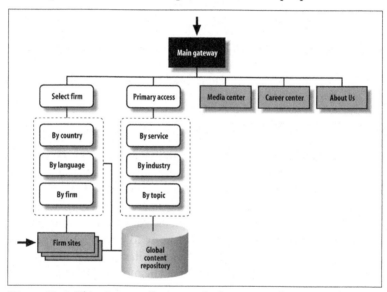

Figure 13-2. This sitemap illustrates the big picture for a consulting firm's public site...

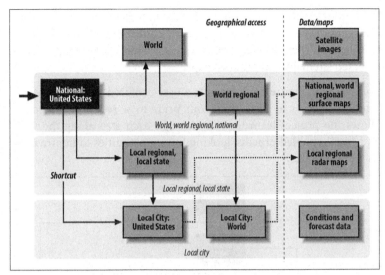

Figure 13-3. ...while this one focuses on geographic hub navigation for The Weather Channel's site...

In Figure 13-4, we see a high-level sitemap for the online greeting card website Egreetings.com. This sitemap focuses on the user's ability to filter cards based on format or tone at any level while navigating the primary taxonomy.

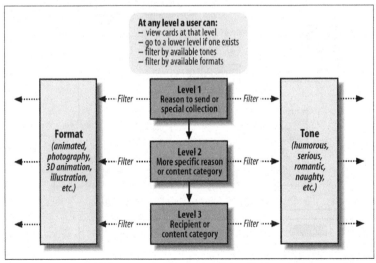

Figure 13-4. ...and this one demonstrates how filtering might work at Egreetings.com

It's important to remind ourselves that information environments aren't just about content; we can also contribute to the design of transactional and task-centered systems. This work requires task-oriented sitemaps and process maps.

For example, Figure 13-5 presents a user-centered view of the card-sending process at Egreetings.com prior to a redesign project. It allows the project team to walk through each step along the web- and email-enabled process, looking for opportunities to improve the user experience.

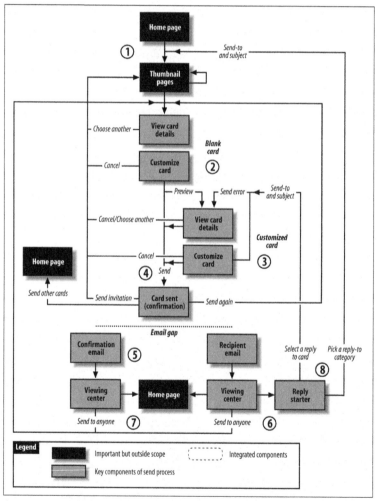

Figure 13-5. A task-oriented sitemap of the card-sending process

Figure 13-6 demonstrates how casual browsers may become engaged in a political campaign over time by interacting with its website's content. This sitemap is as much about changes in the user's mind as it is descriptive of the site's content and navigation.

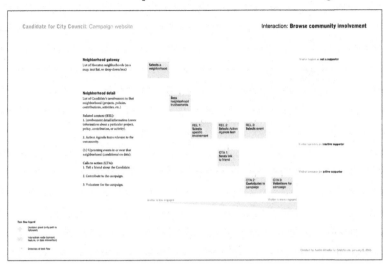

Figure 13-6. A sitemap by Austin Govella depicting growing levels of engagement in a political candidate's campaign

You'll notice that as we dug deeper, we moved from high-level sitemaps toward diagrams that isolated specific aspects of the architecture, rather than communicating the overall direction of the site. Sitemaps are incredibly flexible; while boxes and connectors can't communicate everything about a design, they are simple enough that just about anyone can both develop and understand them.

You should also note that all of these sitemaps leave out quite a bit of information. They focus on the major areas and structures of the site, ignoring many navigation elements and page-level details. These omissions are by design, not by accident. Remember the rule of thumb for sitemaps: less is more.

Keeping Sitemaps Simple

As a project moves from strategy to design to implementation, sitemaps become more utilitarian. At this stage, they are focused more on communicating the information architecture to others involved in design and development, and less on strategy and product definition. "Lower-level" sitemaps need to be produced and modified quickly and iteratively, and often draw input from an increasing number of perspectives, ranging from visual designers to editors to programmers. Those team members need to be able to understand the architecture, so it's important to develop a simple, condensed vocabulary of objects that can be explained in a brief legend. See Figure 13-7 for an example.

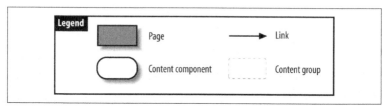

Figure 13-7. This sitemap legend describes an intentionally simple vocabulary

In this figure, the legend describes three levels of content granularity. The coarsest are content groups (made up of pages); these are followed by the pages themselves. Content components are the finest-grained content that it makes sense to represent in a sitemap. The arrow describes a link between content objects; these can be one-way or bidirectional links.

This is a minimal set of objects; we've found that retaining a limited vocabulary helps us avoid the temptation of overloading the diagram with too much information. After all, other diagrams can be used to convey other views of the architecture more effectively.

Detailed Sitemaps

As you move deeper into the implementation stage, your focus naturally shifts from external to internal. Rather than communicating high-level architectural concepts to the client, your job is now to communicate detailed organization, labeling, and navigation decisions to your colleagues on the development team. In the world of "physical" architecture, this shift can be likened to architecture versus construction. You may work closely with the client to make big-picture decisions about the layout of rooms and the location of windows; however, decisions regarding the size of nails or the routing of the plumbing typically do not involve the client. And in fact, such minutiae often need not involve the architect either.

As with physical architecture, these small details often change on the construction site: perhaps the client has changed her mind about the size of her home office, or an electrical fixture is inconveniently located in the kitchen and must be moved. In any case, change is to be expected when abstract diagrams meet the real conditions of the construction site. In our field, agile and lean development methods call for rapid iteration, often based on incomplete information. Detailed sitemaps can (and should) evolve along with the rest of the design to address the new conditions and requirements that come up during the development process in these types of projects.

That said, you should try to map out the entire environment so that the production team can implement your plans as closely as possible when starting the development process. These sitemaps must present the complete information hierarchy from the main page to the destination pages. They must also detail the labeling and navigation systems to be implemented in each area of the environment.

Sitemaps will vary from project to project, depending upon the scope. On smaller projects, the primary audience for your sitemaps may be one or two graphic designers responsible for integrating the architecture, design, and content. On larger projects, the primary audience may be a technical team responsible for integrating the architecture, design, and content through a database-driven process. Let's consider a few examples to see what sitemaps communicate and how they might vary.

Figure 13-8 shows a sitemap from the SIGGRAPH 96 Conference that introduces several concepts. By assigning a unique identification number (e.g., 2.2.5.1) to each component (e.g., pages and content chunks), the diagram presents the groundwork for an organized production process, ideally involving a database system that populates the website structure with content.

There is a distinction between a local and a remote page in Figure 13-8. A local page is a child of the main page on that sitemap, and inherits characteristics such as graphic identity and navigation elements from its parent. In this example, the Papers Committee page inherits its color scheme and navigation system from the Papers main page. On the other hand, a remote page belongs to another branch of the information hierarchy. The Session Room Layout page has a graphic identity and navigation system that are unique to the Maps area of the website.

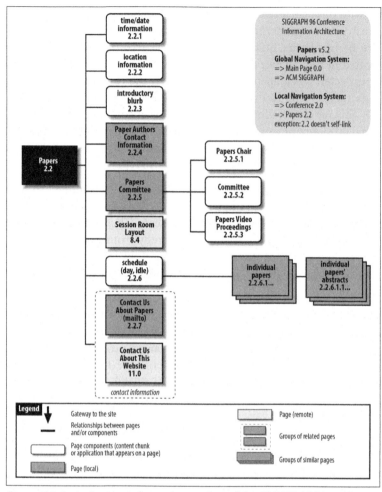

Figure 13-8. A sitemap of a major section of the SIGGRAPH conference website

Another important concept is that of content components or
chunks. To meet the needs of the production process, it is often necessary to separate the content (i.e., chunks) from the container (i.e.,
pages). Content chunks such as "Contact Us About Papers" and
"Contact Us About This Website" are sections of content composed
of one or more paragraphs that can stand alone as independent
packages of information. (We'll discuss content chunking in more
detail later in this chapter.) The rectangle that surrounds these content chunks indicates that they are closely related. By taking this

approach, the architect provides the designer with flexibility in defining the layout. Depending upon the space each content chunk requires, the designer may choose to present all of these chunks on one page, or create a closely knit collection of pages.

You may also decide to communicate the navigation system using these detailed sitemaps. In some cases, arrows can be used to show navigation, but these can be confusing and are easily missed by the production staff. A sidebar is often the best way of communicating both global and local navigation systems, as shown in Figure 13-8. The sidebar in the upper right of this sitemap explains how the global and local navigation systems apply to this area of the website.

Organizing Your Sitemaps

As the architecture is developed, it needs to accommodate more than top-level pages. The same simple notation can be used, but how can you squeeze all of these documents onto one sheet of paper? Many applications will allow you to print on multiple sheets, but you'll find yourself spending more time taping sheets together than designing. And if a diagram is too large to print on a single sheet, it's probably also too large to reasonably view and edit on a standard monitor.

In this case, we suggest *modularizing* the sitemap. The top-level site-map links to subsidiary sitemaps, and so on, and so on. These diagrams are tied together through a scheme of unique IDs. For example, in the top-level diagram in Figure 13-9, major pages are numbered x.0. For instance, the one representing "Committees and officers" is numbered 4.0. That page becomes the "lead page" on a new diagram (Figure 13-10), where it is also numbered 4.0. Its sub-sidiary pages and content components use codes starting with 4.0 in order to link them with their parent.

Using a unique identification scheme to tie together multiple diagrams helps us to somewhat mitigate the tyranny of the 8.5" × 11" sheet of paper, although you may still find that your architecture requires dozens of individual sheets of paper. This scheme can also be helpful for bridging a content inventory to the architectural process—content components can share the same IDs in both content inventory and sitemap. This means that in the production phase, adding content is not much different from painting by numbers.

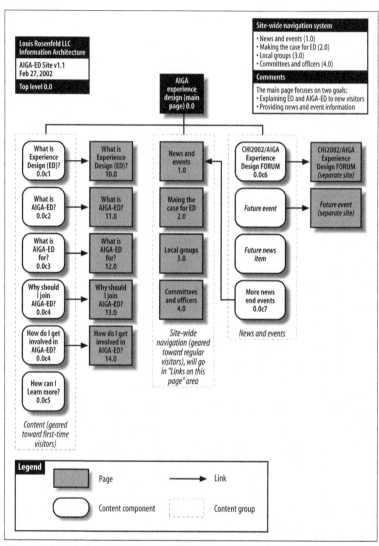

Figure 13-9. A detailed sitemap illustrating several concepts

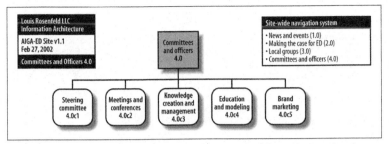

Figure 13-10. This subsidiary sitemap continues from the top-level sitemap

Wireframes

Sitemaps can help you determine where content should go and how it should be navigated within the context of a website, subsite, app, or collection of content. Wireframes serve a different role: they depict how an individual page or template should look from an architectural perspective. Wireframes connect the product's information architecture with its interaction design.

For example, the wireframe forces you to consider such issues as where the navigation systems might be located on the page or screen. And now that you see it on an early layout, does it seem that there are actually too many ways to navigate? Trying out ideas in the context of a wireframe might force you back to the sitemap's drawing board, but it's better to make such changes on paper rather than reengineering the entire system at some point in the future.

Wireframes describe the content and information architecture to be included on the relatively confined two-dimensional spaces (e.g., pages, screens). Therefore, wireframes themselves must be constrained in size. These constraints force us to make choices about what components of the architecture should be visible and accessible to users; after all, if the architectural components absorb too much screen real estate, no room will be left for actual content!

Developing wireframes also helps clarify the grouping of content components, their order, and group priority. In Figure 13-11, "Reasons to Send" is of a higher priority than the "Search Assistant." This priority is made clear by the content's prominent positioning and the use of a larger typeface for its heading.

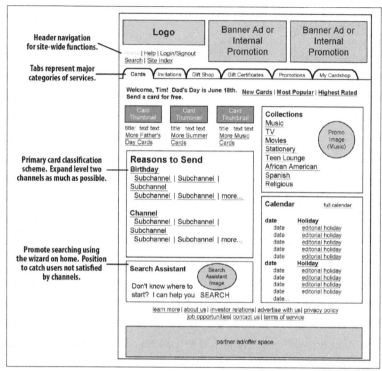

Figure 13-11. A wireframe of the main page of a greeting card site

Wireframes are typically created for the product's most important pages or screens—such as main pages, major category pages, and the interfaces to search—and other important applications. They are also used to describe templates that are consistently applied to many pages, such as content pages. And they can be used for any page that is sufficiently vexing or confusing to merit further visualization during the design process. The goal is not to create wireframes for every page or screen in your system, but only for the ones that are complicated, unique, or that set a pattern for others (i.e., templates).

Wireframes are a convenient way of exploring how page structure varies depending on screen size. Figure 13-12 shows a responsive design that accommodates reflowing for display in phone, tablet, and desktop browsers.

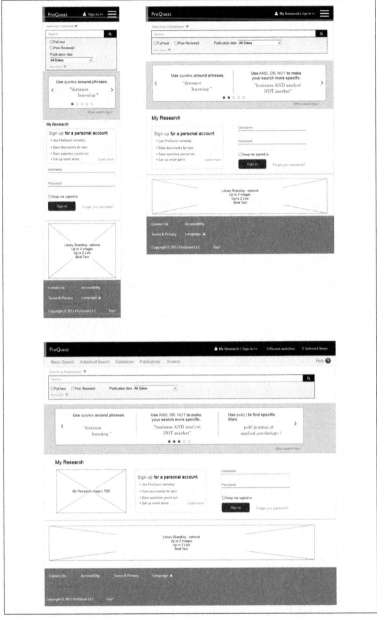

Figure 13-12. Wireframes can help designers explore the implications of varying screen sizes (wireframe developed for ProQuest LLC by Chris Farnum; reproduced with permission of ProQuest LLC—further reproduction is prohibited without permission)

Wireframes represent a degree of look and feel, and straddle the realms of visual design and interaction design. Wireframes (and page design in general) represent a frontier area where many web design–related disciplines come together and frequently clash. The fact that wireframes are produced by someone not necessarily experienced in visual or interaction design, and that they make statements about visual design (despite sometimes being rather ugly), often makes graphic designers and other visually oriented people very uncomfortable.

For this reason, we suggest that wireframes come with a prominent disclaimer that they are not replacements for "real visual design." The fonts, colors (or lack thereof), use of whitespace, and other visual characteristics of your wireframes are there only to illustrate how the site's information architecture will impact and interact with a particular page. Make it clear that you expect to collaborate with a graphic designer to improve the aesthetic nature of the overall product, or with an interaction designer to improve the functionality of the page's widgets.

We also suggest making this point verbally, while additionally conveying how your wireframe will eliminate some work that visual designers and interaction designers might consider unpleasant or not within their areas of expertise. For example, just as you'd prefer that a designer select colors or placement for a navigation bar, you've relieved the designer of the task of determining the labels that will populate that navigation bar.

Finally, because wireframes do involve visual design, their development presents a perfect opportunity for collaboration with visual designers, who will have much to add at this point. Avoid treating wireframes as something to be handed off to designers and developers, and instead use them as triggers for generating a healthy bout of interdisciplinary collaboration.

Types of Wireframes

Just like sitemaps, wireframes come in many shapes and sizes, and the level of fidelity can be varied to suit your purposes. At the low end, you may sketch quick-and-dirty wireframes on paper or a whiteboard. At the high end, wireframes may be created in HTML or with a tool like Adobe Illustrator. While the level of fidelity you use will vary depending on the stage of the development lifecycle

---

(with earlier stages calling for less precision), most wireframes will fall somewhere in the middle: neither too sketchy nor too precise. Let's review a few samples from the work of information architect Chris Farnum of ProQuest, a former colleague at Argus Associates and a wireframe expert. The first example (Figure 13-13) is a low-fidelity wireframe.

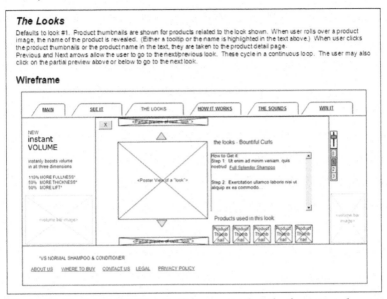

Figure 13-13. A low-fidelity wireframe; note that the focus is on layout of content and visual elements over content accuracy

Figure 13-14 shows a medium-fidelity wireframe with a high degree of detail. This wireframe was intended to introduce several aspects of content, layout, and navigation into the discussion, and was one of many wireframes used to communicate the information architecture to managers, graphic designers, and programmers.

Figure 13-14. A medium-fidelity wireframe by Chris Farnum and Katherine Root; more detail, more explanation, and more unique content (wireframe developed for ProQuest LLC; reproduced with permission of ProQuest LLC—further reproduction is prohibited without permission)

Finally, Figure 13-15 is a relatively high-fidelity wireframe that presents a close approximation of what the page will actually look like. This is about as far as you can go without bringing a graphic designer into the picture.

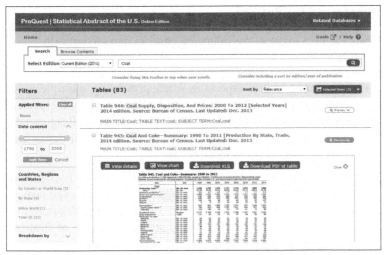

Figure 13-15. A high-fidelity wireframe (wireframe developed for Pro-Quest LLC by Chris Farnum; reproduced with permission of ProQuest LLC—further reproduction is prohibited without permission)

Such a high-fidelity wireframe has the following advantages:

- The content and color bring the page to life, helping to capture the attention of your clients or colleagues.
- By simulating actual page width and font size, the wireframe forces you to recognize the constraints of an HTML page.

The fidelity is sufficient to support paper prototype testing with users. On the other hand, some disadvantages are:

- Higher fidelity requires greater effort. It takes a lot of time to design such a detailed wireframe. This can slow down the process and increase costs.
- As you integrate visual elements and content into a structured layout, the focus may shift prematurely from information architecture to interface and visual design.

Provided that you recognize the strengths and weaknesses of these varying levels of fidelity, wireframes can be extremely powerful tools for communication and collaboration during the information architecture design process.

Wireframe Guidelines

Chris Farnum suggests the following best practices to consider when creating wireframes:

- Consistency is key, especially when presenting multiple wireframes. It ensures that clients will be impressed by the professionalism of your wireframes. More importantly, colleagues take wireframes quite literally, so consistency makes their design and production work go more smoothly.

- Visio and other standard charting tools support background layers, allowing you to reuse navigation bars and page layouts for multiple pages throughout the site. Similarly, Visio's stencil feature allows you to maintain a standard library of drawing objects that can be used to describe page elements.

- Callouts—small notes placed around and over your wireframes—are an effective way to provide details about the functionality of page elements. Be sure to leave room for them at the sides and top of your wireframes.

- Like any other deliverable, wireframes should be usable and professionally developed. So, tie your collection of wireframes together with page numbers, page titles, project titles, and last revision dates.

- When more than one team member is creating a project's wireframes, be sure to establish procedures for developing, sharing, and maintaining common templates and stencils (and consider establishing a wireframe "steward"). Schedule time in your project plan for synchronizing the team's wireframes to ensure consistent appearance, and for confirming that these discrete documents do indeed fit together functionally.

Content Mapping and Inventory

During research and strategy, you are focused on the top-down approach of defining an information structure that will accommodate the mission, vision, audiences, and content of the information environment. As you move into design and production, you complete the bottom-up process of collecting and analyzing the content. Content mapping is where top-down information architecture meets bottom-up.

The process of detailed content mapping involves breaking down or combining existing content into content chunks that are useful for inclusion in your environment. A content chunk isn't necessarily a sentence or a paragraph or a page. Rather, it is the most finely grained portion of content that merits or requires individual treatment.

The content, often drawn from a variety of sources and in a multitude of formats, must be mapped onto the information architecture so that it's clear what goes where during the production process. Because of differences between formats, you cannot count on a one-to-one mapping of source page to destination page; one page from a print brochure does not necessarily map onto one page on the Web. For this reason, it is important to separate content from its container at both the source and the destination. In addition, when combined with a database-driven approach to content management, the separation of content and container facilitates the reuse of content chunks across multiple pages. For example, contact information for the customer service department might be presented in context within a variety of pages throughout the system. If the contact information changes, the modification need only be made to the database record for that content chunk, and it can then be propagated through the system at the push of a button.

Even when you are creating new content, content mapping is still necessary. It often makes sense to create content in a word processing application, because tools like Microsoft Word tend to have more powerful editing, layout, and spell-checking capabilities. In such cases, you'll need to map the Word documents to HTML pages (or whatever format they are stored in in the system). The need for careful content mapping is even greater when new content is created by multiple authors throughout your organization; the mapping process then becomes an important managerial tool for tracking content from these disparate sources.

The subjective process of defining chunks should be determined by asking the following questions:

- Should this content be divided into smaller chunks that users might want to access separately?
- What is the smallest section of content that needs to be individually indexed?

- Will this content need to be repurposed across multiple documents or as part of multiple processes?

Once the content chunks have been defined, they can be mapped to their destinations or means of delivery to your audience, which can be web pages, feeds, or some other medium. You will need a systematic means of documenting the source and destination of all content so that the production team can carry out your instructions. As discussed earlier, one approach involves the assignment of a unique identification code to each content chunk.

For example, the creation of the SIGGRAPH 96 Conference website required the translation of print-based content to the online environment. In such cases, content mapping involves the specification of how chunks of content in the print materials map to pages on the website. For SIGGRAPH 96, we had to map the contents of elaborately designed brochures, announcements, and programs onto web pages. Because it wouldn't have made sense to attempt a one-to-one mapping of printed pages to web pages, we instead went through a process of content chunking and mapping with the content editor. First, we broke each page of the brochure into logical chunks of content, inventoried the results, and then devised a simple scheme tied to page numbers for labeling each chunk (Figure 13-16).

As you saw in Figure 13-9, we had already created a detailed information architecture sitemap with its own content chunk identification scheme. We then had to create a content mapping table that explained how each content chunk from the print brochure should be presented on the website (Figure 13-17).

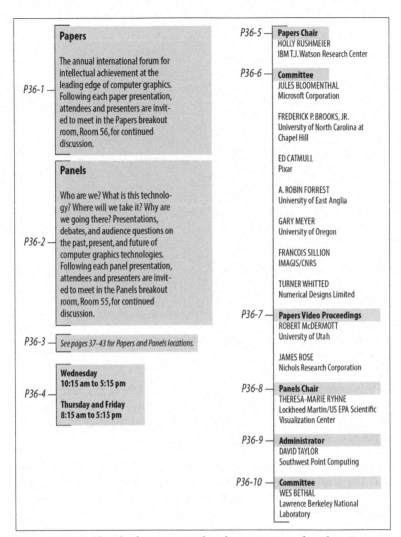

Papers

P36-1 —
The annual international forum for intellectual achievement at the leading edge of computer graphics. Following each paper presentation, attendees and presenters are invited to meet in the Papers breakout room, Room 56, for continued discussion.

Panels

P36-2 —
Who are we? What is this technology? Where will we take it? Why are we going there? Presentations, debates, and audience questions on the past, present, and future of computer graphics technologies. Following each panel presentation, attendees and presenters are invited to meet in the Panels breakout room, Room 55, for continued discussion.

P36-3 — See pages 37-43 for Papers and Panels locations.

P36-4 —
Wednesday
10:15 am to 5:15 pm

Thursday and Friday
8:15 am to 5:15 pm

P36-5 — **Papers Chair**
HOLLY RUSHMEIER
IBM T.J. Watson Research Center

P36-6 — **Committee**
JULES BLOOMENTHAL
Microsoft Corporation

FREDERICK P. BROOKS, JR.
University of North Carolina at Chapel Hill

ED CATMULL
Pixar

A. ROBIN FORREST
University of East Anglia

GARY MEYER
University of Oregon

FRANCOIS SILLION
IMAGIS/CNRS

TURNER WHITTED
Numerical Designs Limited

P36-7 — **Papers Video Proceedings**
ROBERT McDERMOTT
University of Utah

JAMES ROSE
Nichols Research Corporation

P36-8 — **Panels Chair**
THERESA-MARIE RYHNE
Lockheed Martin/US EPA Scientific Visualization Center

P36-9 — **Administrator**
DAVID TAYLOR
Southwest Point Computing

P36-10 — **Committee**
WES BETHAL
Lawrence Berkeley National Laboratory

Figure 13-16. Chunks from a print brochure are tagged with unique identifiers (e.g., "P36–1") so that they can be mapped out and inventoried

Content Mapping Table

Source (print brochure)		Destination (website)
P36-1	-----------------------------	2.2.3
P36-2	-----------------------------	2.3.3
P36-3	-----------------------------	2.2.2
P36-4	-----------------------------	2.2.1
P36-5	-----------------------------	2.2.5.1
P36-6	-----------------------------	2.2.5.2
P36-7	-----------------------------	2.2.5.3
P36-8	-----------------------------	2.3.5.1
P36-9	-----------------------------	2.3.5.2
P36-10	-----------------------------	2.3.5.3

Figure 13-17. A content mapping table matches content chunks with their destinations

In this example, P36–1 is a unique ID that refers to the first content chunk on page 36 of the original print brochure. This source content chunk maps onto the destination content chunk labeled 2.2.3, which belongs in the Papers (2.2) area of the website.

Armed with the original print documents, architecture sitemaps, and the content mapping table, the production staff created and populated the SIGGRAPH 96 Conference website. As you can see in Figure 13-18, the contents of this web page (2.2) include three content chunks from P36.

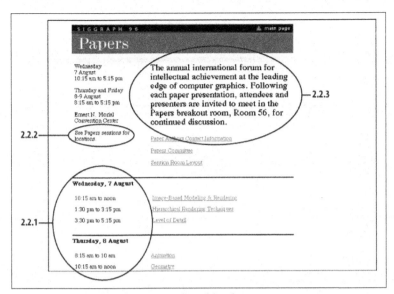

Figure 13-18. The web page produced by the content mapping process; P36–1 maps to 2.2.3, P36–3 maps to 2.2.2, and P36–4 maps to 2.2.1

Another important product of this process is a content inventory, which describes available content and where it can be found (e.g., the current site or the annual report), as well as content gaps that need to be filled. Depending upon the size and complexity of the website and the process and technologies in use for production, there are many ways to present this inventory. For larger environments, you might require a document or content management solution that leverages database technology to manage large collections of content. Many of these applications also provide a workflow that defines a team approach to page-level design and editing. For simpler systems, you might rely on a spreadsheet (see Figure 13-19). Sarah Rice of Seneb Consulting has created an excellent spreadsheet (*http://bit.ly/ex_content_inv*) that you can download and use; in this example, she's applied it to the site of the Information Architecture Institute (formerly AIfIA).

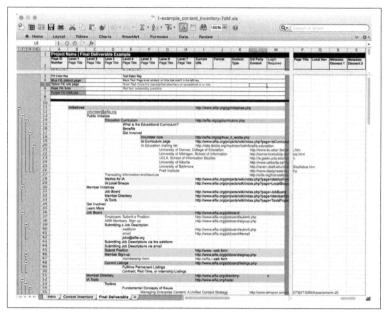

Figure 13-19. Section of a content inventory managed in Microsoft Excel

Or, if you're feeling a bit more ambitious, you can create a web-based inventory that presents the titles and unique identification numbers of each page in the site, such as that shown in Figure 13-20. Selecting the hypertext numbers pops up another browser window that shows the appropriate web page.

You can create a content inventory as soon as you have completed the content mapping process, or vice versa. And once you have an inventory of your content, you can produce a content audit: an understanding of content that needs to be created, page mockups that need to be designed, and designed pages that need to be reviewed before integration into the final product.[3]

---

3 For a good introduction to content inventories, see the aforementioned *Content Strategy for the Web, Second Edition,* by Kristina Halvorson and Melissa Rach (San Francisco: New Riders, 2012).

1.0	Pilot Site: Main Page
1.1	Pilot Site: Why Digital
1.2	Pilot Site: About this Pilot Program
2.0.1.A	Gateway (for subscribers)
2.0.1.B	Gateway (for non-subscribers)
2.0.2	Browser Compatibility Test
2.0.3	Browser Incompatible
2.0	Main
2.1.1	The Dissertation Abstracts Database
2.1.2	The UMI Digital Library of Dissertations
2.1.3	Future Enhancements
2.1.1.1	Submitting Electronic Theses and Dissertations
2.1.4	Feedback
2.1.5	Thank You
2.2.1	Search Results: Quick Search, Less Than 20 Hits
2.2.1.A	Search Results: Quick Search, Greater Than 20 Hits

Figure 13-20. A web-based content inventory

Content Models

Content models are information architectures made up of small chunks of interconnected content. Content models support the critical missing piece in so many information environments: contextual navigation that works deep within the product. Why is this so often a missing piece? Because it's easy—maybe too easy—for an organization to accumulate units of content, but extremely difficult to link those units together in a useful way.

Why Do They Matter?

We encounter content models all the time. A recipe is a great example. Its objects are a list of ingredients, directions, a title, and so on. If you render a recipe as "lorem ipsum,"[4] it'll still be recognizable as a recipe. But change the logic—by putting the steps before the ingredients or leaving out an important object—and the model collapses. Content models rely on consistent sets of objects and logical connections between them to work.

---

4 "Lorem ipsum" refers to a Latin text that is often used by designers as filler to illustrate content in presentations. For more information, see *http://en.wikipedia.org/wiki/Lorem_ipsum*.

Supporting contextual navigation

Imagine that you've found your way deep into a clothing retailer's website in a quest for a snazzy new blue oxford shirt. As a user, you've just clearly stated an incredibly specific information need. Such a need is far more precise than that of a user who has reached a site's main page. Wouldn't it be silly for the retailer not to apply this knowledge to your benefit (not to mention to its advantage)?

That's why most online retailers will, at this point, introduce you to some matching pants or other accessories. "You might also be interested in...." This is far more reasonable than a retailer expecting you to (1) guess that it sells these related items and (2) actually find those items using the top-down organization and navigation systems. Horizontal hopping across the hierarchy is a form of contextual navigation, where your movement is based more on your needs as a user than on the environment's structure. Content models exist primarily to support such navigation, whether for cross-selling retail products, connecting baseball fans to the story behind the box score, or introducing potential customers to a product's specifications.

Coping with large amounts of content

Content models also help us deal with scale. When inventorying content, it's not uncommon to stumble upon large bodies of similar information buried in our content management systems and databases. For example, after a content inventory, a company that provides information on mobile phones might find that it owns dozens of content chunks for each model's basic product information, thousands for reader reviews, and many more for information on related accessories. The phone product pages look, work, and behave the same. So do the review pages and the accessory pages.

If each type of content chunk works the same, why not take advantage of this predictability by linking them? Allow users to move naturally from a specific phone's page to its product reviews and accessories. Better yet, do this in an automated fashion so the links can be generated instantly, rather than having an army of coders deciding what should be linked to what. Automating the creation of links between content chunks means your users benefit from more and better ways to navigate contextually, and your organization derives greater value from its investment in the content.

So, content models can be especially helpful when we've got a lot of high-value content chunks that are similar to one another and aren't well linked, and some technology on hand—like your friendly neighborhood content management system—to automate the expression of those links. You can certainly create content models for smaller numbers of content chunks—for example, information associated with the dozen or so people that serve on your company's board—but it's pretty easy to manually connect these objects. You could also create content models for all of your content, but the process is a bit involved, so we recommend doing so for only your most valuable content (with value defined as a judicious combination of both user and organizational needs, of course).

An Example

Let's say you work for a media organization that has invested lots of resources in assembling information on popular music. Certain content chunks—such as artist descriptions and album pages—number in the thousands, and they all look and work in the same way. You might sense that there is potential here for a content model that serves fans of popular music. Instead of having those fans rely on the system's hierarchy to find content relevant to a particular artist or album, why not create a content model?

Based on a content inventory and audit, there are a few music-related content objects that may emerge as good candidates for a content model, shown in Figure 13-21.

Album "pages"

Album descriptions

Artist bios

Album reviews

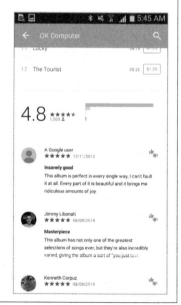

Figure 13-21. Content objects that might be the basis of a content model for album information

How should these objects be linked? We can certainly decide that an album page ought to link to its corresponding review, artist bios and descriptions should link to each other, and so on. But it won't always be so easy to come up with the most obvious links, and even if it is fairly obvious, you may need to produce some user research to validate your work.

In such cases, consider a variation of the card sort exercise. Print out a sample of each content object and cut out the navigation options (to prevent biasing users with the current information architecture). Then ask subjects to look at each content object and consider where they'd want to go next. Then have them cluster the objects and draw lines between them that indicate navigation (they can do this with string, or they can tape the content object samples to a whiteboard and use dry-erase markers to draw their lines). Arrows indicate whether users wish to navigate in both directions or prefer a one-way link.

To perform a simple gap analysis, ask subjects which missing content objects would be nice to include in the mix. By doing so, you'll get a sense of what should be added to your content model. If you're fortunate, the missing objects might already exist somewhere else in your site. Otherwise, you'll at least have some guidance in deciding which content to create or license.

At the end of the process—whether based on user research or your own hunches—you'll have an idea of how your content model ought to work. The result might look like Figure 13-22.

You've now identified new content objects, like a discography, that you might need to create. And you've linked to other content, like YouTube videos of the band and events in a concert calendar, that is a logical extension of the content model (and possibly, a connection to candidates for future content models). You've also identified logical "tops" or common points of entry to this content. And ultimately, you have a sense of how users might want to navigate an area deep in the guts of your site.

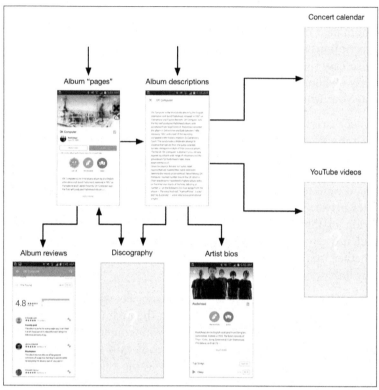

Figure 13-22. An ideal content model, showing navigation and missing content objects

Unfortunately, you're not quite done. How do these links between content objects get made?

If you're Amazon, you've got reams of usage data to draw from. Amazon employs customer behavior data to make connections between related products in its content model; familiar examples are the products listed under "Customers who bought this item also bought" and "What do customers ultimately buy after viewing this item?" But not every organization has the traffic volume from which to cull this kind of useful data.

So, the rest of us typically rely on metadata as the basis of the logic that connects our content chunks. Shared metadata does the work of linking a pair of content chunks. For example, if we want to link an album page and an album review, the logic might look like this:

```
IF ALBUM PAGE'S ALBUM NAME = ALBUM REVIEW'S ALBUM NAME
THEN LINK ALBUM PAGE AND ALBUM REVIEW
```

Now, this rule might suffice for albums with unique titles, like *OK Computer*. But what if the title is the ubiquitous *Greatest Hits*? If you're lucky, the object has a unique identifier, like an ISBN, that can be used as connecting metadata:

```
IF ALBUM PAGE'S UNIQUE ID = ALBUM REVIEW'S UNIQUE ID
THEN LINK ALBUM PAGE AND ALBUM REVIEW
```

But as that's often not the case, your linking logic will likely need to get a little more complicated, and additional metadata attributes will be necessary:

```
IF ALBUM PAGE'S ALBUM NAME = ALBUM REVIEW'S ALBUM NAME
AND ALBUM PAGE'S ARTIST NAME = ALBUM REVIEW'S ARTIST NAME
THEN LINK ALBUM PAGE AND ALBUM REVIEW
```

As you can see, these rules rely on metadata. Do the required metadata attributes exist? The bad news is that you'll probably need to invest in creating new metadata from scratch (or acquiring it).

Of course, metadata availability is a consideration with just about any information architecture project of any size. And the good news is that the content modeling process will help you decide which metadata attributes to invest in by helping you select the most useful from the wide range of possibilities.

Consider our arrows in Figure 13-22. Which metadata will be necessary to drive the logic behind each link? You can make a simple table listing each content object, which other objects it should link to, and the metadata attributes required to make those connections. It might look something like Table 13-2.

Table 13-2. Content object linking table

Content objects...	link to other content objects...	by leveraging common metadata attributes
Album page	Album review, discography, artist	Album Name, Artist Name, Label, Release Date
Album review	album page	Album Name, Artist Name, Review Author, Source, Pub Date
Discography	Album review, artist description	Artist Name, Album Name, Release Date
Album description	Artist bio, discography, concert calendar, TV listing	Artist Name, Desc Author, Desc Date

Content objects...	link to other content objects...	by leveraging common metadata attributes
Artist bio	Artist description	Artist Name, Individual Artist Name
Concert calendar	Artist description	Artist Name, Tour, Venue, Date, Time
YouTube listing	Artist description	Video Title, URL, Amount of Views

Notice a pattern here? Certain metadata attributes show up more frequently than others. These are the attributes that are most necessary for the content model to succeed. If you're operating with limited resources (and who isn't?), now you'll have an excellent way to prioritize your investment in metadata attributes.

A Valuable Process

As you can see, content models are as much an exercise as a deliverable. While the primary output is a useful IA deliverable that informs the design of contextual navigation deep within an information environment, the process also generates two invaluable, if secondary, benefits.

First, content modeling forces us to determine which content is the most important content to model. As you can see, it's work. Most likely you can't create content models for all of your content. So you'll have to ask yourself: which content fulfills the requirements of homogeneity, high volume, and, most of all, high value? You might find a set of priorities falls out of this exercise; for example, perhaps this year you'll develop a product area content model, next year a support area content model, and later you'll link those two models together for even greater benefit.

Second, content modeling also forces you to choose which of the many metadata attributes are the ones that will make your content model operational. The combination of focusing on and narrowing down to critical content and critical metadata means a huge simplification and clarification of a large and complex problem space.

Controlled Vocabularies

There are two primary types of work products associated with the development of controlled vocabularies. First, you'll need metadata matrices that facilitate discussion about the prioritization of vocabularies (see Table 13-3 for an example). Second, you'll need a tool to manage the vocabulary terms and relationships.

Table 13-3. A metadata matrix for 3Com

Vocabulary	Description	Examples	Maintenance
Subject	Terms that describe networking	Home networking; servers	Difficult
Product type	Types of products that 3Com sells	Hubs; modems	Moderate
Product name	Names of products that 3Com sells	PC Digital WebCam	Difficult
Product brand	Brands of products that 3Com sells	HomeConnect; SuperStack	Easy
Technology	Types of technologies associated with products	ISDN; broadband; frame relay	Moderate
Protocols	Types of standards and protocols associated with products	TCP/IP; Ethernet	Moderate
Hardware	Types of devices that products are used in	PDA; wireless phone; Internet appliances; PC	Moderate
Geographic location: region	Name of geographic region	Europe; APR	Easy
Geographic location: country	Name of country	Germany; Czech Republic	Easy
Language	Name of language	German; Czech	Easy
Technology applications	Names of applications for technologies	Call center; ebusiness	Moderate
Industries	Types of industries that 3Com works with	Healthcare; government	Easy
Audiences	Kinds of audiences the 3Com site attracts	Consumers; first-time visitors; media	Easy
Customer group: workplace	Type of workplace that customers work in	Home; office	Moderate
Customer group: business	Size or scale of business that customers work in	Small business; large enterprise; service provider	Moderate
Roles	Type of role that people have in their business	IT manager; consultant	Moderate
Document type	Purpose of content object	Form; instructions; guide	Easy

As you can see from Table 13-3, there's no shortage of possible vocabularies. Your job is to help define which vocabularies should be developed, considering priorities and time and budget constraints. A metadata matrix can help you to walk clients and colleagues through the difficult decision-making process, weighing the value of each vocabulary to the user experience against the costs of development and administration.

As you shift gears from selecting vocabularies to building them, you'll need to choose a database solution to manage the terms and term relationships. If you're creating a sophisticated thesaurus with equivalence, hierarchical, and associative relationships, you should seriously consider investing in thesaurus management software (see Chapter 10 for further discussion). However, if you're creating a simple vocabulary with only preferred and variant terms, you should be able to manage with just a word processor, spreadsheet program, or basic database.

When we created a controlled vocabulary to be used by thousands of representatives at AT&T's inbound call centers, we managed the accepted and variant terms in Microsoft Word (see Table 13-4).

Table 13-4. Excerpt from a controlled vocabulary database created for AT&T

Unique ID	Accepted term	Product code	Variant terms
PS0135	Access Dialing	PCA358	10–288; 10–322; dial around
PS0006	Air Miles	PCS932	AirMiles
PS0151	XYZ Direct	DCW004	USADirect; XYZ USA Direct; XYZDirect card

For this project, we were dealing with 7 distinct vocabularies and around 600 accepted terms:

- Products & Services (151 accepted terms)
- Partners & Competitors (122 accepted terms)
- Plans & Promotions (173 accepted terms)
- Geographic Codes (51 accepted terms)
- Adjustment Codes (36 accepted terms)
- Corporate Terminology (70 accepted terms)
- Time Codes (12 accepted terms)

Even given the relatively small size and simplicity of these vocabularies, we found Microsoft Word was barely sufficient for the task. We created one very long document with tables for each vocabulary.

This document was "owned" by a single controlled vocabulary manager and shared via our local area network. Our team of indexing specialists were able to search against accepted and variant terms in the "database" using MS Word's Find capability. And we were able to output tab-delimited files to assist the programmers who were building the site at AT&T.

Design Collaboration

Once you've developed sitemaps, wireframes, content models, and vocabularies, you'll find yourself collaborating more with other people involved in developing the product—visual designers, developers, content authors, or managers. You'll move from capturing and communicating your own design concepts to integrating them with the visions of other members of your team. Naturally, this is as challenging as design gets—everyone wants his own ideas to play a role in the final product, and because the group's members often come from interdisciplinary backgrounds, there are often competing vocabularies and breakdowns in communication. But if each person goes in with an open mind and good tools for collaborating, this difficult phase is also the most gratifying one, ending with a shared vision that's far better than anyone was likely to arrive at individually. Design sketches and web prototypes are just two tools for merging differing ideas.

Design Sketches

In the research phase, the design team developed a sense of the desired graphic identity or look and feel. The technical team assessed the information technology infrastructure of the organization and the platform limitations of the intended audiences, and they understood what was possible with respect to features such as dynamic content management and interactivity. And, of course, the architect designed the high-level information structure for the environment. Design sketches are a great way to pool the collective knowledge of these three teams in a first attempt at interface design for the top-level pages of the website or app. This is a wonderful opportunity for interdisciplinary user interface design.

Using the wireframes as a guide, the designer now begins sketching pages of the product on sheets of paper. As the designer sketches each screen, questions arise that must be discussed. Here is a sample sketching-session dialog:

> Developer: "I like what you're doing with the layout of the main screen, but I'd like to do something more interesting with the navigation system."

> Designer: "Can we implement the navigation system using pull-down menus? Does that make sense architecturally?"

> You: "That might work, but it would be difficult to show context in the hierarchy. How about a table of contents? We've had pretty good reactions to that type of approach from users in the past."

> Developer: "We can certainly go with that approach from a purely technical perspective. How would a tear-away table of contents look? Can you sketch it for us? I'd like to do a quick-and-dirty prototype."

As you can see, the design of these sketches requires the involvement of members from each team. It is much cheaper and easier for the group to work with the designer on these rough sketches than to begin with code and finished graphics. These sketches allow rapid iteration and intense collaboration. The final product of a sketching session might look something like Figure 13-23.

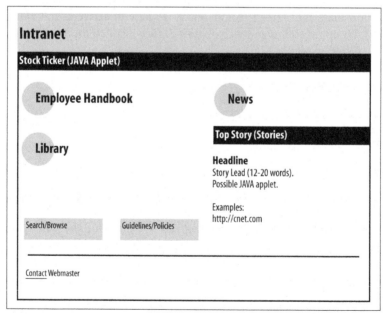

Figure 13-23. A basic design sketch

In this example, Employee Handbook, Library, and News are grouped together as the major areas of the website. Search/Browse and Guidelines/Policies make up the page navigation bar. The News area defines space for a dynamic news panel. This sketch may not look much different from a wireframe. In fact, the team may have begun with a wireframe, then iterated on the design until arriving at this sketch, which in turn may be the basis for a revised and final wireframe.

 Starting with a sketch—whether a formal wireframe or something more "back-of-the-napkin"—is critical to the success of interdisciplinary meetings.

The sketch provides a common focus for each participant, minimizing the attention paid to the individual personalities around the table. It also makes it more likely that participants will be using the same terminology to discuss the design; shared terms for design concepts often emerge directly from the sketch itself.

Finally, note that design sketches aren't necessarily "owned" by the team responsible for the information architecture. For example, sketches that describe functional requirements may be under the purview of the designer or developer. Be wary of getting caught up in ownership issues; contributing to the design, regardless of who is driving Visio, OmniGraffle, or Illustrator, is far more important to the project's outcome.

Interactive Prototypes

A high point of the design process is the creation of interactive prototypes.[5] More than sketches or scenarios, these digital renditions show how the product will look and function. They are concrete and often aesthetically compelling; you can actually see how your work will really come together, and maybe even kick the tires yourself.

While the balance of attention now shifts toward aesthetic considerations such as page layout and graphic identity, the prototypes

---

5 For more on the creation of prototypes, see Todd Zaki Warfel's *Prototyping: A Practitioner's Guide* (Brooklyn, NY: Rosenfeld Media, 2011).

frequently identify previously unseen problems or opportunities related to the information architecture. Once your architecture and navigation system are embodied in an actual interactive system, it becomes much easier for you and your colleagues to see whether they are working.

The designer may begin with two concepts based on a single information architecture. After getting feedback from the client, the design team may work together to adapt and extend the preferred concept. At this point, conceptual design officially ends, and production actually begins. The most exciting challenges for the architecture have been met, and you now begin the days of detail.

Point-of-Production Information Architecture

Ideally, the production process would proceed smoothly in a paint-by-numbers manner, and you could sit back and relax. In reality, you must be actively involved to make sure the architecture is implemented according to plan and to address any problems that arise. After all, you can't anticipate everything.

Many decisions must be made during production. Are these content chunks small enough that we can group them together on one page, or should they remain on separate pages? Should we add local navigation to this section of the environment? Can we shorten the label of this page? Be aware that at this stage, the answers to these questions may impact the burden on the production team as well as the usability of the product. You need to balance the requests of your client against the sanity of the production team, the budget and timeline, and your vision for the information architecture of the environment.

You shouldn't need to make major decisions about the architecture during production, because hopefully these have already been made. Discovering a major flaw in the architecture at this point is a nightmare. Fortunately, if you've followed the process of research, strategy, and design, this is unlikely. You have worked hard to define the mission, vision, audiences, and content for the product. You have documented the decisions made along the way. You have resolved the top-down and bottom-up approaches through content mapping and detailed sitemaps. Through careful planning, you've created a solid information architecture that should stand the test of time.

Still, it's worth reminding yourself that an information architecture can never be perfect. Factors of content, people, and context are constantly changing, and the architecture will, too. It's more important to invest your energy in educating your colleagues that information architecture design is an ongoing process, rather than fighting with them to get it "right."

Putting It All Together: Information Architecture Style Guides

Information environments are always growing and changing. You must help guide their development—even after the product launches—or risk architectural drift, or worse: a decaying user experience that doesn't evolve with its users. It's frustrating to see your carefully and flexibly designed organization, navigation, labeling, and indexing systems get mangled as maintainers add content without heeding the architectural implications. While it may be impossible to completely prevent the effects of entropy, an *information architecture style guide* can steer content maintainers in the right direction.

An architecture style guide is a document that explains how the environment is organized, why it is organized that way, who it's for, and how the architecture should be extended as the system grows. You should begin your guide with documentation of the mission and vision for the product, as it's important to understand the original goals. Continue with information about the intended audiences. Who was it designed for? What are their goals? What assumptions were made about their information needs? Then, follow up with a description of the content development policy. What types of content will and won't be included, and why? How often will it be updated? When will it be removed? And who will be responsible for it?

The "Why" Stuff

Documenting the lessons learned and the decisions made during the research, strategy, and design phases is critical. These underlying philosophies not only drive the design and maintenance of the information architecture, but also guide your product through the zigs and zags of major changes that your organization will surely encounter in the future.

For example, your organization may merge with another or spin off a unit. It may offer new products, or try to reach new markets and go global in the process. Major changes like these often coincide with major organizational changes such as the appointment of new senior managers, many of whom wish to leave their mark in all areas, including the product's design. But do new requirements and major changes to the organization require major changes to the site's information architecture? Ideally, not; a clearly documented rationale explains an information architecture and demonstrates its flexibility, which mitigates against the extremes that plague so many redesigns.

Perhaps the biggest "why" you'll encounter is the one that comes so often from senior vice presidents, marketing managers, and product managers, which in effect boils down to "Why can't my favorite feature/my department's content be made more prominent/become your highest priority?" An information architecture style guide provides you with concrete documentation to help you prioritize the many such requests you'll likely encounter. It'll even provide you with cover when you absolutely have to say no.

The "How" Stuff

Your style guide should include some basic nuts-and-bolts components to help various people maintain the environment. Consider including such sections as:

Standards

There are usually at least a few rules that must be followed while maintaining and changing the environment. For example, newly created documents must be indexed with terms from the appropriate controlled vocabulary before they are published. Or there may be specific procedures that must be followed to ensure that new content is immediately crawled and indexed by the search system. Here's the place to note the rules...

Guidelines

...and distinguish the rules from the guidelines, which suggest—but don't mandate—how the information architecture should be maintained. These may be drawn from information architecture best practices,[6] and often require interpretation for each situation in which you'll find yourself; examples include advice on how to avoid overly long lists of links and page-titling recommendations.

Maintenance procedures
Regular tasks that are required for the environment's survival should be fully documented, such as when and how to add new terms to a controlled vocabulary.

Pattern library
Consider creating a pattern library[7] that documents and provides access to reusable aspects of your product's design—such as a navigation widget that helps users scroll through pages of results—to cut down on reinventing the wheel.

Your style guide should also present the sitemaps, wireframes, controlled vocabulary information, and other documentation that came from the design process and will be reused throughout the environment's lifetime. Because you won't always be there to explain these deliverables, it may be necessary to provide written explanations to accompany the sitemaps. You also need to create guidelines for adding content to ensure the continued integrity of the organization, labeling, navigation, and indexing systems. This can be a challenge. When should a new level in the hierarchy be added? Under what conditions can new indexing terms be introduced? How should local navigation systems be extended as the website grows? By thinking ahead and documenting decisions, you can provide much-needed guidance—a user's manual, really—to the environment's maintainers.

---

6 For a few examples of IA heuristics, check out Lou's "IA heuristics" (*http://bit.ly/ia_heuristics*) and "IA heuristics for search systems" (*http://bit.ly/search_systems*).

7 To learn how Yahoo! developed its excellent library, read "Implementing a Pattern Library in the Real World: A Yahoo! Case Study" (*http://bit.ly/pattern_lib_real_world*), by Erin Malone, Matt Leacock, and Chanel Wheeler.

Keep in mind the different audiences that might use the style guide. For example, in a large organization, content authors working from far-flung parts of the globe may not need to know the site's overall strategy so much as the maximum number of characters they should use for a document title. Conversely, designers may need to understand the rules that guide construction of the `alt` text that a navigation system's mouseovers rely upon. Consider an information architecture style guide as a sort of "how and why" document that should be designed for use, just like any other information system. And remember that your organization may already have a style guide for its branding, its content, and other aspects of its online presence; when possible, integrate information architecture guidelines into existing style guides.

Recap

OK, let's recap what we learned in this chapter:

- In the design phase, the emphasis of the project moves from process to deliverables—it's where the information architecture starts to become manifest.

- That said, these deliverables aren't the whole story—process is as important during this phase as it is during research and strategy.

- Information architectures are abstract and conceptual, which makes it difficult to capture them in diagrams.

- You should provide multiple "views" of your information architecture to display its different aspects.

- These views should be developed for specific audiences and needs.

- IA diagrams define content components and the connections between them.

- Sitemaps show the relationships between information elements such as pages and other content components, and can be used to portray organization, navigation, and labeling systems.

- Wireframes depict how an individual page or template should look from an architectural perspective.

- Content models support contextual navigation that works deep within the product.

- Controlled vocabularies can be conveyed with metadata matrices and applications that enable the vocabulary to be managed.

- As you move through the design phase, you'll find yourself collaborating more with other people involved in developing the product—an open mind and good collaboration tools are essential.

Coda

You've done it! You've reached the end of *Information Architecture: For the Web and Beyond*. Well, not quite. Before we sign off, we'd like to look back to how we got here, recap what we've learned in this edition of the book, and look to what's coming next.

Putting the Arc in Information Architecture

When the first edition of this book came out, the Web was but a few years old. That edition's readers were part of the first generation that had to deal with designing for this new medium. Given the Web's immensity, potential, and radical ways of publishing and navigating information, new approaches were required to make it easy to use and understand. We had few shoulders to stand on. We were all learning—and in many ways, making it up—as we went along. We were like wide-eyed toddlers, inexperienced but optimistic, full of energy, and excited at the prospects of a vast new world before us, waiting to be explored.

By the time the second edition came out, things had seemingly settled down. Within the circles of web designers, information architecture had become a "thing": there were conferences, professional organizations, and passionate people with solid work in their portfolios. These folks were also starting to deal with solving information architecture challenges within the context of *existing* systems with histories of use. We were like children that were starting to mature—but our voices hadn't broken yet.

When the third edition came out, we were starting to deal with the challenges and opportunities inherent in more socially oriented information environments. Tagging and other "people-powered" organization schemes introduced exciting new ways to structure information, and sparked passionate discussion about the role of information architecture. Many of our readers were moving up the corporate ranks, as organizations of all sizes were starting to recognize the strategic importance of information that was easy to find and easy to understand. We believed we had answers for these organizations. There was an evolving discussion at this time about the role of IA in projects: it was either very specifically focused on findability ("small" IA), or more broadly focused on the fuller experience ("big" IA—what today is called UX). Our focus in the third edition leaned heavily toward the latter, making the book very ambitious. We had a shiny new hammer, and were ready to nail so many problems! These were our "teenage" years: we were confident in our perspectives and abilities—perhaps overly so.

This brings us to the book you are holding now. We hope this fourth edition reflects what we perceive to be a new level of maturity in our field. We have moved on from polarizing discussions about the role of IA. We have shed any tribal aspirations that may have been evident in previous editions; information architecture is for *anyone* who is trying to make information easier to find and understand, regardless of what their business cards say. In short, we no longer feel like we have anything to prove to anyone in the broader design world: information architecture is here for all of us to use. Also, we now have a better understanding of the enormity and complexity of the challenges before us—and of our own limitations. Information environments are everywhere; ineffable systems are everywhere. There are more every day, and more pervasively so. As Marc Andreessen has said, "software is eating the world."[1] Things are becoming deeply intertwingled. It's clear that designing an effective information architecture is a difficult task!

Producing the fourth edition of a popular, highly respected technical book is also a difficult IA task. What do we include? What do we leave out? How much do we repurpose? How much must we write anew? How do we structure the narrative to flow in a way that communicates clearly? As an adult, your past is an important part of

---

1 See Andreessen's essay "Why Software Is Eating the World" (*http://bit.ly/soft ware_eating_world*).

who you are. Coming to terms with that past—understanding what it means for who you are now, and who you will be in the future—is a critical ability you gain as you mature. You can't change your past, nor would you necessarily want to: it makes you who you are. In approaching the fourth edition of this book as an information architecture challenge (which includes dealing with its long and venerable history) we have strived to embrace and honor its past, reframing the knowledge accumulated in the book since the first edition so that it can better serve the needs of the present and the immediate future. We think the resulting book is more idiosyncratic (in the best way possible) and richer than one that started from scratch.

A Recap of What We've Learned

So with that bit of introspection out of the way, let's recap what we've learned in this new edition of the polar bear book.

In Part I, we introduced the challenges that information architecture can help us address: information overload and contextual proliferation. We tackle these challenges by thinking about the products and systems that we design as information environments, or places made of information. Users interact with these information environments in various different contexts using different channels of access, and their experience of the environment needs to be coherent between these channels. In order to make this possible, designers need to think about the solutions comprehensively, as part of a system. The outcome we're aiming for is information that is easier to *find* and *understand*. Design for finding is about structuring information so that it can meet people's information needs, so we learned about information-seeking behaviors as developed in the field of library sciences. Design for understanding is about creating contexts that present information in ways that make sense to people, so we learned about placemaking and organizing principles derived from the field of architecture.

In Part II, we discussed basic principles that allow us to structure information for better findability and understandability. We discussed different ways of organizing information environments, including exact and ambiguous organization schemes, hierarchies, structured databases, and free-form hypertext systems. We learned about the importance of labeling: the words we use in links, headings, and more. We also learned about the various types of navigation and search systems, and about "invisible" systems that the user doesn't directly perceive, such as metadata, thesauri, and faceted classification schemes.

In Part III, we learned about the process of designing an information architecture that brings these principles together. We broke this process down into three distinct activities: *research*, in which the team attempts to understand the problem(s) they're solving for; *strategy*, in which they synthesize a comprehensive solution; and *design and documentation*, in which they give the solution form and convey it to the various people responsible for the production of the information environment.

Do we believe this particular content and structure represents the final word in what information architecture is and how it can help make information more findable and understandable? No, we do not. As with all information architectures, there is more than one way to go about it. That said, this one feels good to us: it has the advantage of having evolved over time to respond to the changing needs of designers, their clients, and the broader context of practice. We fully expect that information architecture will continue to evolve as information environments get richer and more complex in the years to come.

Now It's Your Turn

In the time it took the average reader to read this book, our fellow human beings posted 1,180,800,000 pieces of content to Facebook, uploaded 144,000 hours of video to YouTube, pinned 1,666,560 images on Pinterest, downloaded 23,040,000 apps from Apple's App Store, submitted 12,662,400 reviews to Yelp, shared 132,960,000 pithy thoughts on Twitter, and received anywhere between dozens and hundreds of emails that demanded their attention. That's a lot of information!

Take a ride on any major urban public transportation system during rush hour and look around. Your fellow commuters' bodies are there in the train with yours, but most of their minds are engaged elsewhere; they're temporary participants in shared information environments that they enter through the slender slabs of glass, plastic, and silicon in their hands. We increasingly work, play, learn, and communicate in these information environments, and there are more of them—and more in them—all the time.

You are on the receiving end of this information avalanche. But if you are a designer—*any* type of designer—you are on the producing end as well. The stuff you make enters the information stream and either helps cut through the noise, or makes things harder for your fellow humans. This is a vast new world, waiting to be explored... but more importantly, ready to be designed. Helping make information findable and understandable can have an enormous impact on people's lives. Knowing about information architecture—with its strategies and tactics gleaned from both library sciences and architecture—can help you do so most effectively. It's not easy to make these abstract ideas tangible to the people who must act on them, especially when working in fast-moving, agile environments. It is now up to you to employ these strategies and tactics thoughtfully and with an eye to the common good, and to bring others along with you.

References

OK, this really is the end. As you head off into the world to improve its information environments, here are some other books that can help you further hone your practice and a list of professional organizations where you can connect to colleagues and mentors in the field.

Books

- Christopher Alexander, *The Timeless Way of Building* (Oxford: Oxford University Press, 1979)
- Christopher Alexander, Sara Ishikawa, Murray Silverstein, Max Jacobson, Ingrid Fiksdahl-King, and Shlomo Angel, *A Pattern Language: Towns, Buildings, Construction* (Oxford: Oxford University Press, 1977)
- Ricardo Baeza-Yates and Berthier Ribeiro-Neto, *Modern Information Retrieval* (Boston: Addison-Wesley, 2011)
- Benjamin K. Bergen, *Louder Than Words: The New Science of How the Mind Makes Meaning* (New York: Basic Books, 2012)
- Hugh Beyer and Karen Holtzblatt, *Contextual Design: Defining Customer-Centered Systems* (Burlington, MA: Morgan Kaufmann, 1997)
- Nate Bolt and Tony Tulathimutte, *Remote Research: Real Users, Real Time, Real Research* (Brooklyn, NY: Rosenfeld Media, 2010)

- Dan Brown, *Communicating Design: Developing Web Site Documentation for Design and Planning, Second Edition* (San Francisco: New Riders, 2010)

- Alan Cooper, *The Inmates Are Running the Asylum: Why High Tech Products Drive Us Crazy and How to Restore the Sanity* (Carmel, IN: Sams Publishing, 2004)

- Alan Cooper, Robert Reimann, David Cronin, and Christopher Noessel, *About Face: The Essentials of Interaction Design* (Hoboken, NJ: Wiley, 2014)

- Abby Covert, *How to Make Sense of Any Mess: Information Architecture for Everybody* (printed by CreateSpace, 2014)

- Thomas Davenport and Lawrence Prusak, *Information Ecology: Mastering the Information and Knowledge Environment* (Oxford: Oxford University Press, 1997)

- Elizabeth Goodman and Mike Kuniavsky, *Observing the User Experience: A Practitioner's Guide to User Research, Second Edition* (Burlington, MA: Morgan Kaufmann, 2012)

- Dave Gray, *Gamestorming: A Playbook for Innovators, Rulebreakers, and Changemakers* (Sebastopol, CA: O'Reilly, 2010)

- Joann Hackos and Janice Redish, *User and Task Analysis for Interface Design* (Hoboken, NJ: Wiley, 1998)

- Kristina Halvorson and Melissa Rach, *Content Strategy for the Web, Second Edition* (San Francisco: New Riders, 2012)

- Andrew Hinton, *Understanding Context* (Sebastopol, CA: O'Reilly, 2014)

- James Kalbach, *Designing Web Navigation* (Sebastopol, CA: O'Reilly, 2007)

- Steve Krug, *Don't Make Me Think: A Common Sense Approach to Web Usability* (San Francisco: New Riders, 2014)

- George Lakoff, *Women, Fire, and Dangerous Things* (Chicago: University of Chicago Press, 1990)

- George Lakoff and Mark Johnson, *Metaphors We Live By* (Chicago: University of Chicago Press, 2003)

- Thomas K. Landauer, *The Trouble with Computers: Usefulness, Usability, and Productivity* (Cambridge, MA: MIT Press, 1996)

- William Lidwell, Kritina Holden, and Jill Butler, *Universal Principles of Design, Revised and Updated: 125 Ways to Enhance Usability, Influence Perception, Increase Appeal, Make Better Design Decisions, and Teach through Design* (Beverly, MA: Rockport Publishers, 2010)
- Karen McGrane, *Content Strategy for Mobile* (New York: A Book Apart, 2012)
- Donella Meadows, *Thinking in Systems: A Primer* (White River Junction, VT: Chelsea Green Publishing, 2008)
- Peter Morville, *Ambient Findability* (Sebastopol, CA: O'Reilly, 2005)
- Peter Morville, *Intertwingled: Information Changes Everything* (Ann Arbor, MI: Semantic Studios, 2014)
- Peter Morville and Jeffery Callender, *Search Patterns: Design for Discovery* (Sebastopol, CA: O'Reilly, 2010)
- Bonnie Nardi and Vicki O'Day, *Information Ecologies* (Cambridge, MA: MIT Press, 2000)
- Jakob Nielsen, *Designing Web Usability* (San Francisco: New Riders, 1999)
- Don Norman, *The Design of Everyday Things* (New York: Basic Books, 2013)
- Miranda Lee Pao, *Concepts of Information Retrieval* (Westport, CT: Libraries Unlimited, 1989)
- Steve Portigal, *Interviewing Users: How to Uncover Compelling Insights* (Brooklyn, NY: Rosenfeld Media, 2013)
- Andrea Resmini and Luca Rosati, *Pervasive Information Architecture: Designing Cross-Channel User Experiences* (Burlington, MA: Morgan Kaufmann, 2011)
- Louis Rosenfeld, *Search Analytics for Your Site: Conversations with Your Customers* (Brooklyn, NY: Rosenfeld Media, 2011)
- Donna Spencer, *Card Sorting: Designing Usable Categories* (Brooklyn, NY: Rosenfeld Media, 2011)
- Sara Wachter-Boettcher, *Content Everywhere: Strategy and Structure for Future-Ready Content* (Brooklyn, NY: Rosenfeld Media, 2012)

- Gerald Weinberg, *An Introduction to General Systems Thinking* (New York: Dorset House, 2001)
- Richard Saul Wurman, *33: Understanding Change & the Change in Understanding* (Flushing, NY: Greenway Communications, 2009)
- Richard Saul Wurman, *Information Anxiety* (New York: Bantam, 1989)
- Indi Young, *Mental Models: Aligning Design Strategy with Human Behavior* (Brooklyn, NY: Rosenfeld Media, 2011)
- Todd Zaki Warfel, *Prototyping: A Practitioner's Guide* (Brooklyn, NY: Rosenfeld Media, 2011)

Professional Organizations

- Association for Information Science & Technology (ASIS&T) (*https://www.asist.org*)
- The Information Architecture Institute (IAI) (*http://iainstitute.org*)
- The Interaction Design Association (IxDA) (*http://ixda.org*)
- User Experience Professionals Association (UXPA) (*https://uxpa.org*)

Index

automatic stemming, 229
autosuggest, 257

B

Baeza-Yates, Ricardo, 266
Bates, Marcia, 47, 293
BBC, 88-90, 244
benchmarking
  before-and-after, 331
  competitive, 331
  defined, 330
berry-picking model, 46
Best Bets strategy, 94, 336
books, 13
bottom-up information architecture,
  85-88, 357
Brand, Stewart, 67
Bray, Tim, 266
Brenners-Lee, Tim, 11
Broader Term (BT), 284
browsing aids
  browser navigation features, 178
  types of, 91

C

call to action, 250
Callender, Jeffery, 266
card sort exercises
  benefits of, 343
  in content modeling, 425
  open vs. closed, 344
  possible formats, 344
  qualitative analysis of, 345
  quantitative analysis of, 345
  set up for, 343
  types of, 166
  used in strategy development, 364
case studies, 371
channels
  coherence across, 18, 59
  effect on information environ-
    ments, 59
  possible formats, 36
chunks
  assigning unique IDs to, 416
  defined, 93, 415
  process of defining, 415

sitemaps and, 404
citation searching, 230
classification schemes
  ambiguous language and, 99
  faceted, 303-308
  heterogeneity and, 101
  historical application of, 98
  internal politics and, 103
  overview of, 279-282
  perspective and, 102
  polyhierarchies, 301
  in social media, 127
  social/political perspectives of, 97
clustering, 248
collaboration
  point-of-production, 434
  prototypes, 433
  sketches, 431
  tools for, 431
collaborative categorization, 127
collaborative filtering, 230
components
  browsing aids, 91
  categories of, 90
  in content/tasks, 93
  invisible, 94
  search aids, 92
comprehensiveness, 156
conceptual diagrams, 372
configurators, 200
consistency, in labeling systems, 155
content
  defined, 36
  documenting source and destina-
    tion of, 416
  dynamism of, 37, 69, 216
  factors affecting, 36
  interdependency with users and
    context, 32
  labeling systems and, 154
  management team meetings, 320
  metadata descriptions, 37
  ownership of, 36
  possible formats, 36
  possible structures for, 36
  representational vs. descriptive,
    234
  researching, 323-332

Educational Resources Information Center (ERIC) Thesaurus, 162
embedded links, defined, 93
embedded metadata, 93
endorsements, 128
entity extraction tools, 163
entity relationship diagram (ERD), 124
equivalence relationship, 283, 295
equivalent terms, 271
ethnoclassification, 127
executive-centered design, 316
extensibility, 67

F

Facebook
    algorithms for ordering posts, 114
    bottom-up architecture of, 86
    Facebook groups, 58
    social classification via, 127, 206-208
faceted classification, 303-308
Farnum, Chris, 411, 414
Fast, Karl, 308
fat footers, 184
fields, 122
findability, defined, 25
focus groups, 341
free tagging, 127
free-listing method, 168
functional metaphors, 368

G

gap analysis, 425
Garrett, Jesse James, 393
Gehry, Frank, 59
general navigation systems, 91
global navigation systems, 183-186
Google
    factors affecting indexing by, 151
    Google AdWords, 171
    Google Analytics, 334
    Google Chrome, 178
    Google Forms, 168
    Google Play Developer signup, 147
    Google Search, 86

Google Shopping, 205
Google Trends, 336
hybrid approach to sorting, 248
local search/directories services, 108
PageRank algorithm, 92, 245
relevance algorithm used by, 253
subsites offered by, 69
"Similar pages" search results, 49
Gore, Al, 367
GOV.UK, 142-142
granularity, 101, 156, 196, 345
guided navigation, 307
guides, 91, 177, 198

H

hashtags (#), 127
headings
    defined, 93
    labels as, 140, 144-147
heterogeneity, 101, 218, 345
heuristic evaluation, 324
hierarchical relationship, 283, 296
hierarchies
    benefits of, 117
    breadth vs. depth in, 118
    establishing with labels, 144-147
    for growing information environments, 121
    historical application of, 117
    mutually exclusive vs. polyhierarchical, 118
    in navigation systems, 182
    polyhierarchies, 301
    sitemaps and, 194
    vs. other systems, 122
    website example, 120
Hinton, Andrew, 17
homographs, 300
hypertext
    components involved, 126
    embedded inline links, 189
    in navigation systems, 182

I

iconic labels, 152
identifiers, defined, 93

natural language processing tools,
232
navigation systems
advanced
personalization and customization, 202
social, 205
visualization, 205
avoiding clutter in, 183
browser navigation features, 178
challenges of creating, 178
by common qualities, 49
defined, 90
design strategy, 358
embedded
contextual, 188
global, 183-186
implementing, 191
local, 186
types of, 183
guided, 307
hierarchical nature of, 61
importance of, 175
improving flexibility in, 182
labels representing choices in,
140, 147
overview of, 208
placemaking and, 179
sitemaps and, 405
supplemental
configurators, 200
guides, 198
indexes, 195-198
role of, 193
search, 201
sitemaps, 193
types of, 193
types of, 91, 176
website example, 82
Netflix, 260, 280

0

online communities, 369
Online Thesauri and Authority Files,
163
organization schemes
ambiguous/subjective
appeal of, 109

audience-specific, 112
defined, 108
hybrid, 114
metaphor-driven, 113
successful implementation of,
109
task-oriented, 110
topical, 110
value of, 109
defined, 104
differences in, 104
exact/objective
alphabetical, 105
chronological, 106
defined, 105
geographical, 107
organization structures
database model, 122-126
defined, 104
examples of, 116
hierarchies, 117-122
hypertext, 126
social classification, 127
types of, 117
organization systems
challenges of creating, 98-103
components of, 103
creating cohesive, 129
defined, 90
goals of, 98
organization schemes, 104-115
organization structures, 116-127
overview of, 130
strategy and, 357
types of, 91
organizational metaphors, 368
organizing
defined, 25
example structure, 70, 82
importance to understanding, 97
principles of, 59
relationship to system development, 104
rhythm principle of, 61
role in information environments,
60

Rowley, Frederick A., 293

S

scenarios, 370
Scope Note (SN), 284
screen size, 408
search, 201
search aids, types of, 92
search algorithms, 227-232
search analytics, 49, 334
search interface
  defined, 92
  designing, 431
search queries, analyzing, 170
search results
  acting on
    call to action, 250
    selecting subset of, 251
  defined, 93
  human-curated, 89, 94, 246, 336
  presenting
    determining how many docu-
      ments to display, 238
    determining which content to
      display, 234
    grouping, 248
    lists, 240-248
    main issues, 233
search systems
  anatomy of, 216
  choosing what to index
    by topic, 222
    determining search zones, 219
    heterogeneous content and,
      218
    highlighting quality content,
      218
    navigation vs. destination, 220
    recent content, 223
    selecting components for, 224
    specific audiences and, 222
    structured content and, 218
  defined, 90
  determining need for, 212-213
  information retrieval resources,
    266
  overview of, 267
  presenting results

    call to action, 250
    determining how many docu-
      ments to display, 238
    determining which content to
      display, 234
    grouping, 248
    lists, 240-248
    main issues, 233
    saving searches, 251
    selecting subset of, 251
  query builders, 232
  search algorithms, 227-232
  search interface
    advanced search, 258
    autocomplete/autosuggest, 257
    dealing with dead- ends, 264
    designing, 431
    evolution of, 253
    factors to consider, 252
    search boxes, 253-257
    supporting revision, 260-263
  website example, 83
  when to implement, 214-216
search zones
  benefits of, 218
  creating by audience breakdown,
    222
  defined, 92
  determining, 219
  navigation vs. destination, 220
search-log analysis, 170, 336
semantic relationships
  associative, 298
  equivalence, 295
  hierarchical, 296
  in thesauri, 283
sequential aids, defined, 93
seven plus- or -minus two rule, 119
shopping cart feature, 251
silos, 246
Similar pages command, 49
site-wide navigation systems, 183
sitemaps, 373
  detailed, 402-405
  high-level, 395-397
  organizing, 405
  purpose of, 91, 395
  simple, 402

About the Authors

Louis Rosenfeld is an independent information architecture consultant. He has been instrumental in helping establish the field of information architecture, and in articulating the role and value of librarianship within the field. Lou played a leading role in organizing and programming the first three information architecture conferences (both ASIS&T Summits and IA 2000). He also presents and moderates at such venues as CHI, COMDEX, Intranets, and the web design conferences produced by Miller Freeman, C|net, and Thunder Lizard. He teaches tutorials as part of the Nielsen Norman Group User Experience Conference.

Peter Morville is president of Semantic Studios, an information architecture, user experience, and findability consultancy. Since 1994, he has advised such clients as AT&T, Harvard, IBM, the Library of Congress, Microsoft, the National Cancer Institute, Vodafone, and the Weather Channel. Peter is best known as a founding father of information architecture, having coauthored the field's best-selling book, *Information Architecture for the World Wide Web*. Peter has served on the faculty at the University of Michigan's School of Information and on the advisory board of the Information Architecture Institute. He delivers keynotes and seminars at international events, and his work has been featured in major publications including *Business Week*, *The Economist*, *Fortune*, and *The Wall Street Journal*. You can contact Peter Morville by email (*morville@semanticstudios.com*). You can also find him online at *semanticstudios.com*, *findability.org*, and *searchpatterns.org*.

Jorge Arango is an information architect with 20 years of experience designing digital products and services. He is a partner in Futuredraft, a digital design consultancy based in Oakland, CA, and has served the global UX community as president and director of the Information Architecture Institute and as managing editor of *Boxes and Arrows* magazine.

Colophon

The animal on the cover of *Information Architecture: For the Web and Beyond* is a polar bear (*Ursus maritimus*). Polar bears live primarily on the icy shores of Greenland and northern North America and Asia. They are very strong swimmers and rarely venture far from the water. The largest land carnivore, male polar bears weigh from 770 to 1,400 pounds. Female polar bears are much smaller, weighing 330 to 550 pounds. The preferred meal of polar bears is ringed seals and bearded seals. When seals are unavailable, the bears will eat fish, reindeer, birds, berries, and trash.

Polar bears are, of course, well adapted to living in the Arctic Circle. Their black skin is covered in thick, water-repellent white fur. Adult polar bears are protected from the cold by a layer of blubber that is more than four inches thick. They are so well insulated, in fact, that overheating can be a problem. For this reason they move slowly on land, taking frequent breaks. Their large feet spread out their substantial weight, allowing them to walk on thin ice surfaces that animals weighing far less would break through. Because food is available year-round, most polar bears don't hibernate. Pregnant females are the exception, and the tiny one- to one-and-a-half-pound cubs are born during the hibernation period.

Polar bears have no natural enemies. They are extremely aggressive and dangerous animals. While many bears actively avoid human contact, polar bears tend to view humans as prey. In encounters between humans and polar bears, the bear almost always wins.

Many of the animals on O'Reilly covers are endangered; all of them are important to the world. To learn more about how you can help, go to *animals.oreilly.com*.

The cover image is from a 19th-century engraving from the Dover Pictorial Archive. The cover fonts are URW Typewriter and Guardian Sans. The text font is Adobe Minion Pro; the heading font is Adobe Myriad Condensed; and the code font is Dalton Maag's Ubuntu Mono.

Have it your way

Get even more for your money.

CPSIA information can be obtained
at www.ICGtesting.com
Printed in the USA
BVOW05s0716100117
473043BV00004B/5/P